*Rooting For the
Home Team*

Rooting For the Home Team

Sport, Community, and Identity

Edited by

DANIEL A. NATHAN

University of Illinois Press
URBANA, CHICAGO, AND SPRINGFIELD

Library of Congress Cataloging-in-Publication Data
Rooting for the home team : sport, community, and identity /
edited by Daniel A. Nathan.
pages cm.
Includes bibliographical references and index.
ISBN 978-0-252-03761-0 (hardcover : alk. paper) —
ISBN 978-0-252-07914-6 (pbk. : alk. paper) —
ISBN 978-0-252-09485-9 (e-book)
1. Sports—Social aspects—United States.
2. Sports—United States.
I. Nathan, Daniel A.
GV706.5.R66   2013
306.4'83—dc23   2012036559

For my number one fans,
Sol and Irene Nathan.
And SBZ, always.

Contents

Acknowledgments

This book was a team effort. So it gives me great pleasure to acknowledge those who played important roles in publishing it.

First and most obvious, I need and want to thank the book's contributors. They are all professionals, bright, talented, patient men and women who understand that sport is an important cultural institution and practice, not just fun and games. Carlo Rotella and David Wiggins, in particular, provided useful counsel in terms of moving this project through its various phases. The same is true of our editor, Bill Regier, director of the University of Illinois Press, who deftly kept the book on track. We also received constructive criticism that improved this book from three anonymous reviewers. Several other people at the University of Illinois Press helped make this book happen: Walt Evans, Tad Ringo, and Vijay Shah all did first-rate work.

I first discussed this project with Bill Regier at an annual meeting of the North American Society for Sport History in Lake Placid, New York. In many ways and for many years, NASSH and its members have been supportive of my work and career. As its members know and appreciate, NASSH is a valuable community. It provides people from all over the world with a venue to discuss and debate ideas and methods—at its annual conference, in the pages of the *Journal of Sport History,* and online—and to share a sense of fellowship. It's no accident that I first met some of this book's contributors at NASSH. Myriad NASSH members have influenced this book, too many to list here, so a collective thank you will have to suffice.

Likewise, Skidmore College, my academic home for more than ten years, helped bring this book to fruition. Skidmore did so by supporting interdisciplinary work and creativity, and by nurturing a vibrant, engaged group of faculty and students. Many of their ideas and insights appear in these pages. In particular, I'm grateful for the collegiality and friendship of Erica Bastress-Dukehart, Beau Breslin, John Brueggemann, Beck Krefting, Mary Lynn, Pat Oles, Greg Pfitzer, and Jeff Segrave. They are all superb colleagues and even better people.

Skidmore also supported this work in the form of Faculty Development grants and Dean of the Faculty ad hoc grants. In particular, thanks are extended to Skidmore's Faculty Development Committee and its former chair, Peter Stake, and to Associate Dean of the Faculty Paty Rubio.

Blessed with tremendous familial support, I need to thank Margaret Taylor, the Burrs, the Farahs, and the Kelley clan for their good cheer; Marilyn Nathan and Wes Porter for the steady stream of newspaper clippings and e-mails; and my parents—Ron and Jerry Matthews, and Irv Nathan and Judy Walter—for their encouragement, which came in many forms. No one could ask for more supportive, generous, or loving parents.

My gratitude to Susan Taylor, for supporting this project and me, in innumerable ways, is boundless. She and Ben and Zoë Nathan are the lights of my life, and the Four Family is my favorite team.

Introduction

Sport, Community, and Identity

DANIEL A. NATHAN

Many years ago, I lived in Iowa City, Iowa, a vibrant university town with more than sixty thousand residents. The town is surrounded by seemingly unending miles of corn and soybean fields, and lots of hog farms. One of the things I liked best about living in Iowa City was being part of a graduate student cohort that regularly played pickup basketball games at the Field House and on various playgrounds. For a few years, we also played in a city recreation league. Our team was called the Sport Boys. One season we wore black tank tops with hot-pink lettering that read "Vamos Boys" on the back. Those games were good times, even when we lost, which was frequently. Like many Hawkeyes, I have fond memories of and affection for Iowa and the people who befriended me, but I'm not nostalgic for the place where I experienced the coldest winters and hottest summers of my life.

When I lived in Iowa, Dan Gable, Hayden Fry, C. Vivian Stringer, and Tom Davis were the most successful and prominent coaches at the university and probably in the state. They were all icons—well, maybe not Dr. Tom, whom I always liked, despite the incessant passing around the perimeter. These coaches were iconic for many reasons. It was not just that their teams won, especially Gable's, whose record over his twenty-one years as wrestling coach is unprecedented in any American sport. With Gable at the helm, the Iowa wrestling team won fifteen NCAA national titles (nine of them consecutively) and twenty-one straight Big Ten conference championships.[1] Fry, Stringer, and Davis experienced success, too. But beyond the wins, which created opportunities to bask in reflected glory, many Iowa fans connected with, liked, and even admired these people because they personified things that we valued—hard work, preparation, intensity, determination, perseverance, integrity, charm, and humility, at least in public, most of the time. They all had some of these qualities, some more than others. For different reasons, and to different degrees, these coaches brought people—athletes, students, and fans of all ages from all over the state—together. In the process, they helped us differentiate ourselves from others: from, say, Cyclones and Cornhuskers, Badgers and Buckeyes.[2]

This book explores that complicated, double-edged process of inclusion and exclusion, of rooting for the home team. It is about the ways different American communities (big cities, small rural towns, suburbs, college towns, and so forth) used or use sport to create and maintain a sense of their collective identity. This book is predicated on the idea that rooting for local athletes and home teams often symbolizes a community's preferred understanding of itself, and that doing so is an expression of connectedness. It's an expression of public pride and pleasure, a source of group and personal identity. It's about sharing something, about belonging. "People need shared stories and rituals to bring them together and reinforce social solidarity," writes sociologist Stephanie Coontz.[3] Better than most institutions, sport does this well. It provides people and communities with common reference points and can foster solidarity and the creation of social identities, things that many people need and cherish. In different ways, the essays collected here are about how sport brings people together and also divides them, sometimes simultaneously, sometimes profoundly. As historian Mark Dyreson puts it, sport "can build and destroy community in the very same moment. It can unite and segregate in the same instant."[4] These are not trivial matters. They inform the way different communities have shaped and maintained their identities and how they interact and compete with others.

This complex process of coming together and separation, or what political scientist Shelia L. Croucher calls "the politics of belonging," pervades sports.[5] For millions of Americans, sports are the subject about which they're the most knowledgeable and enthusiastic. For better or worse, probably worse, many Americans care about sports more deeply than they care about any other aspect of public life. In some instances, sports appear to be (or are constructed as) a kind of social glue that holds together heterogeneous and contentious communities. "In this fragmented age," *Newsweek* reporter Mark Starr wrote more than ten years ago, "it often seems that only sports can bind together the nation—across its divides of class, race and gender—in common cause and celebration."[6] (Of course, the same has been said about other countries; this sport, community, and identity nexus is not unique to the United States.)[7]

Yet sport has not and does not *just* bring us together, *e pluribus unum*–like. Rather, the history of American sports is also one of exclusion, of segregation, that has forced some people—African Americans and women, most obviously, but many others, too—to play apart. My sense is that Americans tend to avoid dwelling on this. When not ignoring this fact, people have found ways to spin it to good effect.

For all the celebration of individualism in American culture, which is ubiquitous and relentless, many people and institutions (like big universities and rural high schools) stress the ways in which sports promote teamwork and community. More than thirty years ago, political scientist Richard Lipsky argued: "Sports is the 'magic elixir' that feeds personal identity while it nourishes the bonds of communal solidarity."[8] Or as a functionalist might say, "sport functions as a means of integration, not only for the actual participants, but also for the represented members of such a system."[9] Sports have what seems to be or feels like a unique ability to enable disparate people to experience something approximating *communitas,* by which cultural anthropologists following Victor Turner's lead mean an intense community spirit, a feeling of solidarity and togetherness.[10] Admittedly, this sense of belonging is often shallow and ephemeral. It's here and it's gone, like the smell of fresh pig manure in the Iowa wind (which I sometimes miss). For dedicated fans, it can last for a few weeks if their team is in the midst of an end-of-the-season championship drive. Or it can last a few hours, during a specific game. Most of the time, though, when the game is over, fans file out and head home or downtown, with only the most minimal sense of connectedness.

Yet sports-related *communitas* can also be deep and long lasting. For athletes, perhaps especially for teammates who practiced and played together for many years under difficult conditions, "the thrill of victory and the agony of defeat" can last a lifetime.[11] Examples abound. Think about how teammates—say, the Baltimore Colts who played in and won the 1958 NFL championship game—stay in touch and reminiscence about their glory days.

The same is true for fans. Sometimes a form of *communitas* can span and connect generations. Consider the sense of solidarity that a single game can generate, particularly a dramatic one with an unexpected outcome or a sudden reversal of fortune. Many of us can recall at least a few of these games, emblazoned as they are in our memories. Numerous Boston Red Sox fans, a heterogeneous group from all over New England and beyond, are still emotionally scarred, if not psychologically damaged, by the ground ball that went between Bill Buckner's legs that lost game six of the 1986

World Series against the New York Mets.[12] For citizens of Red Sox Nation, twenty-five years and two championships have not erased the painful memory of that event—which was joyous for the Mets and their fans. It created different kinds of *communitas* in two communities.

If *communitas* is an intense form of solidarity and togetherness, then perhaps community is a more ordinary lived reality—which does not mean that it is easy to define, create, or sustain, or that it is not idealized. On the contrary, though we use the term all the time, community is a more complicated phenomenon than most of us probably realize. "The term 'community' implies something both psychological and geographical," explains economist-turned-sociologist Roland Warren, in his classic book on the subject. "Psychologically," he continues, community

> implies shared interests, characteristics, or association, as in the expression "community of interest," or "the business community." Geographically, it denotes a specific area where people are clustered. Sociologically, the term combines these connotations. It relates to the shared interests and behavior patterns which people have by virtue of their common locality. Mere similarity of interest does not in itself make a sociological community, nor does mere geographic proximity of residence.[13]

Community is difficult to define, partly because of the term's polysemic quality. For some time now, I've been cataloging different definitions and conceptions of community and agree with historian Thomas Bender that, when most people use the term, they attach "many layers of emotional meaning" to it, and thus the word "means more than a place or local activity. There is an expectation of a special quality of human relationship in a community, and it is this experiential dimension that is crucial to its definition. Community, then, can be defined better as an experience than as a place. As simply as possible, community is where community happens."[14]

To complicate matters further, let us concede that community is multifaceted, that it takes myriad forms, macro and micro. We talk of "the international community" and of our personal cliques as communities. We talk of the university as a community and still frequently cite Benedict Anderson's argument that the nation-state is an "imagined community." The nation is imagined, Anderson contends, "because the members of even the smallest nation will never know most of their fellow-members, meet them, or even hear of them, yet in the minds of each lives the image of their communion."[15] By "communion," I take Anderson to mean something secular, that is, simply "the sharing or exchanging of intimate thoughts and feelings."[16] These are the kinds of "thoughts and feelings," for example, stirred by the image of a flag or the playing of an anthem or a fight song. The point is, whether via communal celebration or commiseration, community is about coming together; it's the process of sharing something.[17]

Communities share things besides space, such as, say, a common language and history, religion and values, ideas and icons. These and other things can sometimes create a complicated skein of what political scientist Robert D. Putnam calls "social connectedness."[18] But there is something else, too: stories, which are fundamentally social transactions that can reinforce group solidarity. "Community," remarks media studies scholar Peter Dahlgren, "is in part built upon members sharing the same stories."[19] Again, there are different kinds of narratives: creation myths and cautionary tales, stories of triumph and tragedy, sacrifice and suffering, perseverance that pays off. These are among our national favorites, the kinds of narratives that are repeated daily in the media, local and national, and in everyday conversations. If community "is best defined as a network of social relations marked by mutuality and emotional bonds," these things are largely built and maintained by people telling and retelling stories that matter to them.[20]

"Them," though probably not "us." These are important pronouns, because an inescapable feature of most communities is separation, dividing "us" from "them." In 2007, the *New York Times* reported that two high schools in Uniontown, New Jersey, were merging, thus ending their traditional Thanksgiving Day football game against one another. The paper's headline read: "After 88 Years of Rivalry, the Last as Us and Them."[21] Communities exist, in part, by contradistinction. Here, not there. Iowa, not Illinois. The Department of English, not the Department of History. Like most disciplines, the majority of (but not all) communities are predicated on boundaries, literal and figurative. "Borders," writes feminist theorist, critic, and poet Gloria Anzaldúa, "are set up to define the places that are safe and unsafe, to distinguish *us* from *them*. A border is a dividing line, a narrow strip along a steep edge."[22] There are, of course, individuals and small groups that sometimes negotiate that steep edge, or try to cross over, or try to blur if not obliterate dividing lines. Other communities reside in the interstices, neither here nor there. Additionally, membership in one community does not preclude membership in others; clearly people are members of many different groups simultaneously: racial and ethnic groups; groups based on sex, gender, and sexual orientation; religious, linguistic, and political groups, and on and on. We all have multiple identities, interests, and allegiances, some of which may seem contradictory but are more likely paradoxical. I know a feminist scholar who is a gun-toting hunting advocate and an avid, knowledgeable Green Bay Packers fan who lives in Montana on a bison ranch half the year and teaches religion and ecofeminism courses the other half. There are African American lesbian Republicans; devout, thoughtful Jews and Muslims who eat pork; and passionate Boston Red Sox fans in New York. There is, it seems, a community (and perhaps a team) for everyone.

Nevertheless, we should be careful to not romanticize or uncritically celebrate or embrace community. According to feminist scholar Miranda Joseph:

> Community is almost always invoked as an unequivocal good, an indicator of a high quality of life, a life of human understanding, caring, selflessness, belonging. One does one's volunteer work in and for "the community." Communities are frequently said to emerge in times of crisis or tragedy, when people imagine themselves bound together by a common grief or joined through some extraordinary effort. Among leftists and feminists, community has connoted cherished ideals of cooperation, equality, and communion.[23]

However, Joseph argues that "the discourse of community" can also "legitimate social hierarchies."[24] Community can be coercive and promote conformity. It can mask power relations that disenfranchise and silence people, hindering agency. "Fetishizing community," Joseph says, "only makes us blind to the ways we might intervene in the enactment of domination and exploitation."[25] Furthermore, community can be ugly. To take a relatively mild example, a few years ago *Sports Illustrated* published the following letter to the editor: "The hate between SEC [Southeastern Conference] fans has reached an all-time low. My daughter is an Auburn alum and she attended the Tigers' game against Alabama in Tuscaloosa in November. She wore Auburn colors and was spit on and covered in beer by game's end. And for what? Just because she was a fan of the opposing team?"[26] Well, yes. Community is not always civil society at its best. It can be unbearably chauvinistic, regressive, and even violent. Sport as community has critics, too. In 2009, David P. Barash, a professor of psychology at the University of Washington, wrote a scathing article in *The Chronicle Review* that argues sports fandom represents our "dark desire for deindividuation."[27] He adds: "Spectator sports offer quick and easy entree into an instant community. Never mind that it is ersatz. It is there for the joining; no need to 'make the team.' Instead, just buy a ticket, a T-shirt, or turn on the television or radio. The would-be applicant is immediately taken in . . . in more ways than one."[28]

"Instant community" or what sociologists and others have called "contrived community" is superficial and short-lived, and basking in reflected glory sometimes has unintended consequences and unforeseen costs.[29] This is why Miranda Joseph correctly asserts: "To invoke community is immediately to raise questions of belonging and of power."[30]

It also raises issues about identity, about who we are and what we value. This is true individually and collectively. In this book, the contributors emphasize communal identity, how people in specific places understand and represent their communities via sports, but it is of course difficult (if not impossible) to separate one's self from the groups to which one belongs. Not surprisingly, then, many of the contributors here draw on their personal experience and use the first-person. Doing so enriches their storytelling and analysis. It also sheds light on why so many people are invested (sometimes deeply) in specific teams and athletes. "Fan support must be based on one of two criteria," asserts cultural critic and humorist Joe Queenan. "Either you grew up in a specific locality and inherited a congenital municipal connection to the team, or you grew up somewhere else but rooted for your father's team."[31] That's one explanation. There are others. I have long thought, only half facetiously, that sports fandom and identity formation were akin to what animal behaviorists call imprinting, "in which a young animal's early social interactions, usually with its parents, lead to its learning such things as what constitutes an appropriate sexual partner," explains scientist John Alcock.[32] For many people, their sports fan identity is not a choice, at least not one that they made for themselves. In his memoir *Fever Pitch* (1992), novelist and die-hard Arsenal football (soccer) fan Nick Hornby comes to this realization the hard way. After "his" team suffers a particularly disappointing loss, Hornby grasps "that loyalty, at least in football terms, was not a moral choice like bravery or kindness; it was more like a wart or a hump, something you were stuck with."[33] The larger, more serious point is that sports and identity formation are often intertwined, that who we root for represents our communities and us. As a Baltimore Orioles fan, I can testify that this is not always a pleasant experience.

Clearly sport is a place where community and identity come together. Sports are a way that disparate communities define, understand, and represent themselves to themselves and to others. In her contribution in this book, historian Amy Bass writes, "Sports teams contribute to a community's definition, expressing pride, identity, and meaning alongside shared rituals and styles that reinforce belonging." Yes, and at the same time, sports as community contribute to separation, misunderstanding, and antagonism. More than ten years ago, sportswriter Frank Deford argued, "it is time to recognize the truth, that sports in the United States has, in fact, never been so divisive."[34] A trenchant critic, Deford continues:

"Uniquely today, sports has come to pit race against race, men against women, city against city, class against class and coach against player."[35] Deford is in the minority on this matter, but he is not wrong; neither, though, are those who argue that sports create and sustain social cohesion and foster common understanding. It's not an either/or issue. Playing together, playing apart, and rooting for the home team are complicated, multilayered lived experiences.

This book considers some of those experiences, in the past and present. The essays brought together here are wonderfully eclectic, in terms of their subjects and approaches. They discuss professional and amateur sports, from the 1920s to the present, played in different parts of this country, by different kinds of people, for different reasons.

To begin, Mark Dyreson examines the passion for Indiana high school basketball that social scientists Robert and Helen Lynd reported in their celebrated *Middletown: A Study in Contemporary American Culture* (1929). Despite the Lynds' inability to fathom the community's devotion to the game, Dyreson notes that the social scientists "quickly discovered that basketball gave meaning, structure, and predictability to the tribes that inhabited Middletown." David K. Wiggins also revisits the 1920s, specifically the spirited football rivalry between Howard and Lincoln universities. During the 1920s, the annual Thanksgiving Day football game between these historically black universities was more than just a game. It was, Wiggins shows, "an athletic and social event that provided upper-class African Americans the opportunity to exhibit racial pride, measure themselves against the standards of white universities, and come together as a distinct group." Catherine M. Lewis uses 1920s golfing icon Bobby Jones and the sense of southern identity and white privilege that he personified to reflect on the recent Tiger Woods affair. Jones, Lewis asserts, "was marketed as an antidote to Woods's conduct, raising important issues about class, race, and identity in sport," adding that "the golfing world continues to trade on his legend to promote itself as the last gentleman's game, with a distinctly southern flavor."

Like many of the essays in this book, Michael Oriard's connects the past and present. He does so by tracing the history of two deeply entrenched competing views "about the role of high school football in American communities," which he describes as the "Football Town" and the "Friday Night Lights syndrome." These competing mass-mediated visions, Oriard demonstrates, appear to be different sides of the same coin: one (seemingly) wholesome, one troubling. Jaime Schultz and Shelley Lucas are also interested in interscholastic sport, in their case a defunct version of high school girls' basketball known as "six-on-six," a version of the game in which players could not cross half-court, and how it expressed community identity in Iowa. For many reasons, girls' six-player basketball has been relegated to the past, yet Schultz and Lucas show that the game lives on in many places and memories, thanks in part to new technologies and understandings of community. Christopher Lamberti examines a different (if similarly idiosyncratic) midwestern sport, sixteen-inch, no-glove softball, which one enthusiast describes as "Chicago's game" and Lamberti contends is an "important part of the city's heritage." In many ways an expression of traditional class and gender identities and relations, sixteen-inch softball also instilled a distinct sense of community among those who played and followed it.

My essay is about Baltimore and its former, beloved professional football team, the Colts. It focuses on the team's victory over the New York Giants in the famous 1958 "sudden death" championship game, quarterback John Unitas, and the team's clandestine departure for Indianapolis in 1984. In the process it illustrates how the Colts exemplified the city's values and sense of self. Elliott J. Gorn and Allison Lauterbach reflect on and pay homage to another cherished local institution, Los Angeles Dodgers broadcaster Vin Scully, who has provided the team's play-by-play for more than sixty years, with "elegance and ease and seeming effortlessness." Considering Scully from different generational perspectives, Gorn and Lauterbach argue that he "is more than just a well-loved sportscaster. He is the voice of L.A." Evoking a different cadence—that of the Dropkick Murphys, an American Celtic punk band from Massachusetts—Amy Bass scrutinizes the diasporic quality of Red Sox Nation and the effects of winning two World Series on its (formerly "angst-ridden") citizenry. A die-hard fan herself, Bass notes that the Red Sox have "became a national phenomenon, enjoying a community that is rooted to whatever space it occupies at any given moment."

Many of the remaining essays rely on their author's personal experiences, yet all of them are also about sport, community, and identity. David W. Zang reflects on the ways in which Penn State University football "fans draw their sense of community from the shared belief that Happy Valley is not only a mythic place, but a singularly righteous one as well." A Penn State fan, like his father, Zang puts legendary coach Joe Paterno at the center of his narrative and sees "Happy Valley as a fantastical American Brigadoon" that may vanish after Paterno. Focusing on The University of Kansas (KU), traditionally a college basketball powerhouse, Michael Ezra's essay is something akin to a sports fan bildungsroman. He recounts his journey from antagonism for KU basketball to appreciation and pride.

Thanks to superb mentoring and his own maturation, Ezra realizes that some of the values he learned as an American studies graduate student—community building, teamwork, and the pursuit of excellence—explain Kansans' commitment to and love for Jayhawk basketball.

Susan Cahn shares a different kind of sports odyssey. It takes us from suburban Chicago to the West Coast to the upper-Midwest and finally to Buffalo, New York. Cahn's poignant story is about sports played for different reasons in different communities. It's about coming to terms with her lesbian identity, finding supportive spaces comprised of people who respect difference, and a regular pickup basketball game at a community center known as "The Bob." "Basketball at the Bob," she writes, "is about familiarity, a sense of belonging, meaningful activity, and ties that bind." Mike Tanier, too, takes us on a journey. His essay "is the story of Philadelphia after sunset, of the fan life that on-field cameras cannot capture." Traversing different paths that take us from Broad Street to Locust Street, from Pattison Avenue to City Line Avenue, all the way to Bethlehem (where the Eagles have their football training camp), sixty miles north of Philadelphia, Tanier's nocturne is kaleidoscopic. It's the portrait of a massive, eclectic community and some of its many sporting passions. Finally, Carlo Rotella's essay is about the cult of Micky Ward, the Lowell, Massachusetts, boxer whose story is told in the film *The Fighter* (2010). Offering a rich, historically inflected reading of Ward and *The Fighter,* Rotella traces "large-scale flows of resources, power, people, and meanings." He explains: "To talk about Micky Ward is to talk not only about some really stirring ass whippings, but also about major historical transformations that extend far beyond eastern Massachusetts." Among them are "tribal pride," industrial urbanism, and a particular kind of manhood.

Although rich and diverse, the fourteen essays collected here are not intended to be comprehensive. No anthology, no monograph, no encyclopedia can include everything. Every work has gaps or is in some way incomplete. There are many interesting examples of the sport, community, and identity nexus that are unfortunately not in these pages. NASCAR, for example. Clearly millions of people in this country love and deeply identify with NASCAR and constitute a wide-ranging, national community. A number of the people familiar with this project thought that "the country club set," "the polo crowd," sports radio listening communities, Las Vegas and gambling communities, NFL fans, and bowling leagues deserved to be written about. Yes, good points all. Some also mentioned other places where the sport, community, and identity nexus seemed especially vibrant to them: places like Cooperstown, New York; Lexington, Kentucky; and Clarkston,

Georgia.³⁶ One person suggested that it was difficult "to think about spectator sports and community identity in the U.S. without reference to settler colonialism, and to racial discrimination more generally." This person had in mind the Chief Illiniwek controversy at the University of Illinois, "a clear case when 'community' was purchased at the expense of people excluded from it and their 'identity' was suppressed."³⁷ This is an excellent example of Miranda Joseph's central argument: namely, that community is not an unalloyed good. Like all human endeavors, it can be problematic. The same is true of the sport, community, and identity nexus. One would have to be critically naive to ignore how sport is sometimes used reprehensibly, to oppress or diminish individuals and groups, to divide people from one another. The larger point here is that this book and the essays in it have far from exhausted the possibilities of this subject; indeed, my hope is that they illuminate them and inspire others.

One last point. A few years ago, *Sports Illustrated* reported: "Nowhere is the bond between team and town as tight as in Pittsburgh, where four decades of excellence have made the Steelers a civic icon."³⁸ The Steelers are an important civic icon about which many people feel deeply passionate. But nowhere else? How about Green Bay? How about St. Louis or Boston? Lincoln, Nebraska, or Durham, North Carolina? Massillon, Ohio, or Smith Center, Kansas? The point is, pick your place and we can find vivid examples of people cheering with all their heart for the home team. This is not a new phenomenon. Consider what historian and baseball fan Doris Kearns Goodwin has to say in Ken Burns's *Baseball* (1994):

> I think in the past that certainly Brooklyn's character was defined by the Brooklyn Dodgers. I mean, even just the name Dodgers coming from these trolley cars that everybody had to dodge. The idea that Brooklyn felt a stepchild to New York City, and that somehow the Dodgers, the Bums, were stepchilds [sic] too, that were going to show the hoty-toty [sic] New Yorkers that we were really better than them, defined who Brooklyn was. And even in Long Island where I grew up, I felt that sense of Brooklyn, and it was all part of the Dodgers. I don't know that that exists today in the same way, that you define who you are through your team and through your city. And I think it's a loss, it means that people are more fragmented, they've got themselves and a few friends, but they don't have that group sense, unless there's a win, but that's not the same, that's not what this was all about, we hardly ever won and it didn't matter.³⁹

Yes and no. On the one hand, Goodwin is correct. Many people in Brooklyn used the Dodgers to formulate their personal and civic identity, and to solidify their membership in the community, and they did so by contrasting themselves to people living across the river in Manhattan, which seemed to some like a different universe rather than another borough. This theme comes across in many sources, including Roger Kahn's acclaimed *The Boys of Summer* (1972). And yes, there is a great deal of social fragmentation in the United States. On the other hand, Goodwin is wrong to suggest that people no longer define themselves and their communities via sports. People all over the country still do this. For many Americans, sports are an important source of communal belonging, and can provide shared touchstones, contexts in which people can be together.[40] The essays collected here demonstrate this in numerous fascinating ways.

Notes

1. Accessed February 23, 2011, http://www.dangable.com/dangablefacts.html. For more on wrestling's significance in Iowa, see Richard Hoffer, "The Pride of Iowa," *Sports Illustrated*, March 12, 2007, 56–60.

2. For more on Iowa and sport, see Douglas Hochstetler, "'America Needs Farmers': Communal Identity, the University of Iowa Football Team and the Farm Crisis of the 1980s," *International Journal of the History of Sport* 27 (2010): 1360–78.

3. Stephanie Coontz, *The Way We Never Were: American Families and the Nostalgia Trap* (New York: BasicBooks, 1992), 6.

4. Mark Dyreson, "Maybe It's Better to Bowl Alone: Sport, Community, and Democracy in American Thought," *Culture, Society, Sport* 4 (Spring 2001): 26.

5. Shelia L. Croucher, *Globalization and Belonging: The Politics of Identity in a Changing World* (Lanham, Md.: Rowman & Littlefield, Publishers, 2004).

6. Mark Starr, "Blood, Sweat and Cheers," *Newsweek*, October 25, 1999, 42.

7. In *How Soccer Explains the World: An [Unlikely] Theory of Globalization* (2004), for example, journalist Franklin Foer demonstrates that in many places sport "is often more deeply felt than religion, and just as much a part of the community's fabric, a repository of traditions," a source of collective identity. Much of the international scholarship on this subject focuses on the nation-state and national identity, rather than on cities and smaller, local communities. For examples, see below. Franklin Foer, *How Soccer Explains the World: An [Unlikely] Theory of Globalization* (New York: HarperCollins, 2004), 4. Alan Bairner, *Sport, Nationalism, and Globalization: European and North American Perspectives* (Albany: State University of New York Press, 2001); Mike Cronin, *Sport and Nationalism in Ireland: Gaelic Games, Soccer and Irish identity since 1884* (Dublin: Four Courts Press, 1999); Grant Jarvie and John Burnett, eds., *Sport, Scotland, and the Scots* (Easton Linton, Scotland: Tuckwell Press, 2000); Martin Johnes, "Eighty Minute Patriots? National Identity and Sport in Modern Wales," *International Journal of the History of Sport* 17 (December 2000): 93–110; John Nauright, *Sport, Cultures and Identities in South Africa* (London: Leicester University Press, 1997).

8. Richard Lipsky, *How We Play the Game: Why Sports Dominate American Life* (Boston: Beacon Press, 1981), 5.

9. Günther Lüschen, "The Interdependence of Sport and Culture," *International Review of Sport Sociology* 2 (March 1967): 136.

10. Turner writes: "Essentially, communitas is a relationship between concrete, historical, idiosyncratic individuals." Victor Turner, *Ritual Process: Structure and Anti-Structure* (New York: Aldine de Gruyter, [1969] 1995), 131. This is how the OED defines *communitas:* "A strong sense of solidarity and bonding that develops among people experiencing a ritual, rite of passage, or other transitional state together." For more on *communitas,* see Tim Olaveson, "Collective Effervescence and Communitas: Processual Models of Ritual and Society in Emile Durkheim and Victor Turner," *Dialectical Anthropology* 26 (2001): 89–124; Alan G. Ingham and Mary G. McDonald, "Sport and Community/Communitas," in *Sporting Dystopias: The Making and Meanings of Urban Sport Cultures,* ed. Ralph C. Wilcox et al. (Albany: State University of New York Press, 2003), 17–33.

11. The phrase "the thrill of victory and the agony of defeat" means something specific to those of us who remember ABC's *Wide World of Sports,* which was produced by Roone Arledge.

12. Mark Frost, *Game Six: Cincinnati, Boston, and the 1975 World Series: The Triumph of America's Pastime* (New York: Hyperion, 2009).

13. Roland L. Warren, *The Community in America* (Chicago: Rand McNally, 1963), 6.

14. Thomas Bender, *Community and Social Change in America* (New Brunswick, N.J.: Rutgers University Press, 1978), 6.

15. Benedict Anderson, *Imagined Communities: Reflections on the Rise and Spread of Nationalism* (New York: Verso, [1983] 1985), 15.

16. *New Oxford American Dictionary.*

17. The prefix *com* has Latin origins and means with; together; jointly; altogether. For older but still useful studies on community, see Irwin T. Sanders, *The Community: An Introduction to a Social System* (New York: Ronald Press, 1958); Conrad M. Arensberg and Solon Toothaker Kimball, *Culture and Community* (New York: Harcourt, Brace & World, 1965); David W. Minar and Scott A. Greer, *The Concept of Community: Readings with Interpretations* (Chicago: Aldine Publishing, 1969); Gerald D. Suttles, *The Social Construction of Communities* (Chicago: University of Chicago Press, 1972).

18. Robert D. Putnam, *Bowling Alone: The Collapse and Revival of American Community* (New York: Simon & Schuster, 2000), 28.

19. Peter Dahlgren and Colin Sparks, eds., *Journalism and Popular Culture* (London: Sage, 1992), 15.

20. Bender, *Community and Social Change in America,* 7.

21. Winnie Hu, "After 88 Years of Rivalry, the Last as Us and Them," *New York Times,* November 22, 2007, B1.

22. Gloria Anzaldúa, *Borderlands/La Frontera: The New Mestiza,* 2nd ed. (San Francisco: Aunt Lute Books, [1987] 1999), 25.

23. Miranda Joseph, *Against the Romance of Community* (Minneapolis: University of Minnesota Press, 2002), vii.

24. Joseph, *Against the Romance of Community,* viii.

25. Ibid., ix.

26. *Sports Illustrated,* March 21, 2011, 12.

27. David P. Barash, "The Roar of the Crowd," *Chronicle Review,* March 20, 2009, B10.

28. Barash, "The Roar of the Crowd," B8.

29. Alan G. Ingham, Jeremy W. Howell, and Todd S. Schilperoort, "Professional Sports and Community: A Review and Exegesis," *Exercise and Sport Sciences Reviews* 15 (1987): 427–65; Mae Shaw, "Community development and the politics of community," *Community Development Journal* 43 (2008): 24–36.

30. Joseph, *Against the Romance of Community,* xxiii.

31. Joe Queenan, *True Believers: The Tragic Inner Life of Sports Fans* (New York: Henry Holt, 2003), 71.

32. John Alcock, *Animal Behavior: An Evolutionary Approach,* 9th ed. (Sunderland, Mass.: Sinauer Associates, 2009), 69.

33. Nick Hornby, *Fever Pitch* (London: Penguin Books, [1992] 2000), 27.

34. Frank Deford, "Seasons of Discontent," *Newsweek,* December 29, 1997–January 5, 1998, 74.

35. Ibid., 74.

36. The latter is an Atlanta suburb and the subject of Warren St. John's *Outcasts United: A Refugee Team, an American Town* (2009). In the last twenty years, Clarkston has been transformed from a sleepy, mostly white community to the home of a few thousand refugees, from some of the world's most war-ravaged countries: Afghanistan, Bosnia, Congo, Gambia, Iraq, Kosovo, Liberia, Somalia, and Sudan. St. John explains: "the newcomers in Clarkston were not a homogenous linguistic or cultural group of, say, Somalis, whose appearance had transformed some small American towns like Lewiston, Maine, but a sampling of the world's citizens from dozens of countries and ethnic groups. The local high school in Clarkston, once all white, now had students from more than fifty different countries. Cultures were colliding in Clarkston, and the result was a raw and exceptionally charged experiment in getting along." One of the few things this heterogeneous collection of refugees had and has in common is sport, specifically soccer. For many of the ten- to eighteen-year-old players on three boys teams and a newly formed girls team, the Fugees are more than a sports club; it is a haven for young people "caught between worlds, first as teenagers moving from childhood to adulthood, but also as resettled refugees, transitioning from one culture to another." The Fugees have developed important relationships among themselves, with coach Luma Mufleh, and with the volunteers who serve as their academic tutors. Still, at its core, the Fugees is a soccer team. Its members play to have fun, for the camaraderie, and to win. Far from their native lands, they play together and in the process have developed what St. John describes as "a new type of community." Warren St. John, *Outcasts United: A Refugee Soccer Team, an American Town* (New York: Spiegel & Grau, 2009), 9, 221.

37. The "Chief Illiniwek controversy" is a specific example, at the University of Illinois, of the larger issue of athletic teams using Native American names and imagery in ways that many people find racist. For more on Chief Illiniwek, see *In Whose Honor?: American Indian Mascots in Sports,* DVD, produced by Jay Rosenstein (Ho-ho-kus, N.J.: New Day Films, 1997). For more on this subject, see C. Richard King and Charles Fruehling Springwood, ed., *Team Spirits: The Native American Mascots Controversy* (Lincoln: University of Nebraska Press, 2000) and Carol Spindel, *Dancing at Halftime: Sports and the Controversy over American Indian Mascots* (New York: New York University Press, 2000).

38. Tim Layden, "We Are Family," *Sports Illustrated*, February 2, 2009, 45.

39. Quoted in *Baseball*, "5th Inning: Shadow Ball, 1930–1940," produced by Ken Burns and Lynn Novick (Florentine Films, 1994, videocassette).

40. Hornby, *Fever Pitch*, 8.

1. Basketball and Magic in "Middletown"

Locating Sport and Culture in American Social Science

MARK DYRESON

Tales of "Primitive" Argonauts and Heartland Tribes

In the 1920s a team of social scientists descended on a "typical" American city. They were determined to unravel the secrets of communal identity and discover the laws that governed culture change. Using methodologies originally practiced by anthropologists to catalog the lifeways of non-Western cultures in locales far from the urban-industrial core of the twentieth-century Occident, the scientific observers settled among the heartland townsfolk and got to work.[1] They set out to chronicle, in their words, "the life of the people in the city, selected as a unit complex of interwoven trends of behavior."[2] Their study imitated the anthropological methods invented by Bronislaw Malinowski in *Argonauts of the Western Pacific* (1922) and Alfred Reginald Radcliffe-Brown in *The Andaman Islanders* (1922). Those two pioneering works captured the imaginations of both the world's leading social scientists and the general public with tales of the exotic habits of so-called primitives and their explanations of the novel concept that something they labeled as "culture" defined human-ness. The books made their authors famous and rich.[3]

Hoping to replicate the success of Malinowski and Radcliffe-Brown, the Lynd-led scientific team embedded itself in a modern American tribe. The team gave the small heartland city a pseudonym, dubbing it "Middletown" to connote their assessment that the site represented an archetype with the power to explain patterns in any American community. They charted work and leisure, home and family, religion and government. The researchers analyzed coming-of-age rituals and patterns of community. The team argued that they had found a culture that had been radically transformed in just a decade by the automobile and the radio. The new technologies and the culture of consumption in which they were embedded, the researchers feared, had frayed the communal fabric of Middletown to the breaking point.[4]

Certitude in a Capricious Universe:
The Function of "Magic Middletown"

Counteracting the corrosive forces of the car and the airwaves, the scientists discovered another "technology" that built communal solidarity.[5] That technology inhabited the largest structure on the campus of the key institution designed to transform children into adults—the high school gymnasium, where "the five boys who wear the colors of 'Magic Middletown,'" as the scientists colorfully put it, performed regular civic rituals that animated the essential "being" of the city. The anthropological interlopers contended that in this magical ritual "no distinctions divide the crowds which pack the school gymnasium for home games and which in every kind of machine crowd the roads for out-of-town games. North Side and South Side, Catholic and Kluxer, banker and machinist—their one shout is 'Eat 'em beat 'em, Bearcats!'" They reported that the denizens of "Middletown" identified the "meanest man" in town as a grouch who hated basketball.[6]

In 1929 the research team leaders, Robert and Helen Lynd, published their findings as a book titled *Middletown: A Study in Contemporary American Culture*. The first *Middletown* volume became an instant hit among social scientists, media pundits, and general readers. The Lynds, happily returned from their fieldwork to Manhattan, were overjoyed to discover their book on the "best seller" table at Brentano's, the New York City bookstore that served as a favorite haunt of the American intelligentsia.[7] Over the next half-century, *Middletown* grew in stature. One 1970 study ranked it among the twenty-five most significant books in the history of the republic.[8] In their study the Lynds revealed that Middletown was a real place—Muncie, Indiana. The Bearcats was the actual name of the high school basketball team at Muncie Central High School. Basketball, they marveled, captured the magical essence of Muncie. The Lynds insisted that "Magic Middletown," the cultural essence of the community, appeared more fully on the high school basketball court than in any other realm of heartland tribal life.[9]

The Dearth of Sociological Imagination on Sport

The Lynds' work on "Magic Middletown" marked a turning point in American social science and placed the idea that sport forged community firmly into the scholarly lexicon. Before the Lynds put basketball at the center of Middletown's lifeways, a variety of American thinkers had pondered the links between sport and communal identity, but the topic had remained on the margins of social science research. That oversight reveals an astonishing lack of "sociological imagination" in the field. The concept of a "sociological imagination," a theory coined by the mid-twentieth-century American sociologist C. Wright Mills, refers to a fundamental premise in modern social science scholarship, the notion that linking large-scale social forces to the lives of real people to explain how specific social structures produce certain social outcomes rests at the heart of their intellectual endeavor.[10] That most American sociologists failed to appreciate what many Americans had known for centuries, or at least since the founding of the Schuylkill River Colony Fishing Club in 1732, when the political leadership who inhabited William Penn's sylvan landscapes had created a sporting club to advertise their identity as the best and brightest in the American colonies, represents a serious shortcoming in the sociological imaginations of professional social scientists.[11]

From the colonial period until the Lynds' dramatic 1929 announcement that high school basketball shaped communal identity in Indiana, Americans without doctorates in sociology had been busy creating all manner of identities through sport, as participants, spectators, and patrons.[12] Americans forged gender, ethnic, racial, and class identities through sport. They built local, regional, and eventually national identities around their sporting pastimes, as politicians such as Theodore Roosevelt, who used sport to win favor with the masses and to outline his political ideas, and entrepreneurs such as Albert Goodwill Spalding, who used baseball to build a national community of consumers to exploit, understood innately. Some scholars outside of sociology—in theology, literature, philosophy, and the emerging disciplines of physical education and public health—had by 1929 already written extensively about the crucial role of sport in shaping national identity. Indeed, that basic idea had been the central attraction of Thomas Hughes's novel *Tom Brown's School Days* (1859) that in the English-speaking world stood as a literary rite of passage for a century of generations of boys.[13]

Only an occasional social scientist had even bothered to play around the edges of the idea prior to 1929, most notably the delightfully disturbing

Thorstein Veblen in his classic *The Theory of the Leisure Class* (1899), but also the brilliant pragmatist William James, the dour laissez-faire fundamentalist William Graham Sumner, and the encyclopedic enthnographer Edward Stewart Culin.[14] Professional sociologists came very late to sport-as-community-identity party, joining the sportswriters, journalists, politicians, and athletic boosters of all stripes who had been making such claims for more than a century.[15] With the publication of *Middletown* in 1929, followed by Robert Lynd turning those parts of that project, which he supposedly wrote without wife Helen Lynd's aid, into his dissertation for a Columbia University doctorate in sociology in 1931, the idea that sport possessed the magic to conjure the mysterious bonds of community found its permanent shelf in the tool cabinet of modern social science.[16]

Of Magic and Social Science

The Lynds' use of the term "magic" illuminates several crucial aspects of their Middletown ethnography. The term had a history. In the early 1900s Muncie's civic boosters had labeled the town "Magic City" to highlight its rapid growth and to advertise its commercial and cultural wares to the world. The Lynds knew that "Magic City" had become the community's unofficial nickname for itself.[17] Magic as a concept also held important anthropological connotations for the Lynds. The works of Malinowski and Radcliffe-Brown offered modern voyeurs extensive surveys of the magical practices of Pacific Islanders.[18] The two anthropologists offered logical explanations for the function of what from modern perspectives seemed like illogical practices. In their new anthropological formula, magic was transformed from an irrational superstition into a logical response to the reality of an unpredictable universe.

The Lynds' Middletown study made basketball appear as magical as the sorcery practiced by Malinowski's Western Pacific Argonauts or Radcliffe-Brown's Andaman Islanders. Basketball seemed a magical apparition to the husband and wife team. The Lynds were not basketball fans and had no discernible connection to or knowledge of the sport, even though they were great admirers and supporters of the Young Men's Christian Association (YMCA) and ran in the same Protestant Social Gospel circles where basketball had been invented as a missionary game.[19] To the Lynds, the magic of basketball seemed an inexplicable and alien force, even though Robert spent his childhood in Indiana in the early twentieth century when the initial eruption of "Hoosier hysteria" swept the state. The game sprang to life in 1891 at the YMCA college in Springfield, Massachusetts—a city that ironically had been on the short list for the Middletown study before Muncie had been selected. The game quickly migrated from the YMCA into American schools and colleges. Basketball had already made an imprint at the elite campuses where the Lynds earned their undergraduate degrees. Robert graduated from Princeton in 1914, while Helen graduated from Wellesley in 1919, one of the "seven sisters" where a women's version of basketball designed by Smith College physical educator Senda Berenson thrived in this period.[20]

The Lynds' lack of familiarity with basketball before they shipped out for Muncie seems in retrospect an enormous surprise. Not only did the new game swirl about the schools and colleges they inhabited, but it also gurgled through the intellectual neighborhoods in which they lived. Basketball represented a key invention designed by the Lynds' progressive fellow travelers, the Social Gospelers and social engineers of the neo-benevolent empire who sought to redesign the United States for modernity. The game, as the sagacious scholar of sport Allen Guttmann has observed, "was made to order, cut from whole cloth in response to a specific request."[21]

Scissored specifically to draw the urban masses that the YMCA coveted into the massive chain of gymnasiums the sporting evangelists had recently built for wintertime recreation, the belief that team sports could reanimate the mysterious bonds of democratic community under modern conditions formed the broader pattern underneath the design of basketball.[22] A caption from a 1914 cover of *The Playground* magazine, a canonical text in the gospel of American sporting republicanism during the Progressive Era, captured the ardor of the social architects' faith in the power of athletic endeavors to guarantee the commonweal. "The boy learns that basketball is impossible unless the rules of the game are followed and that civilization, like basketball, is based on the rules of the game," rhapsodized the *Playground* beneath a photograph depicting order being imposed by James Naismith's invention on the asphalt jungle of an unnamed American city.[23]

The Lynds went to Middletown with a plan to measure how modernity, in particular the rise of a consumer society, had fractured the commonweal of the small midwestern cities that they imagined, until recently, stood as bastions of American-style *gemeinschaft,* of communal solidarity based on common tradition. By picking Muncie as Middletown, they sought a site that they thought had once been a singular community centered on the common traditions of the white, Protestant, agrarian culture that the Lynds believed formed the original core of American civilization. They rejected several other cities, including basketball-birthplace Springfield, Massachusetts, as too diverse, too heterogeneous, and too ethnic for their purposes. The Lynds had pondered making South Bend, Indiana, their subject city, but ultimately cast it aside for the same reasons they rejected Springfield.[24] One can only imagine that had they studied South Bend, then Notre Dame's brand of college football—and not Muncie's strain of high school basketball—would have appeared to the Lynds as the "magic" glue that had the potential to produce common traditions in an age of *gesellschaft*, the urban, industrial swirl of modern existence.

They ultimately disembarked for fieldwork in Muncie rather than South Bend, and soon discovered basketball, a sport that had been all around them since their childhoods. No longer blind but rather "basketball-sighted," the Lynds sought to explain the wintertime rituals of "Magic Middletown" on the hardwood floors at the high school's main cathedral. Middletown's passion for basketball seemed to the Lynds a mysterious cultural practice that on the surface did not make any more sense to the trained acumen of a modern social scientist than the magical rituals of Pacific Islanders had, on initial observation, made to Radcliffe-Brown and Malinowski. Though their time in Indiana did not make them converts to "Hoosier Hysteria," the Lynds quickly discovered that basketball gave meaning, structure, and predictability to the tribes who inhabited Middletown. In identifying the cultural function of basketball in Middletown, they followed the lead of their anthropological muses who explained the magic of Western Pacific tribes as a mechanism for making sense of a complex and sometimes unintelligible world—a cultural tool at the heart of the human enterprise. The basketball games that "Magic Middletown" played against its many rivals helped the inhabitants of Muncie make sense of an uncertain universe.

Hoosier Hysteria and Magical Function

Ever since the Lynds first illuminated Hoosier Hysteria for the nation in their best-selling books, American observers have looked at Indiana and have seen a state consumed by a passion for high school basketball that has—to both outsiders and tribal members—bordered on the irrational. A history of Indiana pitched at grade-school children explains it directly: "When basketball season arrives, Indianans go wild. No other state gets quite as excited about its high school basketball teams. As a result, tournament time is called Hoosier Hysteria."[25] Another juvenile textbook takes a more understated approach: "People from Indiana are called Hoosiers. They take their basketball seriously."[26] Explanations for adults take a similar tack. In a volume devoted to excavating the Indiana essence by Indiana natives, the novelist James Alexander Thorn posits: "As everyone knows, Indiana is divided into two parts: 1. Basketball. 2. All That Other Stuff."[27] In the same volume, the writer Hal Higdon admits, "Nobody can deny basketball's magical appeal in Indiana."[28]

Outsiders, like the Lynds, have also for more than a century defined "Indiana-ness" through high school basketball. The New York City–based journalist and novelist John R. Tunis satirically captured "Hoosier Hysteria" in his epic "Ain't God Good to Indiana!" Tunis jested, "Folks there tell you that a Hoosier talks basketball for an hour after he is dead and has stopped breathing."[29] More recently, Hollywood has mined "Hoosier Hysteria" and struck pop cultural gold. As the film critic Roger Ebert admits, in spite of its cloying formulaic melodrama, *Hoosiers* (1986)—the cinematic homage to David beating Goliath in Indiana high school basketball—touched an American nerve. Ebert notes that the film offers nothing original, but acknowledges: "'Hoosiers' works a magic . . . in getting us to really care about the fate of the team and the people depending on it. . . . It's a movie that is all heart."[30]

Even social scientists have fallen under the sway of Magic Middletown. Assessing a 1949 report by the state government warning that basketball had usurped important academic functions in the schools, one of the leading historians of Indiana, Howard Henry Peckham, dismissed the study. "It underestimated the social value of basketball in unifying a community," Peckham retorted. "Regardless of politics, religion, or educational levels everyone can rally around the high school team."[31]

Basketball in Middletown: The Original Version

In their original 1929 study the Lynds commented on the significance of sport in general and the special place of high school basketball in the cultural hearts of their subjects. Charting the rapid transformation of Middletown from tradition to modernity, the Lynds contended that sport had become one of the significant features of the new order. They argued that in 1890 sport had been a sporadic and unorganized pursuit. By the 1920s a remarkable transformation had occurred. The city's leaders established a YMCA and a Young Women's Christian Association (YWCA). Gymnasiums, golf courses, and athletic leagues had sprouted throughout the city. Children, adolescents, and young adults participated in sport with the highest frequency, but members of all age groups sometimes played. Although males dominated the ranks of participants in all age categories, women also played sports. Changes in the volume of press coverage of sport indicated that it was increasingly a *lingua franca* for the modernizing community.[32]

While Middletown played and watched a multitude of sports, high school basketball clearly captured the city's affection. Among the student sub-culture, no higher honor could be attained than the captain's role on the basketball squad. The rest of the team members enjoyed a status nearly as high. The Lynds explained that basketball played a tremendously significant role in intergenerational relations in Middletown society, making the lives of adolescents important even to adults. Even the business elites that held the most power in the culture momentarily bowed to the prowess of the high school basketball stars. "The business man may 'lay down the law' to his adolescent son or daughter at home and patronize their friends, but in the basket-ball grandstand he is if anything a little less important than these youngsters of his who actually mingle daily with those five boys who wear the colors of 'Magic Middletown,'" the Lynds marveled.[33]

The Lynds insisted that high school basketball served as the most im-portant nexus of group solidarity in Middletown, outranking all other economic, social, religious, and political institutions. Their oft-quoted ethnographic limerick—"North Side and South Side, Catholic and Kluxer, banker and machinist—their one shout is 'Eat 'em beat 'em, Bearcats!'"—reinforced the magical power of basketball.[34] The Lynds' study concluded that modernity had fundamentally disenchanted the older communal cos-mos that had bound together the traditional Middletown, driving social fault lines between not only neighborhoods, religious congregations, and economic classes, but also cleaving the bonds between individuals inside those groupings. Only basketball, a game for which the Lynds had no real affinity, remained to re-enchant the mystic chords of commonweal.

Explaining the Magic of Basketball

Magical Middletown basketball thus confounded the Lynds, and they turned to magical interpretations offered by their anthropological muses in earlier studies of Pacific Islanders. Malinoswki and Radcliffe-Brown had argued that magic made sense when it helped the inhabitants of a culture function in a capricious universe. The Lynds combined this notion of magic with the classical sociological truism that the transition from tradition to modernity propelled cultures from stability, predictability, and order to dislocation, uncertainty, and alienation—key elements in the chaos of modernity.[35] High school basketball rituals offered Middletown two crucial necessities, the Lynds posited: "One is assurance in the face of the baf-fling too-bigness of European wars, death, North Poles, ill health, business worries, and political graft; the bigness of it all shrinks at a championship basket-ball game . . . and the whole business of living in Middletown suddenly 'fits' again, and one 'belongs'; one is a citizen of no mean city, and presumably, no mean citizen."[36] Basketball allowed Middletown citizens to escape from the unmanageable complexities of modern life and to find meaning in their existence, a magical process in the Lynds' estimation.

The Lynds identified a second crucial necessity high school basketball supplied that presented itself as a neat corollary to the first finding. The feats of "Magic Middletown" in high school basketball contests produced what a later generation of sociologists would call "other-directedness," a magnetic force that allowed Middletownians to identify their individual well-being with the cohesiveness and success of their community. The team represented the town. Its victories were the town's victories. Through the magical powers of sport "they" became "we" and the sweat and skill of a dozen high school boys became the corporate property of the entire community. The Lynds admitted that this process, which they cited as a form of Bronislaw Malinowski's law of cultural unity, was a "legal fiction" that certain groups used for their own purposes. Nevertheless, it was a "legal fiction" that made culture possible in Middletown just as it did in the Western Pacific.[37] By the magic of basketball, Middletown survived the headlong rush into modernity as a cohesive cultural entity. There was a there there, to spin Gertrude Stein's famous line in a communal direction, at least on winter evenings in the massive gymnasium at the high school where "Magic Middletown's" Bearcats ruled the hardwoods.[38]

Basketball in Middletown Revisited

A decade after their first field trip, the Lynds returned to "Middletown" to measure the dislocations of the Great Depression. They published a 1937 follow-up study titled *Middletown in Transition: A Study in Cultural Conflicts.*[39] In general, the Lynds found that the economic collapse had not substantially altered the basic culture of "Middletown." They insisted in their follow-up study that "Middletown is overwhelmingly living by the values by which it lived in 1925," finding no evidence of a turn to radicalism or fascism or any other signs of the imminent social revolution that many intellectuals had predicted would soon come, not only to bohemian Manhattan but to the American heartland in the midst of the grim capitalist crisis.[40]

The Lynds observed on their return that basketball was still the city's great passion. The Bearcats basketball team still served as the town's "official emblem." Indeed, in the years between visits, the team rose on hardwood courts to statewide fame. In 1928 Muncie Central won the state high school championship, triumphing in the whirl of "Hoosier Hysteria" and cementing its status as the city's communal heart. After that monumental victory the city built an enormous field house that sat nine thousand spectators, the largest high school gymnasium in the nation. "Magic Middletown" filled the arena even as the economy collapsed. The dynamic cagers provided status, solace, and sense of belonging in the midst of the Depression, winning the state high school championship again in 1931. City officials ignored a municipal budget crisis and rewarded the team with gold watches for their second magical victory.[41]

The Lynds, never basketball fans themselves and always suspicious that a mere game rather than social science or the Social Gospel knit "Middletown" together, ultimately failed to grasp the power of the magic they had discovered. In spite of clear evidence to the contrary, they argued that by 1935 the frenzy over basketball had subsided. The Lynds insisted that the high cost of tickets, the onerous loan payments that critics claimed made the field house a "financial white elephant," the opening of a new high school, competition from a new team at the local college, and a widespread program of school and community sports that provided opportunities to a large portion of the population, had eroded the grip that Bearcats basketball had on Middletown's culture. The Lynds insisted that the shine had worn off the varsity elites who represented "Magic Middletown." They concluded that the "depression years have apparently pulled some of the Bearcats' teeth, and there is some question as to whether basketball will ever regain its former frenzied preeminence."[42] Having observed accurately that basketball had become a part of the culture of consumption that the Lynds believed was destroying the traditional communal fabric of American civilization, they concluded, less accurately as it turned out, that the game had lost its essential magic.[43]

"Magic Middletown" in the *Longue Durée*

In retrospect, the Lynds vastly exaggerated any trend toward decline in Middletown's interest in high school hoops.[44] They could not comprehend the full power of magical basketball rituals in Middletown. Though the Lynds hoped Middletownians might gravitate to some more noble pattern of culture than high school basketball, the game remained at the heart of the city's identity over the course of the twentieth century. True, they convinced a few nattering nabobs of sporting negativity, such as the erudite Manhattanite John Tunis, that high school basketball was a shallow imitation of true culture. Tunis, in the final analysis, sided with the Lynds.

"Once upon a time, throughout this vast region which Sinclair Lewis liked to call The Valley of Democracy, there was growth in arts and letters, there were statesmen of note and scholars turning out important work," Tunis preached. "Where are the successors to these creative talents?" he lamented. "They don't exist since basketball has become the folk art of the region."[45]

Middletown residents ignored Tunis's vitriol and continued to consume the folk art of basketball. In the decades following the initial studies, waves of social scientists retraced the Lynds' steps and descended on Middletown. They discovered that high school basketball remained at the center of the city's culture. In 1979, a half century after the publication of the Lynds' first work, a stolid social science study with the classic title "The Measurement of Social Change in Middletown" contended that when it came to basketball, nothing had in fact changed. "High school basketball still provides the community with its occasions of collective excitement," insisted the study's author, Theodore Caplow.[46] Middletown High, more accurately Muncie Central High, won six more state championships, in 1951, 1952, 1963, 1978, 1979, and 1988, ranking it as the all-time leader in the open classification state tournament that from 1911 to 1997 mixed all the state's schools, large and small, in the maelstrom of "Hoosier Hysteria."[47] As a footnote to Muncie Central's stellar hoops history, it played Goliath to Milan High School's David in the famous 1954 game that served as the grist for Hollywood's famous *Hoosiers*. Muncie Central lost again the next year in the quarterfinal of the state tournament, falling to Crispus Attucks High of Indianapolis as future basketball Hall of Famer Oscar Robertson led his squad on a journey that would culminate in a historic first championship for an all-black Indiana high school.[48]

The Mysterious Case of Race in the History of "Magic Middletown"

If the Lynds were ultimately blind to the enduring affinity for basketball in Muncie, they were also clearly deaf on the issue of race. They deliberately chose Muncie because it was overwhelming white and Protestant, not the multiethnic, religiously diverse city, such as basketball birthplace Springfield, that their sponsors at the Institute for Social and Religious Research, a group underwritten by John D. Rockefeller, had wanted as a study site. Muncie, a center of the Ku Klux Klan in the 1920s, had a small but significant African American community.[49] It was at the crossroads of race and basketball that the Lynds missed one of their most important sociological opportunities. In their original study the couple had noted the local YMCA had closed its doors to basketball games featuring racially integrated teams.[50] Later sociological studies of Middletown revealed that basketball represented a hotbed of racial conflict and exclusion. One African American informant related: "I think the first time I really felt the sting of racism it involved basketball."[51] A documentary film series about Middletown in the 1980s used basketball as the vehicle to explore black and white perceptions of the city.[52]

The Lynds' lack of affinity for the deeper meanings of basketball in American culture, in combination with their focus on "whiteness" as the basic color of American *gemeinschaft*, led them to miss a profound sociological opportunity in their deconstruction of "Magic Middletown." Their inattention to racial and social conflicts in basketball prevented the Lynds from anticipating the insights of C. L. R. James just a few decades later in his magisterial exploration of the essential meanings of sport in modern cultures, *Beyond a Boundary* (1963). James deciphered the myriad complexities of the ways in which sport provided mechanisms to define, negotiate, and alter racial, social, and political boundaries in the ages of *gesellschaft*.[53]

Lacking the sociological imagination of James, the Lynds simply ignored the boundaries in sport and society that shaped the communal fabric of Middletown. Their ignorance becomes more profound when the history of basketball in Indiana in the macrocosm and at Muncie Central High School in the microcosm comes into sharp relief. Racial and religious boundaries clove "Hoosier hysteria" from its origins. The Indiana High School Athletic Association, founded in 1903, excluded black and Catholic high schools until the Second World War. By design, high school basketball symbolized the white, Protestant dominion that ruled Indiana culture.[54] The Hoosier schoolboy stars evoked the traditions of the agrarian yeomen who once ruled the American republic against the heterodox challengers from the urban-industrial behemoth of modernity. Those folk had been in the Lynds' historical template the very marrow of the *gemeinschaft* nation's culture. Martinsville's John Wooden, later basketball's most famous coach, typified this rural, Puritan archetype when he led his small-town school to a victory over Muncie Central in the 1927 state title game.[55]

Knowledge of this history could have led the Lynds to a richer translation of whether "Catholic and Kluxer" actually integrated into a sociological whole through magical basketball rituals. The possibilities would have been magnified had the Lynds known that Pete Jolly, Muncie Central's venerated basketball coach and history teacher, who in a five-year span from 1927 to 1931 led the team to four state championship games and won two titles (1927 and 1931), readily confessed to students that he had joined the Ku

Muncie Central High School Basketball Team, 1929–1930. Coach Pete Jolly
is in the upper left of the photo. Jack Mann is front and center. Courtesy of
W. A. Swift photographs, Archives and Special Collections, Ball State
University Libraries.

Klux Klan. Despite Jolly's dalliance with the Klan, a Jewish student later
remembered him as "a great guy who didn't know much about history or
teaching."[56] Still, the reality that a "Kluxer," even a relatively indifferent
one, helmed Magic Middletown's cagers underscores the irony of the Lynds'
identification of basketball as the tool that allegedly dissolved religious and
racial boundaries.

An even greater irony emerges when considering that Jack Mann, a 6' 8"
African American center, led "Magic Middletown" to the 1931 state championship. Indiana newspapers referred to Mann constantly as the "giant
Negro" or even the "titanic Negro" as he dominated the hardwood during
the 1930–1931 season.[57] Mann and another African American center, David
DeJernett of Washington High School, later became, in hysterical Hoosier
mythology, demigods in the first great epoch of Indiana high school basketball. They even battled one another in an epic clash in the 1930 state championship game, with DeJernett and Washington High emerging victorious.[58]

Muncie's team in the post-Klan era after Jolly retired, according to the recollections of the city's African American community, became much whiter in the 1950s and 1960s. Black players recalled an intense and pervasive discrimination that limited black representation on the squad to a handful of players over those decades, as Muncie Central won three more state championships (1951, 1952, and 1963).[59] Ironically, in the film *Hoosiers,* where Muncie Central is re-created by Hollywood as South Bend Central, several stellar black players led the team. In actuality, though Muncie Central did have three black players on the squad that lost the 1954 state championship to all-white Milan, the Bearcats featured predominantly white line-ups for most of their games.[60]

As this brief history of race in Muncie Central basketball reveals, how "they" became "we" in Magic Middletown posed many puzzles that remained far beyond the boundaries of the Lynds' sociological imaginations. Still, despite the many shortcomings of their explorations of basketball and common culture in Middletown, the enormous popularity of their work guaranteed that the riddles of sport and social identity would occupy a more central place in American social science in the future.

Magic Middletown represents not only a place in the landscape of Indiana and a station in the American transition from tradition to modernity, but a locale in imaginations of generations of American chroniclers of their own culture. Scenes of wintertime Friday nights in furnace-hot high school gymnasiums, where shorts-clad young bodies struggle up and down the hardwood while hundreds or thousands of their hometown folk cheer them as they vanquish squads of adolescents from neighboring towns and deliver the magic that animates the bonds of community, have become a standard motif in American ethnographies and memoirs, novels and poems, meditations and histories, films and documentaries. Magic Middletown provides the staple backdrop for cinematic treatments of the American heartland. Magic Middletown even provides a calculus for political pundits and sportswriters seeking to explain how basketball magically connected an urban African American politician to white, small-town voters in traditional "flyover" regions and even helped to produce a historic electoral victory that put Barack Obama in the White House.

"North Side and South Side, Catholic and Kluxer, banker and machinist—their one shout is 'Eat 'em beat 'em, Bearcats!'" marveled the Lynds. In the grand meta-narrative of the American migration from *gemeinschaft* to *gesellschaft,* basketball has indeed bewitched sociological imaginations. The secrets of how "they" become "we" through sport continue to fascinate us. Those secrets remain, as they did for the Lynds, in magical realms rather than social scientific locations.

Notes

1. The team was led by the husband-wife combination of Robert and Helen Merrell Lynd. They alighted in Muncie, Indiana, where they produced one of the great classics of American social science. Robert S. and Helen Merrell Lynd, *Middletown: A Study in Contemporary American Culture* (New York: Harcourt, Brace, 1929).

2. Ibid., 3.

3. Bronislaw Malinowski, *Argonauts of the Western Pacific: An Account of Native Enterprise and Adventure in the Archipelagoes of Melanesian New Guinea* (New York: E.P. Dutton, 1922); Alfred Reginald Radcliffe-Brown, *The Andaman Islanders: A Study in Social Anthropology* (Cambridge, U.K.: Cambridge University Press, 1922). For interesting analyses of the impact of Malinowksi and Radcliffe-Brown's work, see Alan Barnard, *History and Theory in Anthropology* (Cambridge, U.K.: Cambridge University Press, 2000); and Jerry D. Moore, *Visions of Culture: An Introduction to Anthropological Theories and Theorists* (Walnut Creek, Calif.: AltaMira Press, 1997).

4. Lynd and Lynd, *Middletown*. The Lynds' study made Muncie into the leading American laboratory for social scientists, spawning a host of other studies of the community throughout the twentieth century and into the twenty-first. As Arthur Vidich, a leading American sociological theorist, has argued, "Nowhere in the United States is there a comparable archive on a single American community that has been studied in depth over a period of seventy-five years." Vidich adds that the attention focused on the small midwestern city has made Muncie "the mother of 'the science of Muncieology.'" Arthur J. Vidich, "Foreword," in Rita Caccamo, *Back to Middletown: Three Generations of Sociological Reflections* (Stanford, Calif.: Stanford University Press, 2000), ix.

5. I have argued this claim about sport as a "social technology" in several places, most extensively in *Making the American Team: Sport, Culture and the Olympic Experience* (Urbana: University of Illinois Press, 1989).

6. Lynd and Lynd, *Middletown,* 212–14, 485–88.

7. Dwight Hoover, *Middletown Revisited,* Ball State Monograph Number Thirty-Four (Muncie, Ind.: Ball State University, 1990), 7; Helen Lynd, with the collaboration of Staughton Lynd, *Possibilities* (Bronxville, N.Y.: Friends of the Esther Rauschenbush Library, 1983), 40.

8. Robert B. Downs, *Books That Changed American Society* (New York: MacMillan, 1970).

9. Lynd and Lynd, *Middletown,* 212–14, 284–85, 485–88.

10. C. Wright Mills, *The Sociological Imagination* (New York: Oxford University Press, 1959).

11. A search of JSTOR sociological journals such as the *American Journal of Sociology, Social Forces,* and the *Annals of the American Academy of Political and Social Science* through 1930 reveals not a single title with the words "sport" or "sports."

12. For a particularly trenchant examination of nineteenth-century American common-sense notions of sport and community, see Benjamin G. Rader, "The Quest for Subcommunities and the Rise of American Sport," *American Quarterly* 29 (1977): 355–69.

13. Thomas Hughes, *Tom Brown's Schooldays* (orig. pub., Cambridge, U.K.: Macmillan, 1857; reprint ed., New York: Oxford University Press, 1989).

14. Thorstein Veblen, *The Theory of the Leisure Class: An Economic Study of Institutions* (New York: Macmillan, 1899); William James, "The Energies of Men," in *Essays on*

Faith and Morals, ed. Ralph Barton Perry (New York: Longmans, Green, 1943), 216—37; William James, *The Moral Equivalent of War* (New York: American Association for International Conciliation, 1910); William Graham Sumner, *On Liberty, Society, and Politics: The Essential Essays of William Graham Sumner,* ed. Robert C. Bannister (Indianapolis: Liberty Fund, 1992); Stewart Culin, "Games of the North American Indians," *Twenty Fourth-Annual Report of the Bureau of American Ethnology to the Smithsonian Institution, 1902–1903,* W. H. Holmes, chief (Washington, D.C.: GPO, 1907).

15. Dyreson, *Making the American Team;* Mark Dyreson, "Nature by Design: Modern American Ideas about Sport, Energy, Evolution, and Republics, 1865–1910," *Journal of Sport History* 26 (Fall 2003): 447–69. For instance, two special issues of the *Annals of the American Academy of Political and Social Science* (July 1909 and March 1910) sought to connect sport to social theory. The authors, however, were mainly sport and physical education promoters such as Luther Halsely Gulick and Dudley Sargent, rather than "professional" sociologists. The early journals of physical education and "sport studies" such as *The Playground* were replete with "sociological imaginings" about the power of sport, but the mainstream field largely ignored the phenomena. An occasional paper appeared in the *American Journal of Sociology.* W. I. Thomas, "The Gaming Instinct," *American Journal of Sociology* 6 (1901): 750–63; George Elliot Howard, "Social Psychology of the Spectator," *American Journal of Sociology* 18 (July 1912): 33–50. The "psychologist" (to use the term loosely, if appropriately) G. Stanley Hall and his disciples went on forever about the evolutionary play theory, but their work appeared more frequently in popular magazines and "sports" journals than in sociological reviews. For an excellent biography of Hall, see Dorothy Ross, *G. Stanley Hall: The Psychologist as Prophet* (Chicago: University of Chicago Press, 1972).

16. Hoover, *Middletown Revisited,* 7–10.

17. Dwight Hoover, *Magic Middletown* (Bloomington: University of Indiana Press, 1986); Hoover, *Middletown Revisited;* Lynd and Lynd, *Middletown,* 55, 407, 486.

18. For keen analyses of magic and function in the works of Malinowski and Radcliffe-Brown, see George C. Homans, "Anxiety and Ritual: The Theories of Malinowski and Radcliffe-Brown," *American Anthropologist* 43 (April–June 1941): 164–72; and Graham Cunningham, *Religion and Magic: Approaches and Theories* (New York: New York University Press, 1999).

19. Biographical sketches of the Lynds appear in Hoover, *Middletown Revisited,* and Caccamo, *Back to Middletown.*

20. Rob Rains and Hellen Carpenter, *James Naismith: The Man Who Invented Basketball* (Philadelphia: Temple University Press, 2009); Pamela Grundy and Susan Shackelford, *Shattering the Glass: The Remarkable History of Women's Basketball* (New York: New Press, 2005).

21. Allen Guttmann, *Games and Empires: Modern Sports and Cultural Imperialism* (New York: Columbia University Press, 1994), 97.

22. For broader discussions of these issues, see Mark Dyreson, "Icons of Liberty or Objects of Desire? American Women Olympians and the Politics of Consumption," *Journal of Contemporary History* 38 (July 2003): 435–60; and Mark Dyreson, "The Limits of Universal Claims: How Class, Gender, Race, and Ethnicity Shaped the Sporting Republic," and "The Idea of a Sporting Republic: Athletic Technology, American Political Culture, and Progressive Visions of Technology," in *Making the American Team,* 98–126, 180–98.

23. *The Playground,* September 1914.

24. For more on how the Lynds hijacked the original Small City Study financed by the John D. Rockefeller funded Institute for Social and Religious Research, which had been proposed to study a heterogeneous and diverse community, see Hoover, *Middletown Revisited,* and Caccamo, *Back to Middletown.*

25. Ann Heinrichs, *Indiana* (Minneapolis: Compass Point, 2004), 33.

26. *Indiana* (Mankato, Minn.: Capstone, [1997] 2003), 9. The 1997 edition lists for author, Capstone Press, Geography Dept. The 2003 edition lists for author, Ed Pell. There is also a 2000 edition that lists for author, Jeff Barnett, Capstone Press, Geography Dept.

27. James Alexander Thorn, "On Being an Old Stump," in *Where We Live: Essays about Indiana,* ed., David Hope (Bloomington: Indiana University Press, 1989), 97.

28. Hal Higdon, "Indiana Sports," in *Where We Live: Essays about Indiana,* David Hope, ed. (Bloomington: Indiana University Press, 1989), 89.

29. John R. Tunis, "Ain't God Good to Indiana!" in *The American Way of Sports* (New York: Duell, Sloane, and Pearce, 1958), 83.

30. Roger Ebert, "Hoosiers," *Chicago Sun Times,* February 27, 1997, accessed May 15, 2010, http://rogerebert.suntimes.com/apps/pbcs.dll/article?AID=/19870227/REVIEWS/702270303/1023.

31. Howard Henry Peckham, *Indiana: A History* (Urbana: University of Illinois Press, 2003), 185.

32. In 1890 sports had comprised 4 percent of the total news content of the local paper. By 1923 sport took a 16 percent share of the total—the highest rate of increase of any department. Lynd and Lynd, *Middletown,* 283–85.

33. Ibid., 212–14.

34. Ibid., 485.

35. An eclectic set of analyses of the sociology of modernity confirms the essentials of this pattern. See Immanuel Maurice Wallerstein, *The Uncertainties of Knowledge* (Philadelphia: Temple University Press, 2004); Nils Gilman, *Mandarins of the Future: Modernization Theory in Cold War America* (Baltimore: Johns Hopkins University Press, 2003); Thomas Carl Patterson, *Change and Development in the Twentieth Century* (New York: Berg, 1999); Alan Macfarlane, *The Riddle of the Modern World: Of Liberty, Wealth and Equality* (Basingstoke, U.K.: Palgrave, 2001); and Richard D. Brown, *Modernization: The Transformation of American Life, 1600–1865* (New York: Hill and Wang, 1976). In history of sport, the work of Allen Guttmann and others have made modernization theory a scholarly ritual. See Guttmann's totemic *From Ritual to Record: The Nature of Modern Sport* (New York: Columbia University Press, 1978).

36. Lynd and Lynd, *Middletown,* 486–87.

37. Ibid., 485–88.

38. Gertrude Stein, *Everybody's Autobiography* (New York: Random House, 1937), 289.

39. Robert Staughton Lynd and Helen Merrell Lynd, *Middletown in Transition: A Study in Cultural Conflicts* (New York: Harcourt, Brace, 1935), 291–92.

40. Lynd and Lynd, *Middletown in Transition,* 487–510.

41. Ibid., 290–92.

42. Ibid., 291.

43. A more robust understanding of modern sport might have forewarned the Lynds

that in certain ways, games such as basketball had always been well-suited to the rise of modern American consumer culture. Mark Dyreson, "The Emergence of Consumer Culture and the Transformation of Physical Culture: American Sport in the 1920s," *Journal of Sport History* 16 (Winter 1989): 261–81.

44. Basketball flourished in Middletown in the 1930s. Dick Stodghill and Jackie Stodghill, *Bearcats! A History of Basketball at Muncie Central High School, 1901–1988* (Muncie, Ind.: JLT Publications, 1988). The game also flourished in the Great Depression in the rest of Indiana and in rural and small-town environments as well as in urban locales all over the United States. See, for instance, Troy D. Paino, "Hoosiers in a Different Light: Forces of Change v. the Power of Nostalgia," *Journal of Sport History* 28 (Spring 2001): 63–80; and Pamela Grundy, "From Amazons to Glamazons: The Rise and Fall of North Carolina Women's Basketball, 1920–1960," *Journal of American History* 87 (June 2000): 112–46.

45. Tunis, "Ain't God Good to Indiana!" 96.

46. Theodore Caplow, "The Measurement of Social Change in Middletown," *Indiana Magazine of History* 75 (December 1979): 344–57.

47. Stodghill and Stodghill, *Bearcats!*

48. Paino, "Hoosiers in a Different Light," 63–80; Randy Roberts, *"But They Can't Beat Us!": Oscar Robertson and the Crispus Attucks Tigers* (Indianapolis: Indiana Historical Society, 1999).

49. Hoover, *Magic Middletown;* Luke Eric Lassiter, Hurley Goodall, Elizabeth Campbell, and Michelle Natasya Johnson, eds., *The Other Side of Middletown: Exploring Muncie's African American Community* (Lanham, Md.: AltaMira Press, 2004).

50. Lynd and Lynd, *Middletown,* 480.

51. Lassiter, Goodall, Campbell, and Johnson, eds., *The Other Side of Middletown,* 170.

52. "The Big Game," WQED/PBS-TV, Pittsburgh, Pennsylvania, 1982.

53. C. L. R. James, *Beyond a Boundary* (Durham, N.C.: Duke University Press, [1963] 1993).

54. Paino, "Hoosiers in a Different Light," 63–80; James H. Madison, *The Indiana Way: A State History* (Bloomington: Indiana University Press; and Indianapolis: Indiana State Historical Society, 1986), 254–56.

55. Bob Adams, *Hoosier High School Basketball* (Chicago: Arcadia, 2002); Steve Bisheff, *John Wooden: An American Treasure* (Nashville: Cumberland House, 2004); Dick Denny, *Glory Days Indiana: Legends of Indiana High School Basketball* (Champaign, Ill.: Sports Publishing, 2006); Phillip M. Hoose, *Hoosiers: The Fabulous Basketball Life of Indiana* (New York: Vintage, 1986); Emerson Houck, *Hoosiers All: Indiana High School Basketball* (Carmel, Ind.: Hawthorne Publishing, 2009); Jeff Washburn, *Tales from Indiana High School Basketball* (Champaign, Ill.: Sports Publishing, 2004).

56. Dwight Hoover, "To Be a Jew in Middletown: A Muncie Oral History Project," *Indiana Magazine of History* 81 (June 1985): 153.

57. "Sports in Shorts," *Logansport (Indiana) Pharos-Tribune,* December 23, 1931, 5; "Muncie-Alexandria Game This Evening," *Logansport (Indiana) Pharos-Tribune,* January 5, 1932, 5; "Wellsmen Traveling to Play Bearcats Tonight," *Logansport (Indiana) Pharos-Tribune,* February 5, 1932, 5; "Berries Lose to Muncie in Quarterfinal," *Logansport (Indiana) Pharos-Tribune,* February 6, 1932, 5.

58. DeJernet and Mann later starred in the 1930s for the Chicago Crusaders professional team. "Net Knots," *Logansport (Indiana) Press,* December 18, 1936, 12; "History of Indiana's Cage Tourneys Passes in Review," *Logansport (Indiana) Press,* March 24, 1939, 10; "Parade of Champions: Year-by-Year Record of Final Battles in History of Indiana H.S. Basketball," *Kokomo (Indiana) Tribune,* March 20, 1947, 19; Dale Burgess, "First All-Negro School Advances to Final Tourney Four First Time," *Logansport (Indiana) Press,* March 13, 1951, 6; Paul Lynch, "Bearcats Bring Big Tradition," *Kokomo (Indiana) Tribune,* February 5, 1965, 8.

59. Even in the 1930s, Muncie Central continued to use African American players. In 1938, Muncie had another "Jack Mann"—6' 8" center Henry Young. John Whitaker, "Speculating in Sports," *Hammond (Indiana) Times,* February 4, 1938, 17. On the increasing "whiteness" of Muncie teams in the 1950s and 1960s, see the oral histories in Lassiter, Goodall, Campbell, and Johnson, eds., *The Other Side of Middletown,* 170–78.

60. *Hoosiers* (Orion Pictures, 1986); Paino, "Hoosiers in a Different Light," 63–80.

2. The Biggest "Classic" of Them All

The Howard University and Lincoln University Thanksgiving Day Football Games, 1919–1929

DAVID K. WIGGINS

African Americans established a number of successful and important separate sports programs during the latter half of the nineteenth and first half of the twentieth centuries. Banned from most predominantly white organized sport during this period because of racial discrimination, African Americans organized their own teams and leagues behind segregated walls at the amateur and professional levels, in small rural communities and large urban settings, and among both men and women of different social and economic backgrounds. Some of the most important of these separate sports programs were those established at historically black colleges and universities (HBCUs). Since the latter stages of the nineteenth century, HBCUs have competed at a relatively high level in football, basketball, and a number of other sports.[1]

The annual Thanksgiving Day football games played between well-known HBCUs drew a great deal of attention and much enthusiasm from African Americans. The most popular and significant of these games were those pitting Howard University and Lincoln University from 1919 to 1929. Described in 1922 by *Chicago Defender* sportswriter Frank Young as "the most important game in the country as far as we (African Americans) are concerned," the Howard and Lincoln Thanksgiving Day matchups during the 1920s, a decade commonly termed the "golden age of American sport," garnered some attention in the white press, voluminous coverage in the black press and attracted great interest among upper-class African Americans in Philadelphia, Washington, D.C., and other black communities across the country.[2]

The Howard and Lincoln annual Thanksgiving Day football games, along with the accompanying social activities were, like the creation of black All-American teams and naming of mythical national champions, a way for two of the most prestigious HBCUs to exhibit a much-needed sense of racial pride and self-determination while at once measuring themselves against the standards of predominantly white university sport and its attendant rituals. The "classic" was also important in that it enhanced the already elevated prestige of Howard and Lincoln, which, in turn, contributed to intangible strategic advantages for two institutions that were becoming more entrepreneurial and commercialized. The games and their accompanying social activities, moreover, played an important role in the identity of upper-class African Americans in Philadelphia, Washington, D.C., and other locales. For many African Americans, the "classic" was both a salve and a symbol of status, bringing them together while cordoning them off according to their respective social station. And things were in flux. Social changes, resulting from the northern migration of southern blacks during the early decades of the twentieth century, cast racial identity in a new light. With alternative modes of social advancement becoming possible in black communities, and toleration of whites toward upper-class African Americans being diminished because of the geographical expansion and more economically mobile pattern of the black population following the great migration, the "classic" was more than just a test to determine athletic superiority. It was "a social competition between the black populace of Washington, D.C. and Philadelphia" and a highly visible way to help keep African Americans of like kind together.[3]

The first football game between Howard and Lincoln took place in 1894 on Howard's campus in Washington, D.C. Characteristic of the sport in the late nineteenth century, the game was a vicious and bloody affair. Lincoln's right tackle James Harper suffered a broken jaw after colliding with Howard's star halfback "Baby" Jones. This incident, along with several other unfortunate confrontations during Lincoln's 5–4 victory and following the game, including a Lincoln player having a pistol drawn on him by a white man on a Washington, D.C., street, were so serious that the schools did not play each other again until 1904. The games played between 1904 and 1918 attracted relatively little fanfare.[4]

In 1919 the Howard and Lincoln Thanksgiving Day football game, which was played in Philadelphia and ended in a 0–0 tie, was advertised and promoted as the "classic" and "greatest event of the season."[5] It would prove to be an apt descriptor as the game, which attracted a reported ten thousand mostly black fans, the usual composition of the crowds for these contests, was transformed into a grand social affair that combined the traditional gridiron battle between the two institutions with elaborately organized dances, visitor receptions, dinner parties, musical productions, breakfast socials, and alumni gatherings held over a frenetic three to five days.[6]

In 1920 Howard crushed Lincoln, 42–0, in front of what was described as "the largest crowd regardless of race, that ever attended a football game in the capital city."[7] The Lincoln Lions, coached by former Harvard University star Clarence Matthews and Paul Robeson, the great athlete, actor, singer and civil rights activist, were completely outclassed by the Howard Bisons at American League Park in Washington.[8] The tables were turned the following year as Lincoln defeated Howard 13–7 at the National Baseball Park in Philadelphia, with approximately ten thousand spectators in attendance. The Lincoln victory was owed in large part to the outstanding coaching of John A. Shelbourne, former star player at Dartmouth College.[9] In 1922 Lincoln defeated Howard, 13–12, at the American League Park in Washington. The star of the game was Franz "Jazz" Byrd, the speedy and elusive running back considered by many to be the greatest player in Lincoln history.[10] A year later, Howard and Lincoln played to a 6–6 tie in front of approximately sixteen thousand spectators at the National Baseball Park in Philadelphia. The Lincoln team of 1923 was extraordinary for both its athletic accomplishments and the professional success of its players in their postcollege lives.[11]

In 1924 Lincoln humiliated Howard 31–0 in front of a reported crowd of twenty-seven thousand at the American League Park in Washington. Perhaps the most ballyhooed of all the "classics," Lincoln was led once again by "Jazz" Byrd, dubbed by the black press as the "black Grange of football," a reference to Red Grange of the University of Illinois, white college football's boy wonder.[12] In 1925 Lincoln and Howard played to a 0–0 tie at Philadelphia's Shibe Park in front of a reported sixteen thousand fans. Despite its success, the "classic" was marred that year by controversy. Lincoln was expelled from the Central Intercollegiate Athletic Association after refusing to cancel the game against Howard, which had been accused of using an illegal player in previous contests.[13] In 1926, with approximately ten thousand spectators in attendance in the new Howard University Stadium, the home team demolished Lincoln, 32–0. The game's star was Howard quarterback Jack Coles, who repeatedly weaved his way through the Lincoln line for huge gains.[14] In 1927 Howard, with one of its strongest and deepest teams, defeated Lincoln, 20–0, at Shibe Park in Philadelphia in front of an announced fifteen thousand spectators. The game followed by almost two months a temporary strike by the Howard football team, which protested the decision of President Mordecai Johnson to eliminate the customary

The Howard-Lincoln Football Classic, 1926, Howard Stadium.
Courtesy of Moorland-Spingarn Research Center, Howard University.

free training table and living quarters provided players during the football season.[15] In 1928 Howard again beat Lincoln, 12–0, in view of some ten thousand spectators at Howard Stadium. The Howard team received an added boost from the expertise of coach Charles West, the former football and track star at Washington and Jefferson University.[16] In 1929, the final year of the "classic," Howard and Lincoln played, just as they had ten years earlier, to a 0–0 tie in front of approximately ten thousand spectators at Municipal Stadium in Philadelphia.[17]

The "father" of the Thanksgiving Day football "classic" between Howard and Lincoln, according to former president and historian of Lincoln, Horace Mann Bond, was Dr. Charles A. Lewis, a 1905 graduate of Lincoln and medical doctor from Philadelphia by way of the University of Pennsylvania. A lifelong supporter of all things Lincoln who regularly traveled with the team and sat on the bench tending to injured players, Lewis realized the monetary and intangible strategic advantages that could potentially result from a more highly publicized and commercialized football contest between his beloved alma mater and Howard.[18] And the time was right for such a series of contests: northern blacks were experiencing an increasing number of southern blacks making their way north; a relatively higher standard of living; and a consumer culture and national obsession with sport, were in their early stages—and destined to become much larger.[19]

Emmett J. Scott, Howard's secretary-treasurer and business manager, was highly supportive of Lewis's idea and perhaps the man most actively involved in marketing "the classic" and its ultimate success. A native of Houston, Texas, and former editor of the city's black newspaper, the *Texas Freeman*, Scott had been a close friend, advisor, and private secretary to Booker T. Washington and the man in charge of the "Tuskegee Machine," an elaborate system in which Washington controlled and manipulated African American leaders and the press.[20]

These experiences would bode well for Scott as he set about promoting the "classic." Encouraged by the success of the first designated "classic" between Howard and Lincoln in 1919, Scott took much of what he had learned while working for the *Texas Freeman* and while at Tuskegee to ensure that the following year's game in Washington, D.C., and subsequent contests between the two institutions, were just as successful and generated the same amount of attention and publicity from the African American community. Just as he strove to improve the academic programs and bring financial stability to Howard, Scott worked tirelessly, called in favors from old friends, and utilized his professional contacts in an effort to provide as much publicity as possible for the annual Thanksgiving Day football "classic" between his institution and Lincoln. He was successful in his efforts, making the public aware of the contest, with the notable assistance of Dr. Charles A. Lewis and Dr. W. G. Alexander, Lincoln's graduate manager of athletics, through public announcements and press releases and other media initiatives.[21] "Everyone present realized the tremendous possibilities of the game," wrote the *Chicago Defender* in 1929, recalling the first classic played ten years earlier. "It remained, however, for the business sagacity of Dr. Emmett J. Scott, secretary-treasurer of Howard University, to perfect the details whereby the occasion might be financially profitable to both institutions as well as occasions worthy to be recorded in the annals of our history."[22]

What Scott helped to create was a recurring athletic and social ritual that allowed Howard and Lincoln to exhibit important feelings of self-pride and determination while at the same time comparing themselves against the standards of white college sport. Like the East-West All-Star game in black baseball that had its beginnings in 1933 and any number of other sporting events organized behind segregated walls, the Howard and Lincoln Thanksgiving Day football games between 1919 and 1929 attested to the strength and vibrancy of the two institutions and the African American community more generally, while also providing an opportunity to measure themselves against the more nationally known and famous football contests between predominantly white institutions. Tellingly, the comparisons made were not with just any predominantly white institutions, but typically with one or more of the Big Three universities: Harvard, Yale, and Princeton. Although beginning to be challenged for football superiority by other institutions across the country, Harvard, Yale, and Princeton still represented the very best in higher education and college football, and the black press was quick to point out the relative merits of the "classic" and by extension the quality of Howard and Lincoln as institutions in comparison to the Big Three.[23] "Dr. Scott has perfected arrangements to such a degree," noted the *Chicago Defender* of 1928, "that the classic takes first place in the games of our schools and to our people it is the Yale-Harvard game of our group."[24] "The football classic of the year is the title justly ascribed to the annual game between Howard and Lincoln Universities," wrote the *Philadelphia Tribune* in 1928. "The importance attached to the game has been likened to the annual classics between Yale and Harvard, Cornell and Penn or Princeton and Yale."[25]

Such heady comparisons could be more readily achieved if the annual Thanksgiving Day black "classic" was hyped, helping create a much-talked-about rivalry. Black weeklies heightened interest by filling a voluminous amount of column space that preceded each of the contests and then followed with additional coverage once the games had been played. Commentators particularly devoted much energy in detailing the rich history and traditions of the "classic." They made clear that each upcoming "classic" was going to be more spectacular, colorful, and exciting than the one that preceded it. "Two years ago," wrote the *Chicago Defender* of 1921, "when the Lincoln management announced that the annual football game between the two ancient rivals, Howard and Lincoln, would be held in Philadelphia at the big National League Park, the pessimists began to shout 'this will be nothing less than athletic suicide,' but the move was without a doubt the most popular venture ever attempted in this country. It was the greatest athletic and social success that has ever been witnessed."[26] "With only seven days intervening, much interest in the annual Turkey Day clash involving the Lincoln and Howard game is being exhibited in Philadelphia and adjacent regions," wrote the *Philadelphia Tribune* in 1928. "As a spectacle and a colorful event little doubt exists that this year's game will rival and perhaps excel in splendor and grandeur those of the past."[27]

Representatives from Howard and Lincoln welcomed the build-up because it added to an already burgeoning rivalry. A rivalry—especially an intense rivalry—these representatives understood, enhanced their respective institutional interests and ensured that the African American community would more closely identify with them and their various constituents. The intense rivalry between the two institutions was born out of the same requisite qualifications for all rivalries; namely, similarities, differences, and contrasts.[28] While Howard and Lincoln were two of the most prestigious HBCUs and both in the business of educating the African American community's "talented tenth" and fielding strong athletic teams, they had different histories, different geographical settings, different student enrollments, different philosophies, and different academic specializations. Lincoln University, located in the small town of Oxford in Chester County, Pennsylvania, was founded in 1854 by white Presbyterian minister John Miller Dickey. During the 1920s it charged $110 in tuition, which was one of the highest of any HBCU in the country. It had a white president, sixteen white faculty, and an all-black male enrollment that by 1927 had reached only 305. The university offered a four-year bachelor of arts degree in liberal arts, a three-year bachelor of sacred theology degree, and a three-year diploma in theology. A committee made up of faculty, alumni, and students administered all athletic activities at Lincoln.[29]

Howard University, on the other hand, was founded in 1866 in Washington, D.C., and named after General Oliver Otis Howard, a philanthropist and commissioner of the Freedmen's Bureau. Although a privately controlled institution since 1879, Howard has received a subsidy from the federal government for both maintenance and capital outlay. It hired its first African American president, Mordecai Johnson, in 1926, employed 171 faculty members (the majority of whom were black), and had a coed enrollment that by 1927 had reached 2,118 students representing thirty-six states and ten foreign countries. The athletic program was governed by a board of athletic control, consisting of faculty, alumni, the secretary-treasurer (Emmett J. Scott), and the director of physical education.[30]

The differences between the two institutions were symbolically displayed on the football field and through distinctive songs, colors, ceremonies, rituals, and logos each Thanksgiving Day during the 1920s. These activities did not simply mimic those that took place in white college sport and in the white sporting world more generally. Students, alumni, and other followers of the "classic" refashioned these activities, like so many other things during this era of the "new negro," in a style and manner that reflected the black experience in Philadelphia and Washington, as well as that of Howard and Lincoln. A ritual of the Lincoln alumnus was to march en masse to the game, which was recorded in the *Chicago Defender* of 1922: "The Lincoln Alumni will hold a get together meeting tonight. Tomorrow morning, headed by a 60 piece band, the alumni headed by Drs. Cannon and Alexander of New Jersey, Prof. Saunders of West Virginia, with their pet lion cub sent from Liberia by the United States minister, an alumnus of Lincoln, will head for the park from the Whitelaw hotel, bedecked in Lincoln's colors, singing their 'Alma Mater' as they go. All Lincoln adherents will follow in the line."[31]

An example of a representative song from the game was recorded in an undated issue of the *Lincoln News*:

Howard has a quarterback,
Who thinks he's mighty cute;
But when he hits the Lincoln line,
He'll do the loop the loop.

He'll ramble off the tackle,
Ramble around the end,
Ramble through the center,
Then ramble back again.

Chorus:
He'll ramble, ramble, ramble all around,
Hey! In and out the town.
Oh! ramble, ramble, ramble 'til ole Lincoln cuts him down.[32]

One of the most original and regular features of the "classic" were the "rabbles," a pregame or halftime improvisational dance where students climbed out of the stands and marched around the field carrying their own musical instruments and singing songs praising their own institutions and denigrating their opponents. The *Howard University Record* of 1921 reported on the "rabble" that took place at halftime of that year's game between Howard and Lincoln: "The ending of the first half was the cue for 'rabble' exhibitions. The rabbles of both schools pounced upon the field in spite of its mud-soaked conditions and the continuous rain. The 'blue and white' rabble headed by its band, executed a wild snake dance while the Lincoln horde did its serpentine dance."[33]

Historian Patrick Miller, in his oft-cited essay "To Bring the Race Along Rapidly: Sport, Student Culture, and Educational Mission at Historically Black Colleges During the Interwar Years," initially made us aware of "rabbles" citing the above-mentioned quote from the *Howard University Record* regarding the Howard and Lincoln contest of 1921.[34] Historian Michael Oriard elaborates further on the "rabbles" in *King Football*. Utilizing the work of William Pierson on "African American Festive Style" and referencing accounts of the Howard and Lincoln games of the 1920s from the *Chicago Defender* and *Baltimore Afro-American,* Oriard makes the point that "rabbles" were representative of "Black Expressive Culture" in that they emphasized improvisation, spontaneity, and the close interplay between performers and spectators. The "rabbles," like various types of dances, funeral processions, and celebrations in the African American South (including different activities in the slave-quarter community, it should be added) can also be seen as a way to satirize the "more formal celebrations" of the ruling class in the country, in this case the "precision marching bands of the big-time football universities." Quoting Pierson, Oriard notes, moreover, "that the marching bands at historically black institutions in the 1990s still retained a 'cake-walking heroic (and comedic) quality' very different from the style at say, the University of Michigan or Ohio State."[35]

The annual "classic" was just as much, in the words of sport historian Raymond Schmidt, "the centerpiece of a social competition between the black populace of Washington, D.C., and Philadelphia" as it was a football rivalry between Howard and Lincoln.[36] Washington, D.C., referred to by historian Willard B. Gatewood as the "capital of the colored aristocracy," was a segregated southern city with a black population that had reached more than 132,000 by 1930.[37] Among this population was a relatively large and influential black elite made up of civil servants, schoolteachers, college professors, lawyers, and doctors who had made their way to Washington, D.C., to take advantage of the jobs available with the federal government and because of the superb educational opportunities provided by Howard. Though Seventh Street housed important business and entertainment establishments and was the center of social life for the black masses, the U Street corridor harbored the very best in Washington, D.C.'s African American community.[38]

Philadelphia had a black population of more than 219,000 by 1930, which ranked it third behind only New York City and Chicago.[39] Unlike African Americans in Washington, D.C., who were largely confined to limited segregated areas, African Americans in Philadelphia lived in several large integrated districts in the north, south, and western parts of the city. Perhaps the most wealthy and prestigious integrated neighborhood in Philadelphia during the 1920s was located west of Fifty-Third Street and north of Market Street in an area now known as Haddington. Black Philadelphians, both alumni and those who were not, adopted Lincoln University as their own. Located some forty-five miles from Philadelphia, Lincoln became the hometown college team for the city.[40]

Each year of the "classic," the black upper crust in the host city vied for social supremacy by staging elaborate dances, parties, receptions and other affairs. Chartered trains would bring the very best of black America to Washington, D.C., and Philadelphia to watch the game and to participate in many accompanying social activities. For upper-class blacks of both cities, prestige was at stake as well as bragging rites and reputations. William H. Jones, in his 1927 study *Recreation and Amusement Among Negroes in Washington, D.C.: A Sociological Analysis of the Negro in an Urban Environment,* wrote that the annual Thanksgiving football game between Howard and Lincoln "has given to the negro life of Washington a prestige among other cities and a magnetic influence over vicinal districts which no other field of negro life in the capital can approximate. Every day for approximately a week scores of important social affairs are held. These consist of break-fast, matinee and evening dances, poker games, bridge parties, slumming, cabaret parties, and numerous other entertainments."[41] "The visitor within our gates," noted the *Philadelphia Tribune* in 1929,

> will evidently go home wondering who was the person that invented the saying "Philadelphia is a slow town," for with the Chi Delta Mu dance on Wednesday night, the breakfast and dance given [by] Mrs. George Deane and Mrs. Hobson Reynolds on Thursday morning, the game, cocktail par-ties, followed by dinner and the Japelmas dance on Thursday night, not to mention the Frogs and innumerable "official dances," the matrons matinee dance on Friday afternoon, the second annual supper dance of the cos-mopolitan club which distinguished itself last season by giving the finest affair of the year on Friday night, a matinee dance given by the Frogs on Saturday when Mrs. Lawrence Christmas and Mrs. Julian Abele will also give a dance in the afternoon for their friends and visitors followed by several parties on that night there will be, very little sleeping. For while dances are over at 2 o'clock, one immediately transports himself to some-body else's home or his own home where the merriment goes right on.[42]

The competition between Howard and Lincoln, as well as that between Washington, D.C., and Philadelphia, should not blind us to the fact that the "classic" also played a supportive role in both the coalescence of the campus communities at each institution and upper-class blacks more gener-ally during the early decades of the twentieth century, when many poorer southern blacks migrated to northern cities. The annual Thanksgiving Day contests between Howard and Lincoln, while important in bringing additional monies into institutional coffers, were particularly significant because they provided occasions for fostering school spirit and helped bind students, alumni, and to a much lesser extent faculty, closer together on both campuses. *The Howard University Record* of 1921 provided its assess-ment of the significance of the "classic" in particular and football more generally when it wrote that

> the annual clash in football between Howard and Lincoln Universities which took place on Thanksgiving Day in American League Park in Wash-ington served not only to dispel any doubt that may have previously

existed as to the high place of football as the most popular sport among American college and university students, but also showed that such contests are the best means of indicating the true coefficient of college alumni loyalty . . . On no other occasion probably do all unite with one mind, one heart and one voice. The whole college gives a striking instance of group psychology and thousands of students act as one man in urging their struggling heroes on to victory.[43]

The need to unite the campuses of each institution was perhaps never so important than during the decade of the 1920s. Although able to maintain their prestige and national reputations, Howard and Lincoln both experienced well-known internal dissension and turmoil during this crucial ten-year period. As Raymond Wolters writes in *The New Negro on Campus: Black College Rebellions of the 1920s* (1975), Lincoln experienced its share of internal dissension during the decade, particularly concerning its all-white faculty and administration. Influential and angry alumni, including the likes of Langston Hughes and Frances Grimke, made concerted efforts to ensure that African Americans were added to the faculty and the board of trustees and also fought to have more voice in all decisions pertaining to the operation of the university. The situation was so bad that on three separate occasions presidents-elect ultimately decided to turn down offers to lead the university when determining that life would be made miserable for them because of the disgruntlement of alumni who believed they had not been adequately consulted on the new hires.[44]

Life on the Howard campus was not much better and, in some cases, perhaps even worse. For much of the decade, white president Stanley Durkee faced bitter opposition from students, faculty, and alumni who questioned his leadership and the direction in which he was taking the university. Carter G. Woodson, the "father of black history," and Kelly Miller, the distinguished professor of sociology and dean of the College of Arts and Sciences, were just two of the Howard faculty who wrote scathing denouncements of Durkee and bitterly opposed his presidency. In 1925, 1,200 Howard students went on strike in protest over president Durkee's decision to expel anyone who missed a minimum number of courses in R.O.T.C. Two years later, the football team went on strike after President Mordecai Johnson, who would serve the university in that capacity from 1926 until 1960, abolished the football training table and severely reduced the athletic budget. Students walked out of their classrooms to show support for the players, and the Thanksgiving Day game with Lincoln was cancelled until Johnson persuaded the strikers to give him more time while he considered their demands.[45]

The annual Thanksgiving Day games between Howard and Lincoln were not only important for fostering school spirit and binding the campuses of each institution together, but also assisted in uniting upper-class African Americans during the social disruption brought about by the northern migration of southern African Americans during the post–World War I period. Upper-class African Americans were being challenged for their special place in society as the great migration came into existence and as alternative modes of social advancement became possible within the black community. In addition, white America's toleration of upper-class African Americans rapidly diminished as the larger African American population became more geographically and economically mobile.[46] The Howard and Lincoln Thanksgiving Day football "classic," while drifting toward tribal display and exclusivity and a social competition between upper-class African Americans of Washington, Philadelphia, and other parts of the East and Midwest, also helped to keep these same African Americans together. This is evident in the recurrent descriptions of the succession of parties, dances, and other social gatherings that accompanied the games. These descriptions make clear that the annual contests between the two famous institutions was to a great extent about upper-class African Americans reaffirming their special place in society, distancing themselves from lower-class blacks, who they blamed for the rising tide of racism, and an occasion to join with those of similar thoughts and values and mutuality of interest in sports and other social and cultural rituals. "The 1919 game between Howard and Lincoln was augmented," noted the *Philadelphia Tribune,* "by the presence of thousands of fashionable and ultrafashionable visitors from Washington, Baltimore, New York, Atlantic City, and other neighboring cities, the latter coming in several days ahead in order to secure the choicest hotel and private accommodations and to participate in the numerous festivities and social functions preceding the open football classic in the afternoon of turkey day."[47] "It will be the eighteenth meeting of the two elevens," wrote Frank Young of the *Chicago Defender* before the 1922 game between Howard and Lincoln in Washington, D.C. "Every incoming train brings its quota. The vanguard of the hosts who will watch tomorrow's struggle are busy renewing acquaintances. The 'Flapper Special' from New York City is due in early in the morning as is a special from Pittsburgh and one from Philadelphia and early morning trains will bring the balance who will help to make up the gayest throng that ever witnessed a football game anywhere and the largest that has ever witnessed a struggle between any two institutions representing our people."[48]

Unfortunately, by 1929 the "classic" lost some of its luster. It generated far less media coverage, experienced a decrease in attendance, and was devoid of much of the great gridiron talent that had marked the previous nine contests between the two institutions. The weakening financial condition of Howard's and Lincoln's football programs, specifically, and of their athletic programs more generally, a result of the Great Depression, contributed to this state of affairs. Though the two schools would continue to play each other regularly until Lincoln dropped football after the 1960 season, the Howard and Lincoln game would never be as popular or meaningful as it was during the 1920s. At the time, "The Biggest Classic" of them all among historically black institutions was an athletic and social event that provided upper-class African Americans the opportunity to exhibit racial pride, measure themselves against the standards of white universities, and come together as a distinct group. In the process, they reaffirmed their place in a country that had undergone unprecedented geographical and economic changes wrought by the northern migration of southern blacks. To African Americans, the Howard and Lincoln Thanksgiving Day football "classic" during the second decade of the twentieth century was just as important as the annual games between Harvard and Yale and any number of other famous gridiron contests between predominantly white institutions. Maybe more so.

Epilogue

On September 10, 2011, Howard University and Morehouse College played each other in what was billed as the "First Annual AT&T Nation's Football Classic" at RFK Stadium. Rekindling a rivalry that had been scrapped some fifteen years earlier, the game was advertised in the *Washington Post* in much the same way the black press advertised the Howard and Lincoln Thanksgiving Day games between 1919 and 1929.[49] The game could potentially provide a financial boost to both institutions, would contribute to a sense of kinship and camaraderie among the students, friends, and faculty from both institutions, and furnish these same individuals an opportunity to watch outstanding football and enjoy the marching bands that "compete with a unique flair."[50] The game was supplemented with many parties, joint fundraiser dances, a student debate, and an assortment of other social gatherings. To some, the game between Howard University and Morehouse College was less about football and more about the accompanying social activities and the opportunity for alumni to "join students to backslap and trash-talk, holler and rally in maroon and white or blue and red on the campus of Howard University and the streets of Washington."[51]

There appear to be many similarities in the descriptions of the Howard University and Morehouse College AT&T Nation's Football Classic with that of the Thanksgiving Day football games between Howard and Lincoln during the 1919 to 1929 period. In actuality, however, because of the strict racial segregation in this country during the 1920s, the Howard and Lincoln Thanksgiving Day "Classic" was decidedly different in regard to organization and probably far more meaningful and culturally significant to the African American community. With only a very select number of African American athletes able to participate in predominantly white college sport during this period, the Howard and Lincoln Thanksgiving Day games included extraordinarily gifted athletes whose names today would undoubtedly dot the rosters of Division I football powers. But because they participated behind racially segregated walls, the Howard and Lincoln games received little coverage in the white press and no sponsorship from major corporations. Finally, with the hopes of highlighting their athletic accomplishments and by extension their sense of black pride and ability for self-organization and independent business acumen, the Howard and Lincoln Thanksgiving Day Football "Classic" was particularly significant in that it was part of a burgeoning black national sporting culture that would eventually include other well-known Thanksgiving Day games between other HBCUs and such events and organizations as the East-West All-Star game, Gold and Glory Sweepstakes, American Tennis Association, National Negro Bowling Association, and Interscholastic Athletic Association Basketball Tournament. This black national sporting culture, which was fueled by a consumer culture that was a boon to the growth of sport more generally in the United States, brought African Americans from across the country a great deal of pleasure and sense of satisfaction and accomplishment that was not easy to come by during the era prior to integration.

Notes

I would like to thank Chris Elzey, Tom Jable, and Patrick Miller for providing cogent comments and suggestions on an earlier draft of this manuscript. I would also like to thank Pierre Rodgers for sharing copies of the *Philadelphia Tribune* that were secured from the Lincoln University Library.

1. For examples of works that deal with various aspects of sports behind segregated walls, see: Janet Bruce, *The Kansas City Monarchs: Champions of Black Baseball* (Lawrence: University Press of Kansas, 1985); Susan Cahn, *Coming on Strong: Gender and Sexuality in Twentieth-Century Women's Sport* (New York: Free Press, 1994); Nelson George, *Elevating the Game: Black Men and Basketball* (New York: Harper Collins, 1992); Neil

Lanctot, *Negro League Baseball: The Rise and Ruin of a Black Institution* (Philadelphia: University of Pennsylvania Press, 2004); Jennifer H. Lansbury, "'The Tuskegee Flash' and 'The Slender Harlem Stroker': Black Women Athletes on the Margin," *Journal of Sport History* 28 (Summer 2001): 233–52; Pete McDaniel, *Uneven Lies: The Heroic Story of African-Americans in Golf* (Greenwich, Conn.: American Golfers, 2000); Patrick B. Miller, "To Bring the Race Along Rapidly: Sport, Student Culture, and Educational Mission at Historically Black Colleges During the Interwar Years," *History of Education Quarterly* 35 (Summer 1995): 111–23; Troy D. Paino, "Hoosiers in a Different Light: Forces of Change vs. the Power of Nostalgia," *Journal of Sport History* 26 (Spring 2001): 63–80; Rob Ruck, *Sandlot Seasons: Sport in Black Pittsburgh* (Urbana: University of Illinois Press, 1987); Robert Gregg, "Personal Calvaries: Sports in Philadelphia's African American Communities, 1920–60," *Sport in Society* 6 (October 2003): 88–115.

2. *Chicago Defender,* December 2, 1922; William H. Jones, *Recreation and Amusement Among Negroes in Washington, D.C.: A Sociological Analysis of the Negro in an Urban Environment* (Washington, D.C.: Howard University Press, 1927).

3. Raymond Schmidt, *Shaping College Football: The Transformation of an American Sport, 1919–1930* (Syracuse, N.Y.: Syracuse University Press, 2007), 13.

4. See Horace Mann Bond, "The Story of Athletics at Lincoln University" unpublished chapter from Horace Mann Bond, *Education for Freedom: A History of Lincoln University, Pennsylvania* (Princeton, N.J.: Princeton University Press, 1976), 3–26; "History of Athletics," *The Bison,* 1924, N.P.; *Pittsburgh Courier,* November 19, 1924; *Chicago Defender,* November 23, 1929.

5. *Philadelphia Tribune,* October 18 and November 1, 1919. See also the *Washington Post,* November 28, 1919.

6. I did not find any autobiographical accounts of the games and the accompanying social activities. I assume, but am not certain, that further digging in the relevant archives would eventually uncover such accounts.

7. *Philadelphia Tribune,* December 4, 1920.

8. Matthews and Robeson coached this one game on an interim basis, taking over from the head coach, Fritz Pollard, the former Brown University star, who was off playing for the professional Canton Bulldogs. Bond, "The Story of Athletics at Lincoln University," 28–29; *Philadelphia Tribune,* December 4, 1920.

9. Bond, "The Story of Athletics at Lincoln University," 29; *Chicago Defender,* November 19, 26, December 3, 1921; *Howard University Record* 16 (December 1921): 125–26; *Washington Post,* November 21, 25, 1921.

10. Bond, "The Story of Athletics at Lincoln University," 30–31; *Chicago Defender,* November 25 and December 2, 9, 1922; *New York Age,* December 9, 1922.

11. Five players were named to the All-Central Intercollegiate Athletic Association team, six players were selected to either the first, second, or third teams on Fay Young's *Chicago Defender* All-American squad; and following graduation three players took their medical degrees, two took their Ph.D.s, two took their law degrees, and another four took various types of master's degrees. Bond, "The Story of Athletics at Lincoln University," 30–31; *Chicago Defender,* November 17, 24, 1923; *Howard University Record* 18 (January 1924): 199–200, 202; *Philadelphia Tribune,* December 8, 1923; *New York Times,* November 30, 1923; *Boston Daily Globe,* November 30, 1923.

12. Bond, "The Story of Athletics at Lincoln University," 21–37; *Howard University Record* 19 (January 1925): 114–16; *Pittsburgh Courier*, November 1, 24, 29 and December 6, 20, 1924; *Chicago Defender*, November 22, 29 and December 6, 1924; *Philadelphia Tribune*, November, 22, 27, 29 and December 6, 1924; *Norfolk Journal and Guide*, December 6, 1924; *The Crisis* 29 (February 1925): 171–72; *Howard Alumnus* 3 (January 15, 1925): 62.

13. Bond, "The Story of Athletics at Lincoln University," 37; *Chicago Defender*, December 5, 1925; *Pittsburgh Courier*, December 5, 1925; *Washington Post*, November 27, 1925.

14. Bond, "The Story of Athletics at Lincoln University," 37–38; *The Crisis* 34 (March 1927): 7; *Chicago Defender*, November 20 and December 4, 1926; *Pittsburgh Courier*, December 4, 18, 20, 1926; *Philadelphia Tribune*, November 20, 27 and December 4, 1926; *Washington Post*, November 14, 26, 1926; *New York Times*, November 26, 1926. The 1920s witnessed the building of many new stadiums with expanded seating capacities at predominantly white universities across the country. Northwestern University and the University of Missouri also built new stadiums in 1926, with seating capacities of approximately forty to fifty thousand. See Raymond Schmidt, *Shaping College Football: The Transformation of an American Sport, 1919–1930*, esp. chapter 3.

15. Bond, "The Story of Athletics at Lincoln University," 38; *Philadelphia Tribune*, November 24, 1927; *The Crisis* 35 (February 1928): 45; *Chicago Defender*, November 12 and December 3, 1927.

16. *Philadelphia Tribune*, November 22, 29, 1928; *Chicago Defender*, November 24, 1928; *Washington Post*, November 29, 1928; *New York Times*, November 30, 1928.

17. *Chicago Defender*, November 23, 1929 and December 7, 1929; *Philadelphia Tribune*, November 28 and December 5, 1929; *Baltimore Afro-American*, December 14, 1929.

18. Bond, "The Story of Athletics at Lincoln University," 26–27. Finding financial data on the Howard and Lincoln games is difficult, but an "income and expenditures" statement from Howard in 1929 indicated that the school netted $4,256.83 from the "classic" that year. The total income from their four other away games that year was $4,800.00. See "Statement of Athletics: Incomes and Expenditures July 1, 1929 to December 31, 1929." Moorland-Spingarn Research Center.

19. The changing nature of sport and the rise of a consumer culture during the 1920s is nicely analyzed in Mark Dyreson, "The Emergence of Consumer Culture and the Transformation of Physical Culture: American Sport in the 1920s," *Journal of Sport History* 16 (Winter 1989): 261–81.

20. Bond, "The Story of Athletics at Lincoln University," 26–27. For background information on Scott, see: Maceo Crenshaw Dailey Jr., "Emmett Jay Scott: The Career of a Secondary Black Leader." Unpublished Ph.D. dissertation, Howard University, 1983.

21. See Dailey, "Emmett Jay Scott"; Edgar Allan Toppin, "Emmett Jay Scott," 105–6, in Henry Louis Gates Jr. and Evelyn Brooks Higginbotham, eds., *African American National Biography* (New York: Oxford University Press, 2008); Louis R. Harlan, *Booker T. Washington: The Making of a Black Leader, 1952–1901* (New York: Oxford University Press, 1972); Louis R. Harlan, *Booker T. Washington: The Wizard of Tuskegee* (New York: Oxford University Press, 1983). Information on both Lewis and Alexander is limited. See, however, Bond "The Story of Athletics at Lincoln University," 26–28.

22. *Chicago Defender*, November 23, 1929.

23. See Schmidt, *Shaping College Football*, 135.

24. *Chicago Defender,* November 24, 1928.

25. *Philadelphia Tribune,* November 22, 1928. For information on Thanksgiving Day games among predominantly white universities in the late nineteenth century, see Michael Oriard, *Reading Football: How The Popular Press Created An American Spectacle* (Chapel Hill, N.C.: University of North Carolina Press, 1993), esp. 89–101.

26. *Chicago Defender,* November 19, 1921.

27. *Philadelphia Tribune,* November 22, 1928.

28. For information on the characteristics and requisite features of sport rivalries, see David K. Wiggins and R. Pierre Rodgers, eds., *Rivals: Legendary Matchups that Made Sports History* (Fayetteville: University of Arkansas Press, 2010); Richard O. Davies, *Rivals! The Ten Greatest American Sports Rivalries of the 20th Century* (Malden, Mass.: John Wiley and Sons, 2010).

29. Bond, *Education For Freedom;* U.S. Office of Education, *Survey of Negro Colleges and Universities,* Bulletin 1928, No. 7, U.S. Government Printing Office, 1929.

30. Walter Dyson, *Howard University: The Capstone of Negro Education, A History: 1867–1940* (Washington, D.C.: Howard University Press, 1941); Rayford Logan, *Howard University: The First Hundred Years* (New York: New York University Press, 1969); Paul E. Logan, ed., *A Howard Reader: An Intellectual and Cultural Quilt of the African American Experience* (Boston: Houghton Mifflin, 1997); U.S. Office of Education, *Survey of Negro Colleges and Universities.*

31. *Chicago Defender,* December 2, 1922.

32. *Lincoln News,* N.D.

33. *Howard University Record* 16 (December 1921): 126.

34. Miller, "'To Bring the Race Along Rapidly,'" 119.

35. Michael Oriard, *King Football: Sport and Spectacle in the Golden Age of Radio and Newspapers, Movies and Magazines, the Weekly and the Daily Press* (Chapel Hill: University of North Carolina Press, 2001), 321, 323.

36. Schmidt, *Shaping College Football,* 135.

37. Willard B. Gatewood, *Aristocrats of Color: The Black Elite* (Bloomington: Indiana University Press, 1990), especially chapters two and four.

38. For a nice description of Washington, D.C.'s black entertainment and business district during this period, see Brad Snyder, *Beyond the Shadow of the Senators: The Untold Story of the Homestead Grays and the Integration of Baseball* (New York: Contemporary Books, 2003), 5–7.

39. Gatewood, *Aristocrats of Color,* 96–97; Charles Hardy, "Race and Opportunity: Black Philadelphia During the Era of the Great Migration," unpublished Ph.D. dissertation, Temple University, 1989, 131.

40. Hardy, "Race and Opportunity," 178, 441, 445.

41. Jones, *Recreation and Amusement Among Negroes,* 73.

42. *Philadelphia Tribune,* November 21, 1929.

43. *Howard University Record* 15 (January 1921): 133.

44. Raymond Wolters, *The New Negro on Campus: Black College Rebellions of the 1920s* (Princeton, N.J.: Princeton University Press, 1975), 278–93.

45. *Washington Afro-American,* May 16, 30 1925; May 8, 1926; Zora Neale Hurston, "The Hue and Cry about Howard University," in *A Howard Reader,* 138–46.

46. See Hardy, *Race and Opportunity,* 19, 22; Gatewood, *Aristocrats of Color,* 332–48.

47. *Philadelphia Tribune,* November 29, 1919.

48. *Chicago Defender,* December 2, 1922.

49. *Washington Post,* September 9, 10, 2011.

50. *Washington Post,* September 10, 2011.

51. *Washington Post,* September 9, 2011.

3. Bobby Jones, Southern Identity, and the Preservation of Privilege

CATHERINE M. LEWIS

The Bobby Jones Apparel Company Web site promotes its brand of luxury clothing and accessories using the legend of one of golf's most beloved players, explaining: "Bobby Jones epitomized what it meant to be a gentleman, and embodied class, grace under pressure, and style."[1] The company's advertising campaign took on special meaning during the 2010 Masters Tournament, as the sporting world witnessed the return of Tiger Woods, who was still reeling from scandals resulting from more than a dozen extramarital affairs. Woods's conduct, replete with tawdry text messages and late-night television show parodies, threatened the game's most cherished traditions at its most beloved tournament. Not surprisingly, Jones was marketed as an antidote to Woods's conduct, raising important issues about class, race, and identity in sport. Jones's life, legend, and legacy shaped the conception of amateurism in the early twentieth century, and the golfing world (that is, tournament organizers, sponsors, the media, and fans) continues to trade on his legend to promote itself as the last gentleman's game, with a distinctly southern flavor.[2]

Bobby Jones and the Golden Age of Sports

Legendary athletic heroes dominated the 1920s, which is often described as the "Golden Age of Sports." It featured Babe Ruth in baseball, Jack Dempsey in boxing, Red Grange and Notre Dame's Four Horseman (Harry Stuhldreher, Jim Crowley, Don Miller, and Elmer Layden) led by coach Knute Rockne in football, Bill Tilden and Suzanne Lenglen in tennis, and Robert Tyre "Bobby" Jones Jr. in golf.[3] Though a number of male and female golfers excelled in this decade, none captured the public imagination quite like Jones. He popularized golf on an international stage and was lauded for his grace, modesty, sportsmanship, and southern charm. In 1930, after a fourteen-year playing career, he became the first and only golfer to win the Grand Slam, that is, golf's four major tournaments in a single year.[4] In sum, Jones played in thirty-one majors and placed first or second better than 80 percent of the time.[5]

Bobby Jones was born in 1902 in Atlanta, just as golf was becoming popular in the United States. From 1916 to 1922, Jones played in dozens of tournaments but did not win a major title, largely because he was unable to control his temper. Journalist O. B. Keeler called this period in his life "the seven lean years." When Jones beat Bobby Cruickshank in a playoff at the 1923 U.S. Open at Inwood Country Club in New York (his first national championship), he began "the seven fat years."[6]

Jones was an aggressive player, and journalists at the time, like Grantland Rice, predicted that Jones's lack of maturity would overshadow his tremendous skill. Barnstorming around the country with Perry Adair, Elaine Rosenthal, and Alexa Stirling to raise money for the Red Cross's war effort during World War I, Jones recognized that his tantrums were becoming a source of embarrassment. At the 1921 British Open at St. Andrews it came to a head. During the third round, instead of taking a six on the par-three eleventh hole, he pocketed his ball, and thus disqualified himself from the tournament. At the U.S. Amateur later that year in St. Louis, he threw a club and hit a woman on the leg. United States Golf Association President George Walker warned Jones in a letter that he would never play in a USGA event again unless he could control his temper.

Over the next several years, he did. At the 1925 U.S. Open, he called a penalty stroke on himself. Jones's transformation was so complete that he won the Sullivan Award, which honors the outstanding amateur athlete in the United States, in 1930. Twenty-five years later, the USGA established the Bob Jones Award, honoring a person who, by a single act or over the years, emulates Jones's sportsmanship, respect for the game and its rules, generosity of spirit, sense of fair play, and perhaps even sacrifice. In 1966, Jones said that he most wanted to be remembered for his sportsmanship.[7] Today, when I talk to golfers interested in Jones's memory, stories of his modesty and sportsmanship dominate the conversation, and they are frequently invoked as a legacy of southern gentility. Rarely do these casual discussions invoke his class status, education at elite universities, or position in southern society. But these factors are crucial components of his stature in the game today, and were largely unavailable to his fellow professional competitors.

Unlike many athletes during this "Golden Age," Jones was from a mod-
erately wealthy family and was well educated. He had bachelor's degrees
in mechanical engineering from Georgia Tech and in English literature
from Harvard. Jones continued to play in golf tournaments while attending Emory University Law School in Atlanta. Halfway through his second
year, he took the bar exam, passed, and joined his father's law firm.[8] In
contrast to many of his golfing peers—working club professionals such as
Walter Hagen and Gene Sarazen—Jones was part of elite southern society,
dominated by country clubs and junior leagues. Golf was a diversion, never
a profession. That was not a luxury enjoyed by many professional players
in the early twentieth century.

In Jones's era, amateur golf reigned supreme and attracted some of the
world's best players, notably Roger Wethered and Francis Ouimet. Though
there were great professionals of this era, they and their events did not gain
respectability until World War II. Two of the legs of the Grand Slam that
Jones won were not even open to professional players. When Jack Nicklaus
and Tiger Woods strove to match Jones's record, they were competing in a
different set of championships. In addition to the U.S. Open and the British
Open, they were playing in the Masters (established by Jones and Clifford
Roberts in 1934) and the PGA Championship (founded in 1916 exclusively
for professional players).[9]

On November 17, 1930, at the age of twenty-eight, and only a few months
after winning the Grand Slam, Jones stunned his fans and competitors by
announcing his retirement from tournament golf to turn his attention to
his family and law practice. His decision did not diminish his interest in or
contribution to the game. Over the next thirty years, he published three
books, wrote dozens of newspaper articles, did a weekly half-hour radio
show, and became a regular contributor to Grantland Rice's *The American
Golfer*. Five days before his retirement, the world's most famous golfer
signed a contract with Warner Brothers to make *How I Play Golf* (1931), a
series of instructional films that were shown in theaters around the nation
and featured well-known celebrities, including W. C. Fields, James Cagney,
and Edward G. Robinson. These films are regularly broadcast on the Golf
Channel today. Using skills he learned as a mechanical engineer, Jones also
helped A.G. Spalding and Bros. design the first matched set of irons in 1932.
During this same period, he worked with Clifford Roberts to create and
nurture Augusta National Golf Club (ANGC). After serving in World War
II, Jones returned to Atlanta to help Robert Trent Jones design Peachtree
Golf Club in 1948. That same year, he was diagnosed with the degenerative
spinal disease syringomyelia and played his last round of golf at East Lake.[10]

In 1955, to honor Jones's contributions and sportsmanship, the United States Golf Association established the Bob Jones Award. Three years later, St. Andrews honored him by presenting him with the Freeman of the Royal Burgh of St. Andrews. On December 18, 1971, at age sixty-nine, Bob Jones died and was buried in Oakland Cemetery in Atlanta, where visitors to the gravesite often leave balls and tees to honor the legendary golfer. His legacy, though, transcends golf. In 1974, Emory University began the Robert Tyre Jones Jr. Memorial Lecture on Legal Ethics. Two years later, the Robert Tyre Jones Jr. Scholarship Program was established by Emory and the University of St. Andrews as an exchange program to nurture college students who "possess the finest academic and personal qualities."[11] Several museums, notably the USGA's Golf House and the World Golf Hall of Fame, have played an important role in preserving Jones's legacy. The most comprehensive exhibition, *Down the Fairway with Bobby Jones,* is on permanent display at the Atlanta History Center. Additionally, Jones has been the subject of books, articles, newsreels, and feature films. His likeness has appeared on everything from bubble gum cards to golf shirts. In the past decade, interest in his life and legacy has blossomed, and dozens of writers and historians have published books to analyze his role in the history of sports.[12] Two feature films have included Jones as a character: *The Legend of Bagger Vance* (2000) and *Bobby Jones: Stroke of Genius* (2004). His legacy and brand seems to grow with each passing year.

Reflecting on the "Golden Age of Sports," there are no athletic figures that have been as memorialized and admired as Jones. Today, there is no Babe Ruth scholarship, no feature films about Bill Tilden, and no permanent exhibition on Suzanne Lenglen. This does not diminish their accomplishments; it simply suggests that Jones's legacy has a kind of currency that is still meaningful and valuable for contemporary audiences. The question is, why?

Celebrated sportswriter Herbert Warren Wind, writing for the *New Yorker* on the fiftieth anniversary of Bobby Jones's Grand Slam, asked a question that still resonates: "How is it that he remains so alive for us and that what he did in 1930 continues to hold meaning for us and to give us pleasure in 1980?"[13] Beginning to answer Wind's question requires a step back in time. Jones was born in Atlanta, the heart of the New South. Except for a short time in Florida selling real estate, in California making films in the 1930s, and his wartime service in the 1940s, he never moved more than ten miles from his birthplace.

Jones's exploits on the golf course made front-page news, and for many he was the most important public figure to emerge from the South since the Civil War. In 1930, Atlanta was only a few decades removed from the devastating 1906 race riot.[14] The year Jones defeated his father in the Atlanta Athletic Club Championship at East Lake, in 1915, was also the year that Leo Frank, a Jewish pencil factory manager, was lynched in Marietta, Georgia, not twenty miles from Jones's home.[15] Bobby Jones's South was only two generations removed from the destructive legacy of the Civil War. He became one of the best-loved southerners since Robert E. Lee. Yet, unlike Lee, Jones's legacy is not tainted with racism and defeat. Instead, Jones came onto the world stage in 1923 and came to represent the city, and in fact the region, on the cusp of a new prosperity during the Jazz Age. Similar to other golfers of his class of this era, Jones was a consummate amateur. He believed that sports should build character and never be played for money.[16] This was a position of privilege not available to the many athletes of this era who found that competition was their paycheck.

The South and the Preservation of Privilege

Interest in Bobby Jones's legacy is fueled by a single event each year: the Masters Tournament in April in Augusta, Georgia. It is the most famous and the most coveted title in golf, and patrons (as they are called by the club) are required to step back in time to an age of southern gentility that is distinctive among major sporting events. Imagine fans at the Super Bowl, the Stanley Cup, or the NBA All-Star Game given a lesson on conduct, customs, or etiquette, as the Masters does in its *Spectator Guide* issued each year to patrons. On the first page is a message from none other than Bobby Jones (President in Perpetuity):

> In golf, customs of etiquette and decorum are just as important as rules governing play. It is appropriate for spectators to applaud successful strokes in proportion to difficulty but excessive demonstrations by a player or his partisans are not proper because of the possible effect upon other competitors.
>
> Most distressing to those who love the game of golf is the applauding or cheering of misplays or misfortunes of another player. Such occurrences have been rare at the Masters but we must eliminate them entirely if our patrons are to continue to merit their reputation as the most knowledgeable and considerate in the world.[17]

Jones's instructions are but one symbol of how the Masters seeks to "southernize" the sport. Such a bold statement of personal conduct keeps with the tradition of the Masters, which is known as the best-run and most polite sporting event in the world. As it attracts an international audience, the Masters also invokes a kind of southern hospitality, complete with pimento cheese sandwiches, iced tea, and polite gallery guards. But it is also the most expensive, elite, and the whitest of all golf tournaments, and among the most coveted tickets in the world. Badges for the four-day tournament (Thursday–Sunday) can cost as much as $4,000. Practice rounds (Monday–Wednesday) run as high as $500 per day.[18]

Augusta National is a living tribute to Jones as much as it is to the game. The site for Augusta National Golf Club is a 365-acre plot with a rich horticultural history on the west side of the city. In 1853, Dennis Redmond purchased 315 acres, including an indigo plantation, and constructed a large two-story house that is Augusta National's Clubhouse. In 1857 he sold the land to Belgian nobleman Louis Edouard Mathieu Berckmans. Berckmans and his son, Prosper Julius Alphonse, formed P.J.A. Berckmans Company in 1858 and began operating Fruitland Nurseries. Prosper Berckmans died in 1910, and Fruitland lost its charter soon after. In 1925, the land was sold to a Miami developer named Commodore J. Perry Stoltz, who hoped to turn the nursery into a golf resort but was unsuccessful. When Bobby Jones and Clifford Roberts inspected the property in 1930, it had not been used for more than a decade. In 1931, Fruitlands Nursery was purchased for $70,000, and a committee, including Jones, assembled to organize the club. Jones selected Dr. Alister Mackenzie as the architect, an English physician with a Scottish lineage. Augusta National was completed in December 1932 and opened the next month. Unfortunately, Mackenzie died in 1934 and never saw Horton Smith win the tournament that would make his creation famous.[19]

The Augusta National Invitation Tournament began in 1934. Tickets for that first tournament cost two dollars, and several thousand spectators showed up to see Bobby Jones come out of retirement to play with some of the best amateurs and professionals of the time. When the name "Masters" was first proposed, Jones thought it sounded too pretentious; but he relented and the name was officially adopted in 1939.[20] What began as a tournament among Bobby Jones's friends has since become a major cultural and sporting event. The Masters is a four-day, stroke play competition of eighteen holes each day. The invitation-only participants are derived from a list of specific qualifications. The Masters is the only one of golf's four designated majors to be played on the same course each year. Each spring thousands of patrons come to Augusta to see the best professional and amateur players compete for the coveted green jacket. Originally intended for members, this important symbol of achievement was first given to Sam Snead, the 1949 Masters champion.[21]

The Masters is steeped in tradition, and many of the innovations in staging golf tournaments that have been made in the past seventy years began at Augusta National. Though initially intended to accommodate Masters patrons, they have been universally adopted by professional golf tournaments throughout the world. Clifford Roberts pioneered the use of elevated mounds to provide patrons with a better view. In 1946, the first amphitheater-shaped mounds were built near the fifteenth green. In 1960, the Masters began the over-and-under scoring system that represents the number of strokes a player is over (in green) or under par (in red) instead of reporting hole-by-hole scores. The Masters was the first tournament to utilize tee-to-green gallery ropes (1949) and observation stands (1962). Organizers also sought to accommodate patrons who could not attend, becoming the first golf tournament broadcast on nationwide radio (1934), the first telecast in color (1966), and the first broadcast oversees via satellite (1967).[22] It is, indeed, as CBS broadcaster Jim Nantz remarks each year during the broadcast, "a tradition unlike any other."

But it is also a powerful symbol of prestige, privilege, and nostalgia. Four moments in history—in 1957, 1960, 1990, and 2002—involved Augusta National and reflect the complex politics of race, class, and gender that reveal fissures in the image of the new and progressive South. Embedded in these discussions is the subtle, symbolic Jones legacy, evoked by members and admirers as a way to hold on to an uncomplicated time when everyone—black and white, male and female, rich and poor—ostensibly knew their place.

The first incident involved President Dwight D. Eisenhower, who became a member of Augusta National in 1948, and was a close friend of Jones. Eisenhower faced two great crises during his presidency: the desegregation fight at Central High School in Little Rock, Arkansas, in 1957 and the U-2 spy plane incident in 1960. Little Rock placed Eisenhower at odds with many of his southern friends, and he paid a high price for opposing Arkansas Governor Orville Faubus and his segregationist supporters. When he called federal troops to help admit nine black teenagers to Central High School, Eisenhower committed, for many, an unpardonable sin of undermining states rights.[23] It was no surprise, then, that the southern press barbecued Eisenhower, and that his decision to defend the 1954 *Brown v. Board of Education* ruling jeopardized many long friendships from Augusta National. Even though they were not all southern, many ANGC members shared Governor Faubus's outlook on segregation. Privately, so did Eisenhower, but he would be judged by this very bold and public maneuver. There is no record of how Bobby Jones responded or reacted to the Little Rock crisis, but his support of Eisenhower was well known. Surely, this crisis tested even that. Eisenhower hoped his friends and the nation would understand that his decision in Little Rock was made in the interest of protecting federal authority (and, by extension, the office of the president) and in an effort to combat the spread of Communism.[24]

Realizing the symbolic power of Augusta National, three years later, supporters of integration tried to make Augusta National and the president's membership there part of the national dialogue about civil rights. On May 2, 1960, eleven of Augusta's Paine College students were arrested in a series of bus demonstrations and fined $45 for violating a segregation ordinance.[25] On December 10, 1960, sixty students and other demonstrators protested President Eisenhower's visit. They gathered outside Augusta National Golf Club, where they held signs that said, "Wrong will fail, right will prevail."[26] This incident did not immediately transform golf or the ANGC; the Caucasian Race Clause would not be removed from the PGA of America's constitution until 1961 and African American golfer Charlie Sifford would not join the PGA Tour until 1964.[27] But it did begin a national conversation about desegregation in one of the nation's most elite sports in the shadow of its most storied venue.

The ANGC finally admitted its first black member in 1990, in the wake of the public controversy regarding race at another southern club. The PGA of America elected not to host the PGA Championship at Shoal Creek Golf and Country Club in Birmingham, Alabama, that same year because it did not admit African American members.[28] This incident sparked a national conversation about golf, race, and equality in American life that seemed strikingly out of date. ANGC was constantly evoked in much of that debate because of its stature as the nation's premier private club. Yet discussions about Jones and his legacy, usually so inextricably tied to ANGC, were strikingly absent. The controversies that engulfed the golf world never seemed to touch the Jones legacy. He was the "teflon hero," in the spirit of Ronald Reagan's moniker "the teflon president."[29] Jones remained untarnished, and, in the face of the Shoal Creek incident, he was also invisible.

While the ANGC membership eventually bowed to the race question, gender was more complex. Augusta National was once again in the news when Martha Burke, the president of the National Council of Women's Organizations, began a well-organized protest in 2002 of the club's refusal to admit female members. In response, ANGC chairman William "Hootie" Johnson replied that her approach was "offensive and coercive" and explained: "Our membership is single gender just as many other organizations and clubs all across America. These would include junior leagues, sororities, fraternities, Boy Scouts, Girl Scouts, and countless others. And we all have a moral and legal right to organize our clubs the way we wish."[30] One member, Boone Knox, a bank executive, responded, "We have nothing against women," Knox said. "I love them all. I've got some myself. But we're a private club, and I'm all for it staying that way."[31] Augusta was alternately portrayed during the controversy as powerful (a private sanctuary where the all-male membership would not bow to the whims of "political correctness") to old fashioned (a throwback to an era of southern hospitality and gentility), and Jones was consistently evoked as the symbol of the club. Yet he remained, somehow, separated from and above the fray. While Burke's protests seemed largely unsuccessful in the media, her "Women on Wall Street Project" targeted companies whose executives are members of ANGC and have won nearly $80 million in settlements from Morgan Stanley, Smith Barney, and other major corporations.[32]

In each of these historical moments, the ANGC and, by extension, Bobby Jones was seen as a symbol of the South's bygone days, where bourbon was sipped on the porch and the messiness of civil rights was locked outside the gates on Washington Road. ANGC was seen as a sanctuary where time stood still and where there was much to admire, from the legend of Jones to the beauty of the azaleas. It is constantly evoked as the most admired place in golf; no other course, except for possibly the Old Course at St. Andrews, evokes stronger emotions. Much in golf is measured against it, and its founder remains the game's most revered player, untouched by controversy.

The Problem with Tiger Woods

Jones not only floats above the fray in the controversies about race and gender. He is also—with his southern charm, humility, grace under pressure, keen skill, and sportsmanship—rolled out as an antidote or salve to the sporting world's troubled present. This became all the more evident during the 2009 holiday season. Thanksgiving that year presented Tiger Woods with a kind of publicity of which he was unfamiliar and could not control. At 2:25 A.M. on November 27, Woods crashed his Cadillac SUV into a fire hydrant outside his home near Orlando, Florida.[33] What was first described as a minor traffic accident quickly blossomed into one of the decade's most scurrilous media scandals. By December 2, *US Weekly* published a cover story about Jaimee Grubbs, a Los Angeles cocktail waitress who claimed to have been having an affair with Woods. That same day, Woods apologized for what he loosely termed his transgressions on his Web site.[34] Three days later, *Saturday Night Live* presented a three-part skit parodying the golfer's woes, as more women continued to come forward. Throughout the winter, Woods's sponsors, such as Tag Hauer, AT&T, and General Motors, begin to drop him as a spokesperson. On December 17, PGA Tour commissioner Tim Finchem declared that "golf will survive" the scandal. On January 20, the most famous athlete in the world was reportedly photographed by the *National Enquirer* at Pine Grove Behavioral Health and Addiction Services in Hattiesburg, Mississippi, where he was reportedly being treated for what the media dubbed "sex rehab." The scandal so dominated the airwaves and print media that it even permeated the Miss America Pageant. During her introduction, one contestant blurted out: "From the home of The Masters Golf Tournament, where I did not meet Tiger Woods, I'm Emily Cook, Miss Georgia."[35] On June 30, the *London Sun* reported that Woods's divorce from Elin Nordegren was final, with a settlement of $750 million.[36]

The Woods scandal, though not unique to the world of sport, was unusual in the golf community. The occasional exploits of John Daly, a popular and deeply troubled golfer, generate periodic interest in the trade press, but nothing of this scope and scale. In the spring of 2010, Tiger Woods announced he was going to play in the tournament made famous by Bobby Jones. It was no surprise that Woods decided to return to competition at the Masters, the most controlled environment in golf. Jones's instructions about conduct, customs, and etiquette reprinted each year in the *Spectator Guide* worked in Woods's favor. Augusta National was the one place in the golfing world where Woods could expect to find a kinder and gentler audience. Largely lost on the press coverage of the event was that Woods had selected the one place where a generation earlier he would have been banned from competition.

Conversations in country club locker rooms and on the nineteenth hole (the cocktail bar) at public golf courses were buzzing with the news of Tiger's comeback. Michael Bamberger, a senior writer for *Sports Illustrated,* speculated on golf scandals in a December 2007 article that anticipated many of the issues raised three years later. As Woods continued to face questions about steroid usage, along with additional infidelities, Bamberger proved only partly wrong. He wrote:

> Nobody does scandal like baseball. Baseball's got it all: sex scandals, drug scandals, gambling scandals, cheating scandals. Many brawls. Guys who do not pay their taxes. No wonder Pete Rose, for a singles hitter, is so famous. Yes, he's the Hit King, but the Scandal King, too. It's all good. When Commissioner Bud Selig was whisked away after his Thursday afternoon

say-nothing press conference at the old Waldorf Astoria, and scores of
reporters reached for their cell-phones to call their bosses, it seemed like
the old days: Bart Giamatti banishing Pete Rose in '89; Kenesaw Mountain
Landis, baseball's first commissioner, doing the same to Shoeless Joe and
his fellow Black Sox after the 1919 World Series. If you're inside these
baseball scandals-du-jour, they're torturous. For the rest of us, they're
part of the fun. Golf has no idea.[37]

Bamberger was correct that the golf world was wholly unprepared for the
scope and scale of the Tiger Woods scandal, but it also raised a conundrum.
Some of golf's (and to some degree, the elite South's) core values—self-
control, modesty, and honesty—were so publicly and blatantly violated
by the sport's most famous and valuable player that few in the industry,
from players to tournament organizers, knew how to respond. How then
could they reconcile golf's central values while supporting its most visible
transgressor? How did this scandal undermine the golfing community,
real or imagined?

Few in the golf industry responded with courage and grace. With the
exception of Swedish golfer Jesper Parnivik, other PGA Tour players replied
with a resounding "no comment" to questions posed by the media. Tournament organizers and sponsors were nearly silent. Only Billy Payne, the
chairman of Augusta National Golf Club, was in a position to scold Woods.
And he did so, on the most public of stages. At a news conference at Augusta National during the 2010 Masters week, Payne compared Woods to
other golfing greats, notably Jones, Jack Nicklaus, and Arnold Palmer and
declared: "As he ascended in our rankings of the world's greatest golfers,
he became an example to our kids that success is directly attributable to
hard work and effort. But as he now says himself, he forgot in the process
to remember that with fame and fortune comes responsibility, not invis-
ibility."[38] Payne, with the authority of the Masters and Bobby Jones behind
him, may have been the only person in a position powerful enough to say
what many were thinking.

But Payne was not the only person to evoke Bobby Jones at the time.
During Masters week, Bobby Jones Apparel Company took a more subtle
approach. It scolded Tiger Woods indirectly. The company's advertisement,
which ran in major newspapers such as the *Wall Street Journal* on Saturday,
read: "It's about grace over ego. It's where style merges with substance. It's
not about what you look like. It's about what you do. Now is a good time
to talk about Bobby Jones."[39] Ironically, many Masters patrons attended to
see Tiger Woods, but they were wearing sportswear with the Bobby Jones

logo. Once again, Jones became the symbol of what sports should be, what it can aspire to be. At Augusta National this symbolism takes on a distinctly southern flavor that is embedded in shared understandings among middle-class patrons about what constitutes gentlemanly behavior—good manners, respect, honesty, kindness, modesty.[40] Woods breached that code, but what was unusual about the public conversation about this scandal was the absence of discussions of race or gender. The trade press treaded lightly on Tiger Woods, maybe because he keeps the sponsors, events, fans, and nearly the entire sport happy and afloat. Yet how his transgressions were framed and largely forgiven tells us much about the sport and the context in which it emerged. Golf is, after all, a business. Civility and honor (the southern values to preserve) and racism and exclusion (the southern values to reject) do not, in the end, trump the almighty dollar.

Notes

1. Bobby Jones Apparel Company, http://www.bobbyjonesshop.com/about/, accessed July 28, 2010.

2. Though Woods's conduct is clearly not a disease, I use the term *antidote* deliberately, as this particular sporting scandal (as with many other historic scandals) was sometimes discussed by fans or the media as a kind of disease that had as its symptoms corruption, deception, or other forms of bad behavior.

3. Elliott J. Gorn and Warren Goldstein, *A Brief History of American Sports* (New York: Hill and Wang, 1993), 188–97.

4. In 1930, the Grand Slam was comprised of the British Amateur, the British Open, the U.S. Open, and the U.S. Amateur.

5. See Martin Davis, *The Greatest of Them All: The Legend of Bobby Jones* (Greenwich, Conn.: The American Golfer, 1997), 192–99.

6. See O. B. Keeler, *The Bobby Jones Story: The Authorized Biography* (Chicago: Triumph Books, 2003), 15–16. For more information about Jones, see Catherine M. Lewis, *Considerable Passions: Golf, the Masters, and the Legacy of Bobby Jones* (Chicago: Triumph Books, 2000).

7. See "Play the Ball Where It Lies," in Lewis, *Considerable Passions,* 6–33. For a broader discussion of his life see, Robert Tyre Jones Jr., *Golf is My Game* (Stratford, Conn.: Classics of Golf, 1997) and Ron Rapoport, *The Immortal Bobby: Bobby Jones and the Golden Age of Golf* (New York: Wiley, 2005).

8. Jones, Evins, Moore & Powers, which is now now Alston + Bird, LLP.

9. Catherine M. Lewis, *Bobby Jones and the Quest for the Grand Slam* (Chicago: Triumph Books, 2005), 51–75.

10. Lewis, *Considerable Passions,* 11.

11. Lewis, *Bobby Jones and the Quest for the Grand Slam,* 114–50.

12. In addition to other texts cited in this chapter, see Stephen Lowe, *Sir Walter and Mr. Jones: Walter Hagen, Bobby Jones, and the Rise of American Golf* (Chelsea, Mich.: Sleeping Bear Press, 2000), Mark Frost, *The Grand Slam: Bobby Jones, America, and the*

Story of Golf (New York: Hyperion, 2005) and Sid Matthew, *The Wit and Wisdom of Bobby Jones* (New York: Wiley, 2003). A number of publishers have also reissued classic texts on Jones, including his early autobiography *Down the Fairway* (Atlanta: Longstreet Press, [1927] 2001).

13. Herbert Warren Wind, "Fifty Years After the Grand Slam," *New Yorker,* May 26, 1980, 81.

14. From September 22 to 24, 1906, white mobs terrorized and killed African Americans on the streets of Atlanta, prompted by an alleged assault by black men on white women. See Clifford Kuhn, "Atlanta Race Riot, 1906," in the *New Georgia Encyclopedia,* http://www.georgiaencyclopedia.org/nge/Article.jsp?id=h-3033, accessed November 13, 2010. See also Rebecca Burns, *Rage in the Gate City: The Story of the 1906 Atlanta Race Riot* (Athens: University of Georgia Press, 2009).

15. The Leo Frank case is one of the most notorious cases in Georgia history. Frank, a Jewish manager of a pencil factory, was tried and convicted of killing Mary Phagan in 1913, and lynched in Marietta two years later. See Steve Oney, *And the Dead Shall Rise: The Murder of Mary Phagan and the Lynching of Leo Frank* (New York: Pantheon, 2003).

16. See Jones, *Golf is My Game.*

17. Augusta National Golf Club, "Conduct, Customs, and Etiquette," message from Robert Tyre Jones Jr. (1902–1971), written April, 1967. *Spectator Guide,* April 2–8, 2001. Author's collection.

18. See BuyMastersTickets.Com, http://www.classictickets.com/orderonline/Results Ticket.asp?evtid=1354736&IcameFrom=BuyMastersTickets.com, accessed December 12, 2010.

19. See Lewis, "Bobby Jones's Architectural Legacy," in *Considerable Passions,* 69. For a broader history of Augusta National and the Masters, see also David Owen, *The Making of the Masters: Clifford Roberts, Augusta National, and Golf's Most Prestigious Tournament* (New York: Simon and Schuster, 1999).

20. Lewis, *Considerable Passions,* 70–71 and Owen, *The Making of the Masters,* 86–99.

21. Ward Clayton, "Honorary Starters Remember Sarazen," *Augusta Chronicle,* April 7, 2000. http://www.augusta.com/masters/review2000/040600/sarazen_remembered _2000.shtml, accessed December 1, 2010.

22. See Lewis, *Considerable Passions,* 68–99. See Owen, *The Making of the Masters,* 183–276.

23. Peter Lyon, *Eisenhower: Portrait of the Hero* (Boston: Little Brown, 1974), 798.

24. Ellis D. Slater, *The Ike I Knew* (New York: Ellis D. Slater Trust, 1980), 161.

25. Kamille Bostick, "Paine Students Worked to End Segregation," *Augusta Chronicle,* February 5, 2005, http://chronicle.augusta.com/stories/020605/met_3201913.shtml, accessed September 11, 2005.

26. Bostick, http://chronicle.augusta.com/stories/020605/met_3201913.shtml.

27. Andy Ambrose, Brooke Bargeron, and Alexis Oliver, "Negroes Cannot Play Here: The Desegregation of Atlanta's Golf Courses," *Atlanta History: A Journal of Georgia and the South* 43(1) (1999): 21–32.

28. Jill Lieber, "Golf Host Clubs Have an Open-and-Shut Policies on Discrimination," *USA Today,* April 9, 2003, http://www.usatoday.com/sports/golf/2003–04–09-club -policies_x.htm, accessed July 1, 2009.

29. Haynes Johnson, *Sleepwalking Through History: America in the Reagan Years* (New York: Doubleday, 1991).

30. Public Broadcasting Corporation, "A web Master's Challenge," PBS Online Newshour, February 20, 2003, http://www.pbs.org/newshour/bb/sports/jan-june03/golf_2–20.html, accessed March 1, 2003.

31. Michael McCarthy and Erik Brady, "Privacy Becomes Public at Augusta," *USA Today,* September 27, 2002, accessed November 29, 2010, http://www.usatoday.com/sports/golf/masters/2002-09-27-augusta_x.htm.

32. William Wolfrum, "Martha Burke's fight against Augusta National's all-male policy gaining momentum, she says." WorldGolf.com, April 11, 2008, accessed August 20, 2010, http://www.worldgolf.com/features/martha-burk-fight-against-augusta-national-all-male-policy-6700.htm. In August 2012, the ANGC announced it will admit Condoleezza Rice and Darla Moore as the first two female members.

33. A timeline of the events surrounding the Tiger Woods scandal can be found at http://nbcsports.msnbc.com/id/34969596, accessed August 22, 2010.

34. Accessed December 30, 2009, http://web.tigerwoods.com/news/dearTiger.

35. Huffington Post, "Miss Georgia: I Didn't Meet Tiger Woods (video)." http://www.huffingtonpost.com/2010/01/30/miss-georgia-i-didnt-meet_n_443379.html, accessed December 2, 2010.

36. A timeline of the events surrounding the Tiger Woods scandal can be found at http://nbcsports.msnbc.com/id/34969596, accessed August 22, 2010.

37. Michael Bamberger, "Could Golf be the Next Sport to Face a Series of Drug Scandals?" accessed August 22, 2010, http://www.golf.com/golf/tours_news/article/0,28136,1695139,00.html.

38. Greg Stoda, "Masters Chairman Billy Payne Calls Out Tiger Woods," *Palm Beach Post,* April 8, 2010, accessed November 9, 2010, http://www.palmbeachpost.com/sports/golf/masters-chairman-billy-payne-calls-out-tiger-woods-535266.html.

39. This advertisement ran in the *Wall Street Journal,* April 10, 2010. Sent to the author by Marty Elgison, Alston & Bird, LLC.

40. This gentlemanly code, a version of which is written by Bobby Jones and printed in the *Master's Patron's Guide* each year, is shared not just by white, middle-class men, but transcends gender, race, class, ethnicity, and even national origin, at least during the Masters. All patrons are expected to adhere to it, and those who have attended the Masters can attest to the civility of the crowd in comparison with other golf tournaments.

4. Football Town under Friday Night Lights

*High School Football and
American Dreams*

MICHAEL ORIARD

In 2003, the prolific best-selling novelist John Grisham took a break from legal thrillers to publish *Bleachers,* a novel about high school football that is a virtual encyclopedia of clichés and stereotypes, including the competing ideas at its center. Has high school football in the southern town of Messina been a source of community identity and pride or a collective pathology? Was the legendary coach Eddie Rake a great man or a monster? Grisham ultimately answered these questions positively, yet until that concession to pop-fiction necessity a convincing sense that the sport and the coach were not one or the other but irreconcilably both gives the novel its power.

The competing views echo familiar narratives about the role of high school football in American communities. One we might call the "Friday Night Lights" syndrome, after H. G. Bissinger's popular and critically acclaimed journalistic account of football at Permian High School in Odessa, Texas, published in 1990, and made into a film in 2004 and a TV series in 2006. The other narrative we can name "Football Town," after a series of portraits in popular magazines in the 1940s and 1950s that have long been forgotten but whose image persists. In some American cities and towns, high school football is simply a sport played by fourteen- to eighteen-year-old boys on teams representing their schools, cheered on by their families and friends. Elsewhere, and to widely varying degrees, it matters much more. "Football Town" casts the high school game as America at its best—communities bonding and celebrating their homegrown traditions through a shared passion for their school team. "Friday Night Lights" casts it as a sign of those communities' spiritual impoverishment, and as a potentially crushing burden borne by mere sixteen- and seventeen-year-olds. Like professional and collegiate football, the high school version is often much more than an innocent game, and Americans have been arguing over what it tells us about ourselves for a very long time.

Interscholastic football began in the late nineteenth century, in tandem with the development of the intercollegiate game. Secondary schools in Boston first adopted the carrying (rugby) version in the 1860s, emulating developments at Harvard. The longest-running high school rivalry, Phillips Academy (Andover, Massachusetts) versus Phillips Exeter (New Hampshire) Academy, began in 1875. Like the college game, interscholastic football spread outward from New England (the dates are moving targets, as researchers keep revising them): to Illinois (Evanston, outside Chicago) by 1879, Ohio (Cleveland) by 1890, California (San Francisco) by 1891, Texas by around 1900.[1] City, state, and national organizations followed in due course: the Public School Athletic League (PSAL) in New York, in 1903, creating a model for other metropolitan areas; state associations in Georgia in 1904, Ohio in 1907, Texas in 1910, Pennsylvania in 1913, California in 1914, and so on; the National Federation of High Schools in 1920.[2]

Again following the college model, geographical diffusion led to intersectional competition by at least 1902, when Hyde Park of Chicago played Polytechnic Prep of Brooklyn in what local sportswriters treated seriously as a measure of eastern and western football prowess. This was the first of some 160 intersectional games played by Chicago-area high schools over the next half-century, in addition to eighty more against schools from Ohio and other nearby states, beginning with a contest in 1901 between Morgan Park Academy of Chicago and University High of Cleveland for an unofficial "private schools Midwestern championship."[3] Intersectional games proliferated in the 1920s in all regions, though trips to and from the West Coast were relatively infrequent. Some of these games were promoted locally as "national championships," but the first "official" high school national champion (from Waco, Texas) was crowned in 1927—by a twenty-one-year-old high school coach in Minnesota, on his own authority, who later made retroactive selections back to 1910. (*USA Today* inaugurated the modern era of national rankings in 1982. The first high school All-America team was selected in 1948, followed by the Sunday supplement *Parade Magazine* in 1963, among others.)[4]

Intersectional contests led by the 1930s to "bowl" games and other postseason invitationals, again modeled on college football, typically in Sun Belt communities through the agency of local promoters or sponsoring newspapers, sometimes on behalf of a Shriners' Hospital, Christmas Toy Fund, or the like. The longest-running of these interscholastic bowls include a Christmas Day game in Miami from 1929 through 1947, with a break for the war, pitting Miami High against a powerhouse from another section; and the Peanut Bowl in Columbus, Georgia, on New Year's Day from 1947 through 1954, with the Georgia state champion taking on an outsider. The Toy Bowl in early December in New Orleans, sponsored by the *Times-Picayune* from 1934 through 1944, matched the New Orleans city champion with a regional champion from Mississippi, before becoming an in-state affair in 1945. Several other postseason "classics" lasted a year or two.[5]

Yet again mirroring big-time college football, these games sparked controversy over distorted priorities, commercialism, and "overemphasis." A year after the landmark Carnegie Foundation report of 1929, which included a chapter on these problems at the high school level, the North Central Association Committee on Athletics in Schools, representing secondary schools throughout the Midwest, reported that three-fourths of its members acknowledged "educationally undesirable" aspects of their athletic programs, including the emphasis on winning, excessive number of games, postseason play, and lax eligibility rules.[6] Over the 1930s and 1940s, school boards and state federations began setting limits on travel and postseason play, leading to sporadic controversies and eventually the disappearance of postseason bowls and most intersectional games by the 1950s.[7]

These contests would likely have ended even without school board restrictions because local rivalries simply mattered more. The interscholastic "bowls" in Miami, New Orleans, and other cities sometimes drew as many as twenty-five thousand but more typically seven to fifteen thousand, in contrast, say, to the seventy-five thousand for Chicago's Catholic-Public league championships in the 1930s and 1940s—an astonishing 120,000 in 1937—and the fifty to sixty thousand for Philadelphia's. Despite their metropolitan settings, these were neighborhood affairs, spiked by broader religious and ethnic partisanship.[8] Whether filling a twenty-two-thousand–seat state-of-the-art stadium in Massillon, Ohio, or a thousand seats on rickety stands in a cow pasture in Pflugerville, Texas, high school football aroused its fiercest passions in small towns without large public universities or professional franchises to provide a competing source of local identity and pride. In towns too small to field eleven-man teams, six-man and eight-man football sometimes played this role. As intersectional games largely disappeared after World War II, postseason in-state competition entered a new era. Several states (North Carolina, California, Texas, Louisiana,

Colorado, and Montana among them) had instituted state championships from nearly the beginning of their statewide associations, but many others began adding them in the 1940s and over the following decades (including Georgia in 1947 and Ohio in 1972), or created divisions to involve more schools of all sizes in existing tournaments. With the creation of three divisions in 1948—adding two more in 1951, and three more (including six- and eight-man) in 1972—the state of Texas established arguably the most intensely followed football playoffs in the nation.[9]

When the national media began paying attention to high school football in the late 1930s, the actual game's place in local communities began to take on larger meanings.[10] The teams from Boys Town (near Omaha, Nebraska)—orphans rescued by football from dead-end lives and given a surrogate family—became a minor phenomenon after the producer of the popular 1938 film starring Mickey Rooney and Spencer Tracy (who won an Academy Award for his performance as Father Flanagan) arranged a game in Los Angeles before a celebrity-studded crowd, with newsreel cameras running. The real Father Flanagan seized this opportunity "to take his football team on the road as a gypsy, bring-on-all-comers sideshow featuring orphans from the world-famous Boys Town."[11] The most famous schoolboy football player of all time, in relative terms, has to be Bill De Correvont of Austin High in Chicago, whose nine touchdowns and 334 yards rushing (on ten carries) in an early season game his senior year in 1937 prompted a syndicated cartoon that led to wire-service attention to his remaining games—including the city championship before 120,000 at Soldier Field and a postseason game in Memphis—followed by network radio coverage of his choice of colleges and a cover story in *Look* magazine marking his varsity debut at Northwestern. (Sadly, schoolboy fame became a leg chain for De Correvont to drag through college. He turned out to be a pretty good player on some decent teams, and afterward had a modest five-year career in the NFL, but nothing short of superstardom could have matched the expectations.)[12]

Boys Town and Bill De Correvont were specific cases. In the 1940s and 1950s, a generic image of high school football also emerged in magazine profiles of "Football Town," a particular place, such as Massillon, Ohio, or Whitehall, New York, but implicitly a symbol of idyllic small-town America everywhere. The term first appeared as the title of a 1937 article in *Collier's* about Green Bay, Wisconsin, the sole remaining small town with a franchise in the National Football League. Yet the idea and variations on the term soon became attached to a series of towns in love with their high school teams: besides Massillon and Whitehall, Amarillo, Texas; Canton,

That Whirlwind From the Windy City

Bill De Correvont received the treatment of a college All-American from the national as well as local press, when Austin High traveled to Memphis at the end of the 1937 season for the second annual Dixie Interscholastic game against the local regional champion. *Memphis Commercial Appeal,* December 5, 1937.

Ohio; Everett, Massachusetts; Alhambra, California; White Plains, New York; Massillon again ("Football Town"); Atchison, Kansas ("Football Crazy Town"); Weymouth, Massachusetts; Donora, Pennsylvania.[13] From its debut in 1954 through the 1970s, *Sports Illustrated* published articles on Massillon (twice); Abilene, Texas; Braddock, Pennsylvania; Valdosta, Georgia (one stop on a "Search for America"); Brownwood, Texas; Hudson, Michigan; and Vicksburg, Michigan.[14]

In Football Town, 100 out of 160 boys in the high school turned out for the team (Whitehall); future prospects were scouted before they reached junior high (Amarillo); "Fathers, brothers and uncles pounce[d] upon chubby youngsters almost as soon as they can walk" (White Plains). Moms, sisters, girlfriends, and cheerleaders baked cookies, painted posters, and hugged their heroes after the games. Booster clubs raised money, sold tickets, met weekly with the coach, and presented awards to the players after the season. Already by 1941, a lower-case term with the indefinite article—Whitehall is "a football town indeed"—designated an entire class of American communities, indistinguishable from each other but collectively unique to the United States.[15] Football Town was benignly patriarchal, class-less, race-less (wholly white), and rarely ethnic—with *Look*'s portrait of multiethnic football at Everett High in 1945 as the striking exception. In a period of profound uncertainty—a Second World War, followed by postwar prosperity *and* accelerating modernization, cold war anxieties, and The Bomb—Football Town celebrated the American Way of Life embodied in the "unchanging" small town.

The actual places designated as Football Towns were of course more complicated than the magazine profiles acknowledged. After all, the all-consuming passions for high school football illustrated the overemphasis on athletics criticized by educators since the 1920s. The season before the *Saturday Evening Post* celebrated White Plains as a Football Town, all but two of its Westchester County opponents dropped the school from their schedules, resulting from disputes over eligibility, financial excesses, and its overall semiprofessional approach to the sport. A year after the article in the *Post*, White Plains agreed to "curb football" to win back its conference rivals.[16]

Other details from the magazine profiles resonate with unacknowledged complications: the overinvolved boosters, costly facilities, inflated salaries of coaches, and relentlessly hard practices—not to mention the rigid gender roles and the fundamental fact of sixteen- and seventeen-year-old boys bearing the hopes of the community. Glimpses of Football Town's dark side began appearing in the 1950s. Jimmy Breslin's portrait of Donora, Pennsylvania, openly confronted the desperation of millworkers' sons to escape their fathers' fate through football scholarships. A high school coach in western Pennsylvania described for the *Saturday Evening Post* the distorted priorities that drove him to quit.[17] Most powerfully, *Life* magazine's 1962 piece on Martins Ferry, Ohio, offered a stunning series of grim photographs: of the molten iron in an open-hearth furnace that the boys were trying to escape; of one of the "smoky riverfront stadiums" set against the backdrop of a grimy mill town; of mud-spattered players with bloody bandaged arms and legs. Football in Martins Ferry meant "transportation out" of a place "where men with missing fingers and legs wander the streets," but the price of escape was submission to "stiff discipline" from parents as well as coaches, reinforced with violence when necessary. The coach's greatest hazard was the Booster Club, which might give him a new car for winning a state championship, then a road map and fifteen dollars for gas after losing a couple of games the next season.[18]

The portraits of Donora and Martins Ferry simply offered Football Town without airbrushing the soot and desperation. Thirty years later in *Friday Night Lights,* H. G. Bissinger cast high school football in Odessa, Texas, as a collective pathology. Odessa was recognizably another Football Town obsessed with its high school team, but Bissinger laid bare the consequences of that obsession: the extravagant spending on football and underfunding of education, the equally grotesque pressures and privileges heaped on adolescents, the stunted lives of adults who can imagine nothing more important than the outcome of a boys' game. Football mattered so much because Odessa—a toxic mix of desolate landscape, volatile oil economy, drunkenness, violence, self-righteousness, and racism—had so little else to offer. Bissinger's book led to a movie in 2004 and a critically acclaimed (but underwatched) TV series in 2006, as well as a reality show on MTV in 2006, *Two-a-Days,* documenting high school football in an Odessa-like Hoover, Alabama, and even a National Public Radio series in 2009 on "Friday Night Lives."[19]

Bissinger's *Friday Night Lights* exposed the dark side of supposed Football Towns and provided a shorthand term for its antithesis. With the disappearance of the great general-interest weekly magazines in the 1960s, *Sports Illustrated* and Hollywood films became the chief chroniclers of high school football at the extreme. Hollywood paid little attention to the schoolboy sport before 1983, when *All the Right Moves* brought the world of Donora and Martins Ferry to the screen—a football scholarship as escape from a dead-end mill town—though with an upbeat Hollywood ending. Among the twenty-odd high school football films that followed, the majority were variations on Hollywood's favorite plot about underdogs or outsiders, but a few at least touched on the game's place in the community. *The Best of Times* (1986) offered an ironic version of Football Town: a godforsaken spot in the San Joaquin Valley, where the only tradition is losing to hated Bakersfield, and a hapless banker has been haunted for thirteen years by a dropped pass that could have won a game. *Varsity Blues* (1999, also a TV series in 2002) re-created *Friday Night Lights*—with an abusive coach and a halftime rebellion by the players that Grisham adapted for *Bleachers*—as of course did the 2004 movie version of Bissinger's book, though with an emotionally tidier ending. More inspiring, or sentimental, *Remember the Titans* (2000) celebrated the power of high school football to transcend a community's racial divisions, although not in the conflict-free manner of a 1940s Football Town.

Initially, *Sports Illustrated* offered mostly benign views of Football Town, with occasional reservations. In 1957, it contrasted, without editorial comment, the high school football played for fun in Hempstead, Long Island, with the deadly serious game played in Massillon and Abilene.[20] In 1970, John Underwood of *Sports Illustrated* left Valdosta, Georgia, and its legendary coach, Wright Bazemore, feeling "ambivalent" about a place where inflated expectations made a tie for the state championship feel like failure.[21] When another writer returned to Massillon in 1985 to describe "A Mauling in Tiger Town"—the firing of a coach with a 79–16–2 record—that ambivalence had deepened. The very thing that made Massillon so appealing—"the town's cradle-to-grave interest in football, the tradition, the avid cross-generational support"—was also "treacherous" for coaches. *Sports Illustrated*'s Jack McCallum wrote: "On an autumn Friday night in the town there is something of America's spirit" in the traditions of a high school football game. "But tradition is a many-headed beast, one that stomps on reality and coldcocks high school football coaches."[22]

As the dark side of Football Town grew darker in *Sports Illustrated*, consistent with the more critical edge to sports journalism generally since the 1960s, the positive version became more idyllic than ever. The effect was to criticize, implicitly rather than directly, by celebrating the vestiges of a vanishing world. When the magazine returned to Valdosta, Georgia ("Winnersville"), in 1988, none of John Underwood's ambivalence remained from 1970. For championship football, Valdosta was to Georgia what Massillon was to Ohio, but *Sports Illustrated* cast Valdosta as an anti-Massillon in ways that mattered more. Massillon was a grimy mill town? Valdosta was "one of the prettiest and most prosperous towns in south Georgia."[23] Massillon was on its fifth coach since 1970? Valdosta was on just its second since Wright Bazemore retired in 1971. Families moved to Massillon so their sons could play at Washington High? Valdosta nurtured its local boys, and outsiders rarely made the team. Massillon won with the best athletes, then sent them on to college with scholarships? High school football in Valdosta was an end in itself. Colleges recruited relatively few Valdosta players, and some of those played poorly "because the game doesn't seem as important in college."[24] Like Massillon, Valdosta had "tradition," but whether its tradition might likewise be "a many-headed beast"—Wright Bazemore had retired at age fifty-five because he was "just tired of it" (tired of coaching state champions in an idyllic setting?)—was left to readers' speculation.[25]

Two years after "Winnersville," *Sports Illustrated* excerpted Bissinger's *Friday Night Lights,* and over the next two decades it swung back and forth between the polar narratives of high school football. In 1993, a team split by factions in Bridgman, Michigan—spoiled "kids [who] won't run through walls anymore" pitted against the arrogant twin sons of an overinvolved father—"ended community social life in Bridgman for the rest of the fall" by cancelling its season.[26] In 2001, *Sports Illustrated* reported that the inter-racial harmony in Alexandria, Virginia, celebrated in Disney's *Remember the Titans,* had vanished.[27] Elsewhere, though, Football Town remained intact: in rural Texas, where six-man football "celebrates an America that didn't die with the social revolutions of the 1960s"; in Anderson, South Carolina, where the team and the town embrace a mentally challenged black man named Radio.[28] High school football in these communities seemed untouched by the celebrity sports culture of twenty-four-hour cable TV; big money and labor conflict in the NFL; continuous scandals in big-time college football, often involving blue-chip high school recruits; and online recruiting Web sites (Rivals.com, Scout.com), where sixteen- and seventeen-year-olds could monitor their college prospects like so many pork futures. Within this new national sports culture schoolboy football seemed both grotesque in itself and merely a stage on the way to wealth, celebrity, and excess for those talented or lucky enough. Except where it remained pure.

Sports Illustrated defined this contrast most sharply in a four-part special report in 2002 on high school sports, whose "disconnection from com-munity" marked a disturbing new era.[29] Young athletes no longer played for school, family, friends, and neighbors, but for themselves, often on travel teams drawn from entire regions rather than single communities, working to get to the next level and the eventual payoff as a professional. Yet against this tidal change, a vestige of Football Town persisted in the traditional Thanksgiving Day game, "redolent of America's all-but-extinct-small-town culture," played for the ninety-sixth time by high schools in Webster Groves and Kirkwood, Missouri, two "leafy, stately," and "gilded" suburbs of St. Louis that clung to "communal memory."[30]

Football Town was the past, rapidly receding from the brave new world of big-time high school football. Yet, alongside its nostalgic evocations of vestigial Football Towns, *Sports Illustrated* contributed its own "High School Football Preview" and weekly "Power Rankings" to the distorted new sports culture in 2006, a year after ESPN and Fox Sports Net added national tele-casts to their regional lineups of high school games. NBC's "The Line of Scrimmage" segments also began appearing during halftime of *Sunday Night*

Football in 2006—two guys traveling around the country in a Toyota pickup to look in on local high school football traditions—and both *Friday Night Lights,* the TV series, and *Two-a-Days,* the reality show on MTV featuring Hoover High School in Birmingham, Alabama, debuted. With print and electronic media shining a brighter light on teenage football players than ever before, Football Town survived even as it became more difficult to find. In a special issue on Texas football in 2008, an uncritical salute to "Texans' soul-sacrificing obsession with the game," *Sports Illustrated* represented the high school sport with the six-man version played in tiny towns like Gordon and Zephyr, where the illusion of Football Town was easier to maintain than in AAAA or even the lower eleven-man classifications.[31]

Football Town and Friday Night Lights: like John Grisham's *Bleachers,* the most recent portrait of Massillon, Ohio, a documentary titled *Go Tigers!* (2001), captures competing images that have now persisted for more than half a century. Boosters still put peewee footballs in the bassinets of newborn males, yet not everyone in Massillon is a football fan. The film gives a voice to alienated antijock students and a critical English teacher, while also revealing a powerful sense of community spirit as citizens celebrate over several city blocks following a victory over Canton McKinley High in the 105th meeting of the two great rivals. Euphoric from the victory, voters finally approve a desperately needed school bond levy. But should viewers be uplifted or appalled that a mere football game could matter so much? Because the film has no narrator, the competing words and images speak for themselves, revealing *both* Football Town and Friday Night Lights—or rather Football Town under Friday Night Lights, inseparable and irreconcilable.

Notes

1. Mel Smith, "1858: A Pivotal Year in Early U.S. Foot-Ball," *College Football Historical Society Newsletter,* February 2010; "List of high school football rivalries (100 years+)," http://en.wikipedia.org/wiki/List_of_high_school_football_rivalries_(100_years%2B) (October 12, 2010); Ray Schmidt, "A Century-Plus of Gridiron Thrills: A History of Illinois High School Football," Illinois High School Association, http://www.ihsa.org/initiatives/hstoric/football_new.htm (October 12, 2010); Timothy L. Hudak, "Looking Back at the OHSAA's Football Championships," Ohio High School Athletic Association, http://www.ohsaa.org/sports/history/Tim_Hudak_Features/Football.htm (October 12, 2010); Mike Bynam, ed., *King Football: Greatest Moments in Texas High School Football History* (Birmingham, Ala.: Epic Sports Classics, 2003). The date for California is from the list of longest rivalries; earlier games might have been played.

2. Dates from association Web sites.

3. Robert Pruter, "A Century of Intersectional and Interstate Football Contests,

1900–1999," Illinois High School Association, http://www.ihsa.org/initiatives/hstoric/football_intersec.htm (October 12, 2010).

4. For a complete list of polls and All-America teams, see Doug Huff, ed., *National High School Football Record Book* (Anaheim, Calif.: Studentsports, 2001), 44–45, 60–61.

5. St. Petersburg and Clearwater, Florida, hosted Christmas Day games in the 1930s; and I have located a Dixie Intersectional in Memphis in 1936 and 1937; a "national championship" game in Baton Rouge in 1938 and 1939; an Oyster Bowl in Norfolk, Virginia, in 1946; a Strawberry Bowl in Hammond, Louisiana, in 1946; an Exchange Bowl in Jackson, Tennessee, in 1946 and 1947; and an Orchid Bowl in Chattanooga, Tennessee, on New Years Day in 1947 and 1948 (some of these regional rather than national). My sources are newspapers from the host cities—this is unexplored territory.

6. Howard J. Savage and others, *American College Athletics,* Bulletin Number Twenty-Three (New York: Carnegie Foundation, 1929), 52–76; E. E. Morley, "Report of the North Central Association Committee on Athletics in Secondary Schools," *North Central Association Quarterly* 5 (December 1930): 332–39.

7. See, for example, the *New York Times* for December 28, 1935, and December 4–8, 1939; Wm. McG. Keefe, "Viewing the News," *New Orleans Times-Picayune,* December 7, 1938; and Pruter, "Century," 25. Miami High sometimes had to go through several choices before finding an opponent.

8. Gerald R. Gems, "The Prep Bowl: Football and Religious Acculturation in Chicago, 1927–1963," *Journal of Sport History* 23 (Fall 1996): 284–302; for the Philadelphia games (which began in 1938), see the *Philadelphia Inquirer.*

9. High school football only in Texas has been fully documented in trade books (as opposed to self-published or online histories). In addition to Bynam's *King Football* cited above, see Al Reinart and Geoff Winningham, *Rites of Fall: High School Football in Texas* (Austin: University of Texas Press, 1979) and Bill McMurray, *Texas High School Football* (South Bend, Ind.: Icarus Press, 1985).

10. For high school football in the Hearst newsreels, synopsis sheets (at the UCLA Film & TV Archive) list games for November 2, 1937, November 5, 1940, November 4, 1941, December 12, 1943, and December 6, 1952. For *Universal News* (at the National Archives in College Park, Md.), see December 13, 1943, December 16, 1946, December 9, 1947, August 14, 1950, December 11, 1950, December 10, 1951, December 7, 1952, and December 7, 1953.

11. Leo Adam Biga, "Boys Town: How Father Flanagan's Barnstorming Sports Teams Gained National Fame," *Nebraska Life* 11 (March–April 2007): 20.

12. Arthur Grahame, "Fame and Bill de Correvont," *Sport Story Magazine,* 1st November issue, 1938. See also *Memphis Commercial Appeal,* December 5, 8, and 12, 1937; *Look,* November 7, 1939; and *Life,* February 14, 1938. *Time,* February 21, 1938; October 17, 1938; October 16, 1939; and October 21, 1940. *Time* repeatedly deflated De Correvont's college accomplishments in contrast to his high school reputation.

13. Quentin Reynolds, "Football Town," *Collier's,* November 6, 1937, 62–65; "The Cradle of Pro Football Cheers a Great High School Team," *Life,* October 2, 1939, 54–55; "Look Goes to a High-School Football Weekend," *Look,* November 18, 1941; "Amarillo's Golden Sandies," *Look,* November 17, 1943; Pete Martin, "Football City," *Saturday Evening Post,* November 20, 1943 20ff; "High School Football," *Look,* October 2, 1945; "High School

Football at Night," *Look,* November 26, 1946; Pete Martin and Ben Carroll, "The Whole Town Made the Team," *Saturday Evening Post,* November 22, 1947, 36 and following; Carl L. Biemiller, "Football Town," *Holiday,* November 1949, 72ff; "Football Crazy Town," *Life,* December 4, 1950, 59–62; "Championship High-School Football," *Look,* September 23, 1952; Jimmy Breslin, "the Town That Spawns Athletes," *Saturday Evening Post,* October 15, 1955, 26 and following. Note: The page references for *Look* are unavailable.

14. Don Parker, "Football in the Backyard," *Sports Illustrated,* November 11, 1957, 22–26; "A Town and Its Team," *Sports Illustrated,* November 2, 1959, 34–37; Walter Bingham, "Football From the Cradle," *Sports Illustrated,* November 13, 1961, 46–51; John Underwood, "A Brief Search for America," *Sports Illustrated,* May 4, 1970, 64–80; Carlton Stowers, "A Pride of Lions in Cattle Country," *Sports Illustrated,* November 1, 1971, 38–42; Douglas S. Looney, "Wave the Flag for Hudson High," *Sports Illustrated,* November 24, 1975, 38–43; Bil Gilbert, "That Senior Season," *Sports Illustrated,* November 14, 1977, 104–22.

15. "Look Goes to a High-School Football Weekend."

16. "Football Now Is a Major Factor in the Life of White Plains High," *New York Times,* November 14, 1946, 31; "White Plains High to Curb Football," *New York Times,* December 17, 1948, 44.

17. Don Group (as told to Harry T. Paxton), "I'm Through with High-School Football!" *Saturday Evening Post,* October 11, 1952, 42 and following.

18. "Rocky Cradle of Football," *Life,* November 2, 1962, 70–78.

19. http://www.nbc.com/friday-night-lights/, accessed October 12, 2010; http://www.mtv.com/shows/2_a_days/series.jhtml, accessed October 12, 2010; http://topics.npr.org/topic/Friday_Night_Lights, accessed October 12, 2010.

20. Don Parker, "Football in The Backyard," *Sports Illustrated,* November 11, 1957, 22–27.

21. See note 15.

22. Jack McCallum, "A Mauling in Tiger Town," *Sports Illustrated,* July 1, 1985, 46.

23. Geoffrey Norman, "Winnersville U.S.A.," *Sports Illustrated,* October 31, 1988, 68–82.

24. Norman, "Winnersville U.S.A.," 75.

25. For a glimpse of the "beast," see Steve Wieberg, "Millions of Dollars Pour into High School Football," *USA Today,* October 6, 2004, accessed July 1, 2011, http://www.usatoday.com/sports/preps/football/2004-10-05-spending-cover_x.htm.

26. Gary Smith, "Generation Gap," *Sports Illustrated,* October 25, 1993, 36.

27. Tim Layden, "Does Anyone Remember the Titans?" *Sports Illustrated,* October 15, 2001, 72 and following.

28. John Ed Bradley, "6 Shooters," *Sports Illustrated,* October 28, 1996, 72; Gary Smith, "Someone to Lean On," *Sports Illustrated,* December 16, 1996, 78–93. Smith's piece on Radio led to the 2003 movie starring Cuba Gooding Jr.

29. Alexander Wolff, "The High School Athlete," *Sports Illustrated,* November 18, 2002, 74 and following.

30. Mark Bowden, "The Game of a Lifetime," *Sports Illustrated,* December 9, 2002, 76 and following.

31. Gene Menez, "A Texas Baptism," *Sports Illustrated,* August 5, 2008, 6–7; John Ed Bradley, "Small World," *Sports Illustrated,* August 5, 2008, 24–28.

5. Girls' Six-Player Basketball

"The Essence of Small-Town Life in Iowa"

JAIME SCHULTZ
AND SHELLEY LUCAS

I grew up playing five-player basketball in Iowa City, attending
coach C. Vivian Stringer's basketball camp nearly every summer
with misguided dreams of one day suiting up for the Hawkeyes.
It was there, amid the sweat-soaked T-shirts, calloused fingertips,
and the sound of rubber soles squeaking against the court, that I
first encountered that strange sub-set of athletes whose game did
not permit them to cross the half-court line. I felt sorry for these
girls, there to develop a "total game" while their regular-season
coaches insisted upon honing either their offensive or defensive
skills, accentuating one set to the detriment of the other. My
view of six-player basketball was from the outside; it afforded me
very little understanding of the game's deep roots, the merits
of its style, and its importance to notions of community and
identity. To think of six-on-six only in terms of its limitations,
I have since learned, is a big mistake.

—Jaime Schultz

My six-player basketball career began in second grade as a
member of a biddy basketball team in Long Grove, a small town
in eastern Iowa, and ended when I graduated from New London
High School in 1985. My senior year was the first year that high
school girls in Iowa were given the option to compete under the
five-player rules. Eleven years later, as a graduate student in
sport history, I discovered that Iowa occupied a unique place in
the history of women in sport. Until that time, I had no idea that
the game I grew up playing was different than what girls in other
states, even just an hour away, were playing. My position in that
classroom was as an "insider" who felt the need to balance my
critique of six-on-six as a game whose imposed constraints on

female physicality were based on sexist assumptions, with my
lived experience as a player who very much identified as a "real"
basketball player and who witnessed firsthand the culture of six-
on-six that celebrated, among other things, female strength and
the power of community.
—Shelley Lucas

Throughout the twentieth century, more than a million Iowa high school
girls played the half-court, two-dribble version of basketball colloquially
known as "six-on-six." Originally conceived to accommodate girls and wom-
en's perceived physical limitations, six-player basketball often lent itself
to fast-paced, high-scoring, crowd-rallying competitions. By the 1970s and
1980s, high schools across the nation, as well as those in larger Iowa cities,
adopted five-player or "boys' rules." Yet the Iowa Girls High School Athletic
Union (IGHSAU) continued to sponsor six-player basketball in the smaller,
rural communities until 1993, at which time, 275 of the state's 409 schools
with girls' basketball programs still offered six-on-six.[1]

Though the six-player game may be gone from the Iowa high school
program, it is anything but forgotten. Former athletes, coaches, adminis-
trators, and fans actively sustain the sport's memory in a variety of ways.
The game has inspired popular and scholarly publications, commemorative
programs, and a staged production of "Six-On-Six: The Musical." In 2008,
the state's public television network aired a documentary titled *More Than
a Game: Six-on-Six Basketball in Iowa,* and the program's official Web site
invites viewers to "Share your Iowa story" on an online discussion board;
contributors reminisce about their uniforms, coaches, teammates, and the
illustrious state tournament. They remember that their communities would
pack the gymnasiums, where girls' contests often drew bigger crowds than
the boys.' Others mourn its loss: "When Iowa went to 5 on 5 basketball for
girls," one person commented, "a part of iowa [*sic*] history died."[2]

To the contrary, we argue that the history of Iowa's six-player basketball is alive and thriving in alternative forms. Although the ties between
traditional notions of community and six-on-six have withered since the
game's discontinuation, new, transitory communities have emerged to sustain its remembrance. For the purposes of this chapter, we are particularly
interested in two sites: a 2003 reunion game in which former players and
supporters gathered, and a Facebook page titled "I Played 6 on 6 Basketball in Iowa," which fosters a virtual kinship of more than seven thousand
members. In the wake of school consolidation, farming crises, urbaniza-

tion, and the decline of rural populations, we argue that these ephemeral communities are essential for not only remembering the six-player game but for simultaneously reasserting small-town exceptionalism.

Six-Player Basketball in Iowa

Shortly after James Naismith invented basketball in 1891, physical educator Senda Berenson adapted the rules for her female students at Smith College in Northampton, Massachusetts. Deemed "suitable" for women, the feminized game quickly spread across the country, passing through several iterations before finally pitting one sextet against another.[3] From the 1930s through the 1990s, Iowa girls competed with three defensive guards and three offensive forwards—the positions separated by the half-court line. The rules restricted players to their designated bisections and to two dribbles per individual possession. Only forwards could score, while the guards tried to prevent their opponents from doing the same at the other end of the court. Six-player basketball thus resembled two games of three-on-three, but with only one game (and half of the players) in action at any given time.[4]

The IGHSAU plays a fundamental role in the sport's history. During the mid-1920s, a national movement of physical educators and other supporters adopted a philosophy of non-competitive athletic opportunities for girls and women, leading most states, including Iowa, to abandon scholastically-sanctioned sports programs. In response, a determined group of twenty-five male superintendents and principals formed the IGHSAU in 1925 with the express intent to continue girls' basketball. In 1926, the organization began holding the state tournament and quickly built "the most vibrant girls' high school program in the nation."[5] Although social and legal pressures in the 1970s pushed girls' basketball to the five-player format, the IGHSAU stuck with the six-player game until the mid-1980s, at which time it presented its member institutions a choice of which style to offer their student-athletes. Consequently, in the state's larger cities girls began playing by "boys' rules" while the smaller, rural schools continued to sponsor six-on-six.

A number of elements made the game special. First, because of its modified rules, it was considered both "acceptable" for girls and different from the game played by boys, crucial elements in the success of six-player ball.[6] It allowed supporters "to deal with girls who are skilled basketball players, but at the same time, girls" by reminding spectators of the athletes' femininity.[7] Certainly, six-player basketball required skill, strength, stamina, and teamwork. But as one former-player remembered, "when we played in high school we were never compared to the boys team because we were so different."[8] The asymmetry with the boys' rules, therefore, did not invite comparability, which helped to garner social support for the girls.

Second, because the six-player game was unique and, ostensibly, gender appropriate, the national media paid attention, finding novelty in the pursuit. At a time when girls' and women's sporting achievements earned scant press coverage, publications such as *Life, Sports Illustrated,* and the *New York Times* "made Iowa synonymous with high school girls basketball."[9] Journalists appeared especially captivated by Iowans' enthusiasm for the popular state tournament held each year in Des Moines' Veterans Auditorium, marveling, "Farm towns from Correctionville to Buffalo Center transform themselves into mobile cheering sections," despite bitterly cold winters and long, cross-state drives.[10] The audience for this game grew exponentially in 1951, when the Iowa girls' state basketball tournament became the first televised high school sporting event—of either sex.[11] In short succession, healthy revenues from basketball encouraged the IGHSAU to add three more sports (softball, golf, and tennis), contributing to the organization's unique status as a benefactor of girls' competitive sports.[12]

The third element that set Iowa girls' basketball apart was its strong association with local communities. In 1993, the *New York Times* observed, "the six-player game represented the essence of small-town life in Iowa."[13] But if the national press conveyed it in ways that generalized what these towns had in common, their citizens used it to celebrate their differences. It fostered a sense of small-town exceptionalism by emphasizing the unique history and identity of each municipality.[14] High schools' teams and their supporters formed intense, competitive relationships in ways that augmented social camaraderie by setting one program in contradistinction to another. As one former player remembers, "Nothing can compare to the rivalries that existed during that time as well as how entire communities would get behind their teams."[15] Girls' high school basketball became a way for towns to pronounce their civic sense of self within the state; the results and records of their local programs were measuring sticks with which to compare themselves to intrastate contenders.

If six-player basketball set one small town apart from another, it also served as a "tangible and unique activity that set the rural school apart from the urban school."[16] This was especially evident each year when the state's sixteen elite teams converged upon Veterans Auditorium. In 1979 a *Des Moines Register* journalist reflected, "They're just ordinary little towns that nobody knows about most of the year—then all of a sudden . . . these towns are on the minds and lips of everyone in the state."[17] Many Iowans might have been unfamiliar with Mediapolis or Maynard or Montezuma save for their perennial powerhouse girls' basketball teams.

Six-on-six could not have survived and prospered as it did without fervent community support. After interviewing thirty-two members of the Iowa Girls' Basketball Hall of Fame, historian Jan Beran found that, "All but one . . . indicated that basketball brought community recognition and most agreed that it unified the community."[18] Correspondingly, the game helped cultivate communal solidarity. It took on a totemic quality, offering a site around which townspeople could rally—rare instances in which girls' sport became a regular setting for constructing the body politic. Concentrated in the bleachers of their home gymnasiums or populating the stands of their opponents, boosters came together to support their local teams and found occasion to gather in ways that the rhythms of everyday life did not allow. Years later, one former player reminisced, "We were what was happening in our small town on Friday nights!"[19] Indicative of the games' popularity and the importance of high schools to their local communities, the capacity of provincial gymnasia frequently exceeded the areas' total population. In the mid-1970s, for example, Lone Tree's leaders built a venue that held 1,200–1,400 spectators, despite a total of 850 citizens, just 150 of whom were high school students.[20]

In retrospect, the end of Iowa girls' six-player basketball was an inevitability that not even the stalwart IGHSAU could ward off. At least two significant historical currents coalesced to induce a switch to five-player rules throughout the state. First, athletes, with the help of women's sports and civil rights activists, launched legal attacks against six-on-six, arguing that it was discriminatory against girls.[21] Critics claimed that because of the game's unique format, players were disadvantaged in their opportunities to earn athletic college scholarships. Second, contracting rural populations jeopardized the viability of their local schools. Ironically, this trend had been instrumental in retaining the half-court game for so long, because area residents united around the cultural symbol that exemplified their independence.

In 1950, 700 of Iowa's 834 high schools offered girls basketball. By 1970, according to historian Max McElwain, that number had dwindled to just 332, "primarily because of school consolidations."[22] Echoing trends throughout the United States, the rural population of Iowa has been in gradual decline since the mid-1900s.[23] As a result, enrollments dropped, forcing struggling schools to pool resources and merge with one another, stripping communities of their central, often defining institutions. To illustrate, by 1994, one year after the IGHSAU voted to discontinue the six-player girls basketball, nine out of ten high schools in towns with fewer than 500 residents had closed; another three out of five towns with populations of 500–999 residents also lost their high schools.[24] In sparsely populated, agricultural areas, schools provide more than educational facilities. They also offer sites for community involvement, where athletics are perhaps the foremost extracurricular activity responsible for bringing people together.[25] The loss of both schools and their associated sports programs threatened the identities of these weakened collectives. Bemoaning the IGHSAU's decision to eliminate the game, one journalist wrote, "If you have to mourn something, mourn the tradition and singularity. Another piece of small-town Iowa is gone. Another piece of the state's identity is vanished."[26]

A Community Reunion

Like many Iowa towns, Montezuma, located slightly southeast of the state's geographical center, experienced a population decline throughout the late twentieth and early twenty-first centuries.[27] For thirty years, Montezuma asserted itself as the "Basketball Capital of Iowa," as advertised on welcome signs at each of its four entry points. These types of signs, argues historian John Bale, serve as a means of "place boosting" and "image projection" for both residents of and visitors to the towns they adorn.[28] City officials erected the markers just after the boys' high school basketball team won the 1971 state tournament. Bolstering the title was their successful girls' program, the Bravettes, which boasted back-to-back state championships in 1969 and 1970. Between 1966 and 1972, Montezuma High School (MHS) sent six girls' teams to Veterans Auditorium. Augmenting their prestige was an eighty-nine-game win streak that began in 1969, only to be snapped with a one-point overtime loss in the quarterfinals of the 1971 state tournament. That Montezuma's identity remains tied to its six-on-six program is evidenced by a successful six-player reunion game that took place twenty-three years after its last state title.

On February 8, 2003, a crowd estimated at one thousand packed the MHS gymnasium.[29] Organized by the school's athletic director, Al Rabenold, thirty-nine former six-on-six players suited up, ranging in age from their mid-twenties to their mid-fifties and traveling from as far as Florida and Oregon for the chance to play again. Rabenold enhanced the experience with a commemorative display highlighting the heyday of Bravette basketball: game footage from the 1969 season and original score sheets from 1969, 1970, and 1971. Organizers also acknowledged the contributions of former coaches and team "moms" who chaperoned the girls on

Montezuma High School Bravettes basketball players from the late 1960s and early 1970s reminiscing on the court with their state tournament trophies after the six-on-six reunion game. Courtesy of J. O. Parker.

the bus and accompanied them in the locker rooms.[30] The event was clearly about more than the athletes: it was an opportunity to recognize all those who lent their support over the years, including the townsfolk who rallied behind them.

Spectators quickly filled the north-side bleachers and so, to accommodate the growing crowd, someone pulled out the south-side seats. Ruth Fleming, who graduated from MHS in 1979 and played in the 2003 reunion game, noted her surprise at the crowd as she arrived at school, for Rabenold had turned the reunion into a "huge community event."[31] Following a good-natured, competitive game, players asked to open the case that held their trophies from 1969 and 1970, which they paraded around the gym in a "victory lap."[32] Athletes and spectators loitered long after the referee's final whistle: visiting, reminiscing, and taking pictures with one another. According to Rabenold, "it was one of those nights that people didn't want to end because they have such fond memories of what girls' basketball was in Montezuma in the 6-on-6 era."[33]

Who packed the gym that night, speculated to be the largest crowd the facility had held since six-on-six ended? Some returned to see their daughters and granddaughters play basketball again, while the players' own children and family, unfamiliar with the antiquated format, watched with curiosity. Liz Gnida, a 1966 graduate and the oldest woman to participate in the game, joked that many citizens turned out to be entertained and to "watch us die!"[34] There were those who supported the highly successful teams of the past and others who just wanted to see the game again. Kathy Bowers, who played for the Bravettes in the late 1960s, remembered the "camaraderie and community support" her team once felt, adding, "in Montezuma, it was not just people that had kids in the school. It was the whole community."[35] The same could be said more than three decades later.

Although billed as a "6-on-6 Basketball Reunion," the event took on larger meaning for those who filled the MHS gymnasium. Fleming described the evening as "a community reunion more so than just a basketball reunion." Indeed, those interviewed repeatedly used the word "community" when discussing both the contest and their memories of Montezuma's six-player acclaim, with recollections such as, "That's what basketball was like when I played. It was a community event. . . . The community's life revolved around the teams of your school and how they performed in athletics."[36] Rabenold admitted that the reunion had been "a much bigger deal to the community" than he had anticipated. It was a way for Montezuma's citizens, past and present, to play out their nostalgia for a time when both the town, as well as six-on-six girls' basketball, prospered.

Social Networking

News of the game reverberates beyond the confines of Montezuma. On a Facebook page titled "I Played 6 on 6 Basketball in Iowa," an attendee of the homecoming shared "Montezuma had a 'reunion' a few years ago. Divided up the returnee's and played a game. The gym was packed and it was awesome!" Facebook, currently the most popular online social network, boasts more than five hundred million active users.[37] Free and available to the public since 2006, the Web site offers users a place to connect and communicate with one another individually and privately, as well communally and publicly. In early 2010, "I played 6 on 6 basketball in Iowa" appeared among its myriad pages. Billed as an online "sorority" for former players and fans of the game, in less than a year, a staggering seven thousand devotees joined the group, finding it a source of "wonderful memories" and a place to declare themselves "proud to be a member of this unique/awesome club!"[38]

Hundreds of patrons have used the site's "Wall" space, where they can openly post their comments. The overwhelming majority substantiate a "love" for the sport with passionate phrasing and emphatic punctuation. It was the "Best game ever!!" one writer maintains, "I wish it would have never changed." Multiple authors mourn its passing, long nostalgically for their athletic glory days, and wax poetic about the many virtues of six-on-six. Users post photographs of high school teams—scanned from newspapers, yearbooks, and personal scrapbooks. Some ardently call for its revival while others temper their memories with good humor, cracker-barrel sentimentality, and self-deprecating disclosures. "I played 6 on 6 basketball in Iowa" thus creates a new type of virtual, ephemeral community built around a sense of "what was" in spite of "what is." Significantly, as one woman writes, "I played 6 on 6 at Boone Valley . . . neither exist now!"

The Facebook group serves multiple purposes. It provides an opportunity for six-on-six enthusiasts to "'relive' the 'good ole days,'" as one member described it. It also gives ex-players a sense of validation, for those who have either moved out of state or shared their athletic pasts with subsequent generations report that they are often met with disbelief. They are glad to find this Web site, they write, and ask if users might share videos to prove the game existed: "I try to explain it to my nephews and kids . . . they think I'm crazy!!" Used to combat both ignorance and misconceptions about the game, Facebook contributors reminisce about the skill it required, the distance one could cover in two dribbles, the remarkable scoring exploits of teams and individuals, and recount multiple, sometimes serious injuries that confirm its physicality.

Most evident in the collection of comments, however, is the role the game plays in forging physical communities in the past, as well as contemporary kinships. One way in which these assertions manifest is in the preponderance of members who identify the high schools for which they played. Place names and mascots like the Centerville Redettes, Bellevue Comets, Sigourney Savages, Graettinger Pirettes, Audubon Wheelers, and the Everly Cattlefeeders proudly affix constituents with badges of small-town exceptionalism. The declarations allow former teammates, now dispersed by time and geography, to reconnect with one another. Online discussion boards—offshoots from the main Facebook page—extend these reunions. Under headings like "Cheers & Song," "What the Coach Said," and "Uniforms," members come together to share their memories of a game that might otherwise fade from collective memory.

They regularly note the years they played the game, their positions (guard, forward, "a GREAT benchwarmer") and titles (coach, statistician, referee). Additional users make connections with former opponents and idols. "I guarded you," read several replies; in one instance, a woman greeted her former adversary, adding: "it is so funny how you can forget people through out your life, but you never forget a high school basketball rival." Another wrote, "Aside from the sheer joy of playing this unique game, it provided lifelong friendships . . . not only with my teammates, but also with players from other teams." Seemingly trivial, fleeting past encounters become foundations for present-day encounters, as in "I remember rebounding for you in the free throw competition." Others share stories and updates about legendary players and coaches who achieve folk-hero status through this collective retrospection. Even those who never met face-to-face forge alliances: "you played with my Aunt" or "against my sisters" or "I'm your old coach's daughter," they share. Spectators praise former players, writing "I was in the stands watching," or "sitting in front of the TV as a kid with the folks watching the state tourney." It is a community now connected by memory and tradition rather than the Friday night gatherings of yesteryear.

Very few commentators criticize six-player basketball. Two wrote that they "hated" it and a third called it "boring," but other members of the group paid them no public attention. One detractor, however, sparked a wave of responses when she entreated, "What were they thinking when they made up the rules?" She continued by contending that six-player ball "was a disservice to the women who played it and watched it . . . probably why NO ONE came to ANY girls games." Significantly, no one challenged her opinion of the game's character, but instead corrected her on the spectators who regularly turned out for their contests: "Don't know where you played basketball—but [we] ALWAYS had a full gym—the entire town came out to support us in 6 on 6 basketball!!!!" They write that they consistently played in front of a "full house" and that their fans "packed the gym" for every girls' game after which "most of the crowd would leave at the beginning of the boys' games." And if a team was lucky enough to secure a state tournament bid, "the WHOLE town went" and "the town basically shut down."

The Facebook site has led to physical revivals as well. Members announce reunions and advertise alumni games and recreational leagues, while others publicize the return of six-on-six to the Iowa Games, a statewide, Olympic-style competition. They form teams, schedule practices, and plan meetings. This seemingly ephemeral community actively sustains the game and promotes occasions to gather, thereby developing new connections, renewing long-lost relationships and, above all, breathing life into a sport that refuses to die.

Reuniting Communities

The six-player teams of the past activated a form of social capital for local citizens, providing important cultural symbols and affording reasons to assemble. High school girls no longer play six-on-six basketball. In fact, consolidation eliminated or reorganized many of the schools that used to sponsor the teams, crippling the towns for which they once provided the hub of community life. Consequently, the uniqueness of particular places is increasingly pronounced by their histories, rather than their current circumstances.

Those who reunite with the six-player game and its adherents, whether by reunion or in cyberspace, appear to have much in common. Ultimately, members of both groups seek to connect or reconnect with those of similar backgrounds, estranged though they may be by time and space. They bask in the reflective glow of a tradition that "made girls basketball special" and "was one of the things that made Iowa unique."[39] They validate their participation in a pastime that might otherwise slip from collective memory. But these are communities built on loss, simultaneously tinged with nostalgia and lament and celebration. Despite their best efforts, the groups and individuals who assemble because of six-player, high school girls basketball can never recapture the connection between the sport and their communities, precisely because the former no longer exists and the latter has changed so drastically in the past decades. It may be that cultural, technological, economic, geographical, and political shifts will forever alter our understanding of community, in its traditional sense, leaving ephemeral stand-ins based on the memories of what once was.

Notes

1. In 1993, just 134 schools offered five-on-five teams for their female students. See "End of Era in Girls Basketball," *New York Times,* February 5, 1993, B9. Also see Max McElwain, *The Only Dance in Iowa: A History of Six-Player Girls' Basketball* (Lincoln: University of Nebraska Press, 2004).

2. Terrimcdaniel1, "Iowa Stories," Iowa Public Television, accessed October 7, 2010, http://www.iptv.org/iowastories/detail.cfm/sixonsix#comments.

3. See Pamela Grundy and Susan Shackelford, *Shattering the Glass: The Remarkable History of Women's Basketball* (New York: The New Press, 2005).

4. See Janice A. Beran, *From Six-on-Six to Full Court Press: A Century of Iowa Girls' Basketball* (Ames: Iowa State University Press, 1994).

5. Grundy and Shackelford, *Shattering the Glass,* 48.

6. Janice A. Beran, "Iowa, Longtime 'Hot Bed' of Girls' Basketball," in *A Century of Women's Basketball: From Frailty to Final Four,* ed. Joan S. Hult and Marianna Trekell

(Reston, Va.: American Alliance for Health, Physical Education, Recreation and Dance, 1991), 190.

7. "Hoops, Dear, in Iowa," *Life*, March 4, 1957, 95–96.

8. Facebook Posting: "I played 6 on 6 basketball in Iowa!!"

9. "End of Era," B9.

10. Kevin Cook, "The Iowa Girl Stands Tall," *Sports Illustrated*, February 13, 1989, 76. See also "Pretty Virginia Harris Leads Hansell to Iowa Basketball Championship," *Life*, April 8, 1940, 41–48; "Hoops, Dear, in Iowa," *Life*, March 4, 1957, 95–96; Rose May Mechem, "Les Girls in Des Moines," *Sports Illustrated*, February 17, 1969, 39; "At Sixes and Fives," *Sports Illustrated*, November 8, 1976, 16.

11. The girls' semifinal and championship games were broadcast live in an effort to accommodate the many fans that could not get tickets to attend the tournament. It was not until the following year that the first boys' basketball tournament in the United States would be televised. By 1966, television coverage of the girls' championship has extended into Minnesota, Nebraska, and South Dakota. Beran, *From Six-on-Six*, 83.

12. The IGHSAU added softball in 1955; tennis and golf in 1956. Beran, *Six-on-Six*, 192.

13. "End of Era," B9.

14. We derive the concept of small-town exceptionalism from theories of American exceptionalism. See, for example, Byron E. Shafer, ed., *Is America Different?: A New Look at American Exceptionalism* (New York: Oxford University Press, 1991).

15. Facebook Posting: "I played 6 on 6 basketball in Iowa!!"

16. Beran, *From Six-on-Six to Full Court Press*, 100.

17. Valerie Monson, quoted in Beran, "Iowa, Longtime 'Hot Bed,'" 190–91.

18. Janice A. Beran, "The Story: Six-Player Girls' Basketball in Iowa," in *Her Story in Sport: A Historical Anthology of Women in Sports*, ed. Reet Howell (New York: Leisure Press), 560.

19. Facebook Posting: "I played 6 on 6 basketball in Iowa!!"

20. Jim Enright, *Only in Iowa: Where the High School Girl Athlete is Queen* (Des Moines, Iowa: Iowa Girls' High School Athletic Union, 1976), 135, 138.

21. Shelley Lucas, "Courting Controversy: Gender and Power in Iowa Girls' Basketball," *Journal of Sport History* 30 (2003): 281–308.

22. McElwain, *The Only Dance in Iowa*, 38.

23. Leland L. Sage, *A History of Iowa* (Ames: Iowa State University Press, 1974), 314.

24. William H. Dreier and Willis Goudy, "Is There Life in Town after the Death of the High School?" Paper presented at the Annual Rural and Small Schools Conference (Manhattan, Kans.: 1994), 1–12.

25. See, as examples, Steve Kay, "Considerations in Evaluating School Consolidation Proposals," Small School Forum 4 (1982) 8–10; Brad Hughes, "Surviving Closing and Consolidations," *School Administrator* 60 (2003): 16–18; Neil G. Stevens and Gary L. Peltier, "A Review of Research on Small-School Student Participation in Extracurricular Activities," *Journal of Research in Rural Education* 10 (1994): 116–20.

26. Marc Hansen, "The Restrictions are Lifted," *Des Moines Register*, February 4, 1993, S1.

27. U.S. Census Bureau, American FactFinder, http://factfinder.census.gov, accessed October 28, 2010.

28. John Bale, *Landscapes of Modern Sport* (New York: Leicester University Press, 1994), 136–37.

29. J. O. Parker, "Heroes of the Hardwood," *Montezuma Republican,* February 19, 2003, 14.

30. Brenda Moore, interview by Shelley Lucas, North English, Iowa, June 11, 2004.

31. Ruth Fleming, interview by Shelley Lucas, Cedar Rapids, Iowa, April 10, 2003.

32. Al Rabenold, interview by Shelley Lucas, Montezuma, Iowa, June 14, 2004.

33. Rabenold interview.

34. Liz Gnida, interview by Shelley Lucas, Iowa City, Iowa, June 9, 2004.

35. Kathy Bowers, interview by Shelley Lucas, Iowa City, Iowa, June 10, 2004.

36. Fleming interview.

37. As of 2009, 28 percent of Facebook users are adults aged thirty-four and older, the demographic of most former six-players. Dan Fletcher, "How Facebook Is Redefining Privacy," TIME.com, May 20, 2010, accessed October 1, 2010, http://www.time.com/time/business/article/0,8599,1990582,00.html#ixzz11tfKsvUT.

38. Before analyzing the Facebook group's comments, we consulted the Institutional Review Board for Human Subjects Research (IRB) at Boise State University. The IRB deemed our study exempt on the grounds that the site's administer allows open, unrestricted, public access to "I played 6 on 6 basketball in Iowa." Although we did not use information identifying the source of individual comments, we did feel an ethical obligation to notify members of our presence and intentions. We thus posted a comment on the "Wall" to make known our intentions, but did not solicit any additional information from users.

39. Facebook Posting: "I played 6 on 6 basketball in Iowa!!"

6. Chicago's Game

CHRISTOPHER LAMBERTI

Some of my earliest memories are of my father playing softball. He manned third base, the hot corner, for a local team in a sixteen-inch ball, no-gloves league. The son of Italian immigrants, my father grew up in a working-class suburb of Chicago in the 1960s. When I was a boy, my grandfather's hands were hardened and calloused from working as a carpenter and maintenance man. My father, a college graduate, sold paper binding and laminate machines. His hands were gnarled from softball; a few of his fingers meandered off at awkward angles past their last joints.

Along with hundreds of thousands of others in and around Chicago, my father played softball in the late 1970s and early 1980s, when the popularity of sixteen-inch, no-gloves reached new heights. At the time, playing softball in Chicago was explicitly about recreation and friendship. Softball strengthened players' and fans' bonds to communities they imagined themselves part of, even if the game failed to bring racially segregated communities together. Softball, some players said, reinforced a "Chicago feeling."[1] But implicitly, Chicago's game was also about class and gender. Although entire communities rallied around their teams, softball in Chicago was a sport dominated by men. Playing and celebrating the sport helped men retain a macho, urban, blue-collar identity in the midst of a dynamically changing city. Some players say that the sport harkened back to a time when men could not afford gloves; twisted fingers reminded middle-class professionals of their family ties to a working-class and immigrant past. Chicagoans still play sixteen-inch softball, but the sport's heyday was the 1960s, '70s, and '80s, years when, for better or worse, "the City that Works" increasingly did so in white collars rather than blue ones.

Virtually unknown outside the city's greater metropolitan area, Chicago-style softball is played with a larger, softer ball called the "Clincher" fielded by ten position players (the tenth usually stationed behind second base) with their bare hands. Fielding the batted softball is difficult and sometimes painful, and hitting requires an emphasis on placement over power. Chicagoans originally played softball on a smaller field, with the bases forty-five feet apart. Baselines eventually expanded to sixty feet, but outfields remain confined in comparison to softball parks outside the city. Over the years, Chicago softball officials have taken measures to contain the game in smaller fields, including limiting the weight of bats and injecting softballs with water. Pitchers rely on angles, rotation, and trajectory to prevent hitters from getting the good part of the bat on the ball. They move several paces off the mound, often hesitate with a pump of the pitching arm before delivering slow, high-arcing tosses to the batter at home plate. At first glance, Chicago softball might be misconstrued as absurd; a group of large men on a miniature baseball field knocking around a ball the size of a melon. But this game is extremely difficult to master, and when played at a high level, it requires technique, cunning, and courage. At all levels, Chicago-style softball is enjoyable, demanding, competitive, and, above all, an important part of the city's heritage.[2]

Softball's past is part history, part folklore. One of the game's creation myths begins in a gymnasium at Chicago's Farragut Boat Club on Thanksgiving Day 1887, when a group of Ivy League alumni gathered around the tickertape machine awaiting the results of the Harvard-Yale football game. At one point, a member of the crowd hurled a boxing glove toward another, who returned the piece of equipment with a swat of a broomstick. The men wrapped the glove in tape and made a game of it. "Indoors baseball" was born. Some softball historians credit Chicago football greats George Halas and Paddy Driscoll with popularizing the game outdoors. Fast pitch and slow pitch softball contests, both played with a fourteen-inch ball, were featured with great fanfare at the city's Century of Progress World's Fair in 1933. The exhibition was such a success that teams were invited back to play a tournament the following year at Soldier Field. The event was held there annually until 1939, by which time softball had caught on and became one of the most popular sports in Chicago to watch and play.[3]

But most stories about the game's origins do not mention tricked-out venues like boat clubs or world's fairs, nor social elites and famous athletes. No, this is a humble sport with humble beginnings. Softball enthusiasts mostly tell stories of the game's coming of age on neighborhood ball fields during the Great Depression. Chicago's game, they say, developed in smaller parks in crowded neighborhoods, and softball without gloves appealed to working men with hardened hands who neither required nor had the money for gloves.[4]

Like other American sports, softball was a means for children of European immigrants to shed the provincialism of their parents. But softball was also a way of maintaining immigrant communities, as teams throughout the city were often identified by the ethnicity of their players. The owner of a local tavern in a North Side Polish neighborhood might stake the local team in a game against South Side Lithuanians. Members of the community would wager on the outcome of the contest, and drop a nickel in the hat being passed around the bar for drinks to celebrate the victory. Native-born Americans of Italian, African, Irish, Jewish, Czech, and other backgrounds all fielded teams, and the names of some of the game's early greats reflected Chicago's ethnic character: "Coon" Rosen, Matthew Ruppert, Vito Yario, Redmond J. Hurter, Vernon Parry, "Lefty" Goldfeder, Lewa Yacilla, "Fat" Heuel, and Morris Pomeroy.[5]

Softball throughout the 1930s and '40s provided Chicago with sports heroes and some of its most colorful sports moments before television. Following the 1933 World's Fair, softball became a professional sport in Chicago. The Windy City League staged games in some of Chicago's largest venues, like Wrigley Field, Bidwell Stadium, and Parichy Park, where cash-strapped patrons might pay a dime to see three games. For the better part of the next two decades, big games drew thousands of spectators who came to witness and wager. The heavy gambling rivaled local racetrack handles, with upward of $10,000 in side bets wagered by players and backers. Local businesses served as sponsors; among the best teams were those supported by Stony Tires, Salerno Cookies, Cool-Vent, First National Bank, and Cinderella Florists. Many early professional softballers went on to make their names in other sports—Bill Skowron, Phil Cavaretta, Milt Galatzer, and Lou Boudreau, in baseball; Ray Meyer and Nat "Sweetwater" Clifton (whose African American team, the Brown Bombers, ruled the professional circuit) in basketball.[6]

Unable to compete with national sports after World War II, the Windy City League closed its doors in 1950. But softball remained popular on a local level throughout the '50s and '60s. The Amateur Softball Association (ASA), founded in Chicago in 1933, took no-gloves softball nationwide in 1963 when it organized a national tournament held in Chicago. During the ensuing decades, Chicago teams dominated play, as sixteen-inch softball remained a Chicago institution almost exclusively.[7]

Chicago sixteen-inch legend Steve Prostran remembers growing up with softball in the mixed Northwest Side neighborhood of Avondale in the

1960s and '70s. Children spent their summers watching games at Brands Park, shagging balls during practices, and idolizing softball players. The better community teams sponsored junior squads, serving both to perpetuate interest in the game and as a farm system meant to groom young talent. For example, the Stompers, a successful local team, recruited players for their youth teams, the Junior Stompers and the Stompers 3. For five months, softball was played nightly in parks throughout the city, and tournaments took place on weekends. Residents of Avondale would catch local contests at Brands Park, and occasionally trek east to Clarendon Park on the lakefront, where some of the best teams in Chicago played in front of swells of spectators.[8]

Softball fever was not exclusive to the Northwest Side; the game permeated life throughout the city. "In every neighborhood," Prostran recalls, "kids grew up in it, and they were playing it." Leonard "Sarge" McKinnon, perhaps the most prolific slugger on a legendary team called the Iron Men, remembers the part sixteen-inch softball played in his youth growing up in the south side African American community of Bronzeville: "If you lived on the east side of Wabash and I lived on the west side there was a softball team on either side of the street. At the school, we would all get together and have a neighborhood softball game. When all the mothers, and the fathers, and the sisters would come out and watch us play ball."[9]

Softball was for everyone, but postgame rituals were for adults only. Gathering after the game at a local bar was an important part of the life for many players, and softball managers widely recognized that teams that got along together off the field played better on it. Known for softball, Chicago was even better known for its saloons, and the relationship between softball and the tavern industry was strong. Many bars sponsored teams and tournaments, and in return enjoyed the nightly patronage of droves of local softball players. Taverns served as the locker room, where players might sip pre-game Old Styles and change into their uniforms, leaving work clothes and valuables with the bartender. During games, a player might rush over to a nearby saloon to restock an empty beer cooler.[10]

After the game, bars welcomed players and fans to chat about the evening's events. Bars were emporia of softball information, the outlets of the softball world. Bibulous players recounted stories of diving catches and game-winning hits; fans bought drinks for the night's heroes; softball bards recounted tales of the game's beginnings, its greatest teams, players, and moments, often until the wee hours of the morning. Many sections of the city and suburbs boasted softball taverns. Among Chicagoland's most famous in the late 1970s were Terry's Parkwood Inn and WGAF on the South Side; Irving O'Brien's near downtown; Andy's, River Shannon, and Yak-Zie's on the North Side; Papa Bears Pub, Bally Much Tavern, Big Banjo, Bojangles, Sportsman Lounge, The Lantern, Vail Lounge, Spring Inn, and Santi's in the suburbs. Many retired softballers say they miss the late night camaraderie more than the playing.[11]

Scenes like these multiplied in the late 1960s through the 1970s as the game's popularity spread. Increased media attention gave the sport greater exposure in Chicago. Mike Conklin began a regular softball column in the *Chicago Tribune,* describing sixteen-inch, no-gloves softball as "Chicago's game." Since its inception in Chicago, "softball has splintered back into several games," Conklin wrote, "But the nearest and dearest to Chicagoans, and the one seen most on local diamonds, is played gloveless with a ball measuring 16 inches in circumference." Other Chicago dailies soon joined the *Tribune* in covering softball, and the sport's bigger tournaments enjoyed local television coverage. Before the 1971 season, park officials estimated that 4,500 teams and about seven hundred leagues would be competing on Chicago's playgrounds. Flashy players on teams with colorful names— Bobcats, Dwarfs, Strikers, Sobies, Bruins, Flamingos—drew numbers of spectators unseen since the days of professional softball in Chicago. Perhaps the city's most popular softball facility was Grant Park in the Loop, or Chicago's commercial district, but the best teams could be found in leagues at Clarendon Park in Chicago's Uptown neighborhood about five miles north of the Loop, and Kelly Park in Chicago's Brighton Park area six miles to the southwest of the Loop. The best of the best vied for the unofficial city title at the annual Andy Frain tournament at Clarendon Park.[12]

In 1975, Mike Conklin noted that big games had been played previously "in dimly-lit neighborhood parks in front of wives and friends." However, that summer Conklin declared that "16-inch softball appears headed for strides that could take it out of the closet and into some daylight for the thousands of persons who play and follow the game." Also that season, Chicago's *Windy City Softball* magazine, with the support of the Winston cigarette company, sponsored a series of eight local tournaments that culminated in a sixteen-inch "World Series" held at Soldier Field. Mayor Richard J. Daley declared the week before the championship game "Softball Week" in Chicago. Conklin remembered becoming aware at this time that "16-inch had struck a nerve" with Chicagoans. Numbers of players were increasing locally. In 1974, 225 teams turned out for softball in Grant Park; by 1978, Grant Park served 360 teams, with many others on a waiting list. And interest was growing citywide, with nearly every park district reporting a growing number of new teams, more than the extant leagues could

Willie Simpson, Bobcats 16 Inch Hall of Fame player, takes a rip
at the clincher in a 1974 home run contest held at Comiskey Park.
Courtesy of Al Maag and the Chicago 16 Inch Softball Hall of Fame.

accommodate. In 1977, park district supervisors estimated that a quarter
of a million people played softball in the Chicago area. Just a year later,
the estimate grew to half a million.[13]

Sixteen-inch softball blossomed in Chicago at a time when the city was
undergoing social and economic change. Between 1967 and 1982, the city
lost a quarter of a million jobs, and in the 1970s 25 percent of all Chicago
factories closed. Chicago's once massive meatpacking industry, followed
by steel and later electric and communications industries, relocated in

response to global economic conditions, union demands, and lower profits. But before the fall of industry, union wages afforded the children of workers a college education. This generation filled new positions in the city's service sector. Unlike other rustbelt towns, a new Chicago rebuilt itself within the shell of the old; as the old industrial economy dwindled, finance, legal services, insurance, and advertising boomed.[14]

While the city was losing its manufacturing jobs, the game with working-class roots helped Chicagoans maintain a blue-collar identity. Sons of factory workers, many now working downtown and in the suburbs, ground it out sans gloves on local softball diamonds, maintaining ties to their parents' working-class neighborhoods. Some played along the lakefront at Grant Park, in the shadows of the skyscrapers towering above the Loop, which now represented the undisputed center of the city's economy. Grant Park still boasted a softball "industrial division," but it was clear the meaning of the term had changed, for within that category, teams faced off in the "Advertising League," the "Accountants League," and the "Architects-Engineers League." It is probably no accident that softball's newfound citywide popularity coincided with the onset of deindustrialization. Softball, I would argue, helped city residents transition to postindustrial urban life. Amid chaotic economic forces beyond workers' control, Chicago's unique brand of softball remained familiar, connecting the city's new guard with the old.[15]

The game once described as "an excuse to get out of the house to go drinking" was, by the 1970s, attracting some of Chicago's best athletes. Softball offered them a prominent urban stage and substantial payoffs in the form of tournament purses and side wagers. When played at a high level, Chicago softball was also tremendously challenging. It may not have been hyperbole when softball great Ed Zolna declared, "The 16-inch softball players are the best bat-and-ball athletes there are." But despite the presence of elite players on the circuit, there was always something implicitly democratic about softball. The game appealed to Chicagoans seeking more affordable, more grounded leisure and recreational activities in contrast to the professional sports that Mike Conklin described as "backed by profit-seeking businessmen and exposed thru [sic] professional public relations."[16]

Out of this mix came another element of the game's mythic appeal. Softball, it was said, brought together athletes and nonathletes alike, and socially the softball field was a great leveler. In the neighborhoods, upwardly mobile white-collar workers mingled with blue-collar ones, and they not only shared the same diamond but also competitive spirit, banter, and six-packs on the bench. Softball helped to mask inequality at a time when real income for working people had stagnated and wealth was becoming more concentrated in the hands of a few. At Grant Park, corporate and municipal employees of varying income levels played together on the same teams and in the same leagues. On the field, it was said, a mailroom employee might comfortably criticize a company executive for misplaying the ball. "It's an equalizer in Chicago," said George Bliss of the Chicago 16 Inch Softball Hall of Fame, "You might be the mayor, you might be a guy that's, unfortunately, homeless, when you're on the 16-inch field it's like you're equal . . . it brings back the Chicago feeling of togetherness." Softball not only reinforced the sense of social equality among coworkers together on the field, but commonality across teams and leagues; no matter what one did for a living or how much money one made, Chicagoans had softball in common.[17]

That "Chicago feeling" was characterized not only by togetherness, but also manliness, or more precisely, the togetherness of shared masculinity. While as late as the 1960s softball served as recreation for the city's factory workers, by the late 1970s it was an important means of perpetuating a blue-collar identity among car dealers, teachers, bankers, lawyers, and other white-collar workers native to "the Chicagoland area," as the city and its suburbs are known. Increasingly, Chicago softball players had their names etched on desk plates rather than embroidered on their work shirts; they shed jackets and ties, not dungarees and work boots before slipping into their stretch-knit pants and T-shirts. Like their predecessors, however, softball players in the 1970s and beyond believed that "the day's really serious business" took place not in the workplace but on the diamond. "Off the field, I was just a regular Joe going to work," says softball great Steve Prostran, "But on the softball field at night, in these parks, I was somebody."[18]

Among Chicago's most notable softball boosters was Pulitzer Prize–winning newspaper columnist and *Chicago Daily News* team pitcher Mike Royko. For Royko, the city's affinity with no-gloves softball and its dominance in the sport nationally affirmed the superiority of hardy Chicagoans. While players outside the city would "slink away, moaning about their twisted fingers and painful booboos on their hands," Chicagoans reveled in the machismo of no-gloves softball.[19] The game was tough and the toughest teams were made up of native Chicagoans. As Royko explained in a 1982 interview:

> If you work for, say, the Chicago Police Department, it's very easy to put together a great team. All-cop teams are good teams because they're made up primarily of native-born Chicagoans who played softball. Macho males. If you play for a company like mine that has a relatively small number of people, and a lot of them are Ivy Leaguers, who aren't very good at softball because they don't want to hurt their hands, then it's very hard to put out a good softball team.[20]

In sixteen-inch no-gloves softball, Royko found both a passion and a cause. The bare-hands rule became the source of much controversy in 1970s softball circles when the sanctioned use of gloves was on the rise. The ASA, at that time headquartered in Oklahoma City, began allowing gloves in 1971 in an effort to draw more teams from outside Chicago to its sixteen-inch national tournament. Gloves and smaller balls became popular in Chicago's sprawling suburbs, where larger fields could accommodate longer fly balls. The number of women's teams was increasing as well, many of them in leagues that allowed gloves. In 1977, Royko filed suit against the Chicago Park District when it sanctioned the use of gloves at Grant Park. The suit claimed that the use of gloves "unfairly penalizes those with talent and calloused hands and gives unfair advantage to those with tender and well-manicured hands." Moreover, the suit contended that members of the *Chicago Daily News* team were "without the economic resources with which to purchase the additional equipment." The judge adjudicating the matter, a former softball player, ruled in favor of the plaintiff.[21]

Outside the courts, Royko used his column to emasculate those who would defile Chicago's game. In the *Daily News,* Royko targeted the ASA, made up of "lazy, small-town bumpkins," who allowed gloves in the 1979 sixteen-inch nationals in Harvey, Illinois, "to satisfy the rustics from other parts of the country who are not skillful or brave enough to play without them." For Chicago's most celebrated columnist, the tournament was "a disgrace, an abomination, an obscenity, and maybe even un-American." "What is billed as the national championship of 16-inch softball," Royko continued, "is nothing but a sissy event." In the effort to maintain the sanctity of Chicago softball, Royko encouraged his readers to shout at any player with the gall to bring a glove out on the field, "If you're gonna wear a glove, you ought to also wear a bra."[22]

Until late in the twentieth century in Chicago, the world of sixteen-inch softball was frequented by women, but dominated by men. Practices, games, and of course postgame activities required extended amounts of time away from families. Many teams competed in multiple leagues, and some teams trained year round. For married men, spousal and family obligations posed a danger to team chemistry and success. League games on weekday nights and tournaments on weekends were the priorities of the summer, and often conflicted with birthdays, weddings, and barbecues. In discussing the impediments to "winning softball," Mike Conklin warned, "It's tough to win the big showdown with the hated rival when your No. 3 hitter has been told by his wife that he'd better be at dinner with the in-laws that same night—or else."[23]

Over the course of one or more seasons, players developed powerful homosocial bonds, further strengthened through postgame rituals, which required tolerant spouses. "I've heard that there are wives of some softball players who say an after-the-game drink isn't necessary," wrote Edward Claflin in *The Great American Softball Book* (1978). "These wives have what is called a bad attitude."[24] The softball life allegedly caused relationship breakups when players preferred the company of their male teammates and the nightly adoration of female fans to wives or steady girlfriends. As Chicago softball great Steve Prostran remembers:

> Softball would ruin a marriage because of coming home from the bar at 3 o'clock in the morning every night. . . . The camaraderie you had with those guys was unbelievable. These guys you were playing with were your friends all year round. You're playing ball, it was just fun, fun, fun. You're in the bar, women all over, let the good times roll. Who cares? But that's what got guys in trouble. I knew guys in marriages with kids who blew it all, because they wouldn't go home.[25]

Women's softball leagues existed in Chicago, but female players were often the subject of titillation. For example, women's teams competed in the Lake Shore Park tavern leagues, where Mike Conklin noted, "the boys would come to ogle the girls, then head off to Rush St. after games." In addition to men's teams, some taverns sponsored women's teams that would mingle with the men in the bar after the game. But while sponsors provided baseball pants and T-shirts for their men's squads, for their women's teams they bought tighter-fitting uniforms made from markedly less material. It was difficult for male spectators to concentrate on the softball game "with 18-year-old girls in halter tops and hip huggers," remarked one female player. "Our sponsors must have a great sense of humor."[26]

Lots of women, however, defied these stereotypes and took the game very seriously by the late 1970s. Many of them were young, had college intramural softball experience, and preferred to play twelve-inch softball with gloves; a number even practiced indoors in the offseason and trained year-round. Chicago's female softballers were part of a larger demographic trend. In 1977 women's squads represented nearly one-quarter of all softball teams nationwide, up 6 percent from the previous year. Chicago's Grant Park hosted twelve women's teams in the early 1970s, and by 1978 the park's women's team quota was full, with an additional twenty-five squads on a waiting list. In suburban Elmhurst, the number of women's teams jumped from nine to twenty-seven in a matter of a few years. Like the men, women enjoyed drinking beer during games, and afterward hanging out at the bars. Although few women played on sixteen-inch teams with men, more women shared the same parks and the same taverns after games. By the late '70s, a larger number of women had entered the softball sphere, taking part in the softball life as players. It is no coincidence that interest in sixteen-inch no-gloves softball, so closely associated with homosocial bonding and masculinity, began to flag during this period.[27]

But the decline in the sixteen-inch game was part of a larger trend. By 1983, Chicago-style softball was failing to attract the city's best athletes, and most recreational players had begun to use gloves. The number of sixteen-inch leagues dwindled during the next two decades, so much so that, by the turn of the century, many former gloveless players feared the game's extinction. The growing presence of women and legitimacy of women's softball does not fully explain the decline in interest in Chicago's game. The ASA introduced gloves into the sixteen-inch national tournament in the early 1970s, and in the 1980s it was devoting more resources and directing more sponsorship dollars toward twelve-inch softball. As a result, gloves became the norm among the city's elite players. Gendered arguments against the use of gloves lost their bite when the city's best and biggest athletes began using them with regularity. "I know a lot of guys think it's not very macho or it's unmasculine to use [gloves]," remarked legendary softball manager Ed Zolna. "Well, let's just say I'd like to see someone say that to one of my players face-to-face. . . . Cheap errors are feminine, not great catches."[28]

No longer did no-gloves softball get the kind of media coverage it enjoyed when the game attracted the city's top players. The Chicago Park District had never done much to promote Chicago softball, and its popularity was largely dependent on local news outlets for citywide exposure. But Mike Conklin stopped writing about softball regularly for the *Tribune* in the late 1970s and Mike Royko's *Daily News* closed its doors in late 1979, which left the *Sun Times* as the only major Chicago newspaper covering softball regularly. Local television shifted from the sixteen-inch to the twelve-inch game, but neither version got much coverage. By the 1980s, the Chicago Park District shifted priorities, emphasizing activities for children that did not include softball, and plowing up neighborhood diamonds.[29]

But maybe the biggest reason for the decline of softball in Chicago was the suburbanization of the metropolitan area. Increasingly, Chicago's suburbs became home to corporate offices as well as to small and mid-sized factories that relocated from the city. Between 1972 and 1981, Chicago lost 10 percent of its private-sector jobs while suburban employment increased 25 percent. Seeking work and spacious residential lots, native white Chicagoans, the base of the city's softball-playing population, left the city for the suburbs. By 1950, the city of Chicago held about three and a half million people, and that number declined slightly over the coming decades. Meanwhile, the suburban population surrounding Cook County boomed. In the twenty years between 1950 and 1970, the number of suburbanites doubled, and by that latter date, it had surpassed the total residential numbers in Chicago.[30]

Increasingly, highways rather than the "El" connected teams and leagues to each other. Serious softball leagues and tournaments sprouted up in the working- and middle-class suburbs of Evanston, Harvey, Blue Island, Des Plaines, Downers Grove, Mt. Prospect, and Forest Park. For a time, the sport linked Chicago with outlying towns, creating fluidity among those who had roots in the city and homes in the suburbs. But gradually, suburbanization meant that interest in sixteen-inch softball became less concentrated, players grew tired of making long cross-county treks to play the game, and boys no longer grew up near sixteen-inch diamonds. At the same time, twelve-inch became more popular on larger suburban fields, which could accommodate the long flight of the smaller ball. Because it had come to seem a bit passé by the 1980s, the children of Chicago's newer immigrants—who began to arrive in droves from Latin America, Asia, and Africa by the 1970s—did not take to softball. Moreover, transplants from midwestern colleges settling in gentrified communities, with little knowledge of Chicago softball culture and cursory ties to their neighborhoods, had little interest in playing softball without gloves.[31]

Now, at the beginning of the twenty-first century, sixteen-inch softball in the city proper remains strongest with its largest group of native Chicagoans, African Americans. In 2009, the "Sunday's Best Softball League" in Washington Park on the South Side held games on Wednesdays, Fridays, and Sundays. On some days, more than fifty teams played on thirteen diamonds in front of three thousand spectators. A 2011 *Chicago Tonight* television report titled "Softball Sundays," referred to the league at Washington Park as "the biggest, busiest, sixteen-inch softball league in the world."[32]

Historically, Chicago has seen its share of great black teams: Brown Bombers, Kuppenheimer, Safari Tigers, and recently Steel Gold and the Young Guns. But Chicago is a segregated city with a long history of racial troubles, and Chicago softball history is no exception. A few black players played on white teams, but because softball was a neighborhood game, for the most part black teams played in black neighborhoods, and white teams in white neighborhoods. Meetings between local ethnic white teams were common, but friendly contests between white and black neighborhood

teams occurred rarely, if ever. The better white and black teams competed in
larger tournaments, and though little evidence exists suggesting prejudice
against black athletes and teams in the past, some players today contend
that discrimination is not new and not abating.[33]

Sarge McKinnon claims that black teams were not invited to the national
tournament known as the World Series of Softball in its early years, despite
the popularity of the sixteen-inch game in Chicago's black neighborhoods
and the prominence of some of the teams and players within them. It was
not until 2005 that an African American team, Gold Steel, triumphed in
the sixteen-inch national championship. For black softball aficionados, the
victory was long overdue. In a recent ESPN interview, Sherman Nelson,
the manager of a successful all-black Chicago sixteen-inch softball team,
suggested that his players routinely have been the victims of racist taunts
and umpire bias, and his team subject to suspect tournament draws that
placed black teams in the same bracket, making an all-black championship
game impossible. Moreover, it has been more difficult for elite black teams
to secure the same level of corporate sponsorships enjoyed by white teams.[34]

On Chicago's South Side, sixteen-inch softball has had a positive impact
on young African American men living in working communities hit hard
by the social and economic effects of deindustrialization, neighborhoods
where violent crime rates have been high. "It's a game that kept a whole
lot of us out of trouble," says Dennis McKinnon, son of Sarge, "It takes us
out of the neighborhood, where all of the trouble is at, and brings you out
here [to Washington Park] where you do something constructive. And you
learn positive things."[35]

For decades, softball helped instill a sense of community among hundreds of thousands of native Chicagoans, many of them wage earners or the
first generation of the city's salaried professionals and college graduates.
As is often the case, Chicago softball players built their communities by
excluding outsiders. And though sixteen-inch softball failed to promote
gender or racial equality, it helped Chicago maintain its reputation as the
city with "broad shoulders" in a postindustrial landscape. Today, the softball
life as old-timers knew it is gone. Mostly nostalgia remains. The nexus of
sixteen-inch softball has shifted to the western suburb of Forest Park, home
of the Chicago 16 Inch Softball Hall of Fame and the "No Glove Nationals"
tournament. While sixteen-inch has made a bit of a comeback in Chicago
Park District leagues—eighty-one thousand people played sixteen-inch
softball in Grant Park leagues in 2009—the game lacks the artistry and
meaning that once defined it.[36]

Notes

Sincere thanks to Elliott J. Gorn for his help with this article, as well as Steve Prostran, Mike Conklin, and Peter Vernon for bringing Chicago's Game to light for the author.

1. George Bliss of the Chicago 16 Inch Softball Hall of Fame mentioned softball and the "Chicago feeling" in a WGN radio interview with Bob Sirott. "WGN RADIO Interview with Bob Sirott," Chicago 16 Inch Softball Hall of Fame, accessed November 10, 2010, http://www.16inchsoftballhof.com/auxfiles/BlissandBobSirottHOFOct142008.mp3.

2. Mike Conklin, "Chicago Teams Have a Lock on Top Spot," *Chicago Tribune,* August 10, 1977, F2; Mike Conklin, "Softball: Made in Chicago and Still Thriving," *Chicago Tribune,* August 26, 1974, C3; Steve Prostran, interviewed by author, Chicago, December 9, 2009.

3. Mike Conklin, "16-inch Softball Comes Back," *Chicago Tribune,* September 4, 1970, C6; Al Maag, "16" Softball History—Chicago's Game," Chicago 16 Inch Hall of Fame, accessed November 10, 2010, http://www.16inchsoftballhof.com/history.asp; Edward Claflin, *The Irresistible American Softball Book* (New York: Dolphin Books 1978), 5, 9.

4. Maag, "16" Softball History—Chicago's Game"; "Mike Royko at the Billy Goat Tavern Chicago 1982," MediaBurnArchive on YouTube, accessed November 10, 2010, http://www.youtube.com/watch?v=qPbp3vMDzQ8; Mike Royko, "An Ode to the 'Softies,'" reprinted from September 2, 1979 in *One More Time: The Best of Mike Royko* (Chicago: University of Chicago Press 1999), 122–24.

5. Conklin, "16-inch Softball Comes Back"; "Mike Royko at the Billy Goat Tavern Chicago 1982."

6. Conklin, "16-inch Softball Comes Back"; Conklin, "Softball: Made in Chicago and Still Thriving."

7. Maag, "16" Softball History—Chicago's Game."

8. Prostran interview.

9. Prostran interview; Jay Shefsky, "Softball Sundays," Chicago Tonight, accessed December 7, 2011, http://chicagotonight.wttw.com/2011/08/15/softball-sundays.

10. Mike Conklin, "Preseason Checklist for Winning Softball," *Chicago Tribune,* March 15, 1978, D2; Mike Conklin, "Bar Guide for Beer Pitchers," *Chicago Tribune,* July 19, 1978, F2; Prostran interview.

11. Conklin, "Bar Guide for Beer Pitchers"; "Mike Royko at the Billy Goat Tavern Chicago 1982."

12. Conklin, "Softball: Made in Chicago and Still Thriving"; Mike Conklin, "On Softball," *Chicago Tribune,* May 25, 1971, B33.

13. Mike Conklin, "Big Strides Ahead for Softball Fans," *Chicago Tribune,* May 6, 1975, C4; Mike Conklin, "Softball on Threshold of New Era?" *Chicago Tribune*, September 3, 1975, E3; Mike Conklin, e-mail interview with author, September 13, 2010; Mike Conklin, "On Softball," *Chicago Tribune,* July 14, 1971, C3; Conklin, "Preseason Checklist for Winning Softball"; Mike Conklin, "Softball: Batting a Thousand as More Get in the Lineup," *Chicago Tribune,* July 19, 1978, F1; Conklin "Chicago Teams Have a Lock on Top Spot."

14. A history of postindustrial Chicago can be found in chapters 10 and 11 in Dominic A. Pacyga, *Chicago: A Biography* (Chicago: University of Chicago Press, 2009). The statistics referenced here are on page 366.

15. Mike Conklin, "On Softball," *Chicago Tribune,* July 14, 1971, C3; Conklin, "Softball: Made in Chicago and Still Thriving."

16. Conklin, "Bar Guide for Beer Pitchers"; Prostran interview; Mike Conklin, "Softball and Chicago: A Long-Running Love Affair," *Chicago Tribune*, June 13, 1980, E1; Mike Conklin, "On Softball," *Chicago Tribune*, May 3, 1972, C3.

17. Prostran interview; Pacyga, *Chicago*, 366; "WGN RADIO Interview with Bob Sirott."

18. Prostran Interview; Conklin, "Softball: Made in Chicago and Still Thriving"; Mike Conklin, "On Softball," *Chicago Tribune*, July 14, 1971, C3.

19. Royko, "An Ode to the 'Softies.'"

20. "Mike Royko at the Billy Goat Tavern Chicago 1982."

21. *Edwardsville Intelligencer*, April 27, 1977, 5; Mike Royko, "An Ode to the 'Softies.'"

22. Mike Royko, "An Ode to the 'Softies.'"

23. Conklin, "Preseason Checklist for Winning Softball."

24. Claflin, *Softball Book*, 63.

25. Prostran interview.

26. Conklin, "Softball and Chicago: A Long-Running Love Affair"; Conklin, "Softball: Batting a Thousand as More Get in the Lineup"; Prostran interview.

27. Conklin, "Softball: Batting a Thousand as More Get in the Lineup"; Claflin, *Softball Book*, 71–73.

28. Mike Conklin, "Chicago's Game Gets a Facelift," *Chicago Tribune*, July 11, 1983, ND1; Conklin e-mail interview; Prostran interview; Mike Conklin, "Chicago's Game," *Chicago Tribune*, August 31, 1979, E2.

29. Conklin e-mail interview; Prostran interview.

30. Pacyga, *Chicago*, 366–67.

31. Mike Conklin, "'City Game' Spreads to Evanston," *Chicago Tribune*, May 24, 1973, C3; Conklin "Chicago Teams Have a Lock on Top Spot"; Conklin, "Chicago's Game Gets a Facelift"; Conklin e-mail interview.

32. "Sunday's Best Softball Leagues," accessed November 10, 2010, http://insandouts.webs.com; Jay Shefsky, "Softball Sundays," *Chicago Tonight*, accessed December 7, 2011, http://chicagotonight.wttw.com/2011/08/15/softball-sundays.

33. Chicago 16 Inch Softball Hall of Fame, accessed November 10, 2010, http://www.16inchsoftballhof.com/hof.asp; Jay Shefsky, "Softball Sundays," *Chicago Tonight*, accessed December 7, 2011, http://chicagotonight.wttw.com/2011/08/15/softball-sundays.

34. "Sunday's Best Softball Leagues," accessed November 10, 2010, http://insandouts.webs.com; "Hall of Fame," Chicago 16 Inch Softball Hall of Fame, accessed November 10, 2010, http://www.16inchsoftballhof.com/hof.asp; Jay Shefsky, "Softball Sundays," *Chicago Tonight*, accessed December 7, 2011, http://chicagotonight.wttw.com/2011/08/15/softball-sundays; Scoop Jackson, "The Young Guns Story: Quest for a Title," ESPN, accessed November 10, 2010, http://sports.espn.go.com/espn/blackhistory2008/columns/story?columnist =jackson_scoop&id=3271178.

35. Jay Shefsky, "Softball Sundays," *Chicago Tonight*, accessed December 7, 2011, http://chicagotonight.wttw.com/2011/08/15/softball-sundays.

36. "Chicago 16 Inch Softball Hall of Fame," accessed November 10, 2010, http://www.16inchsoftballhof.com; "Softball Leagues," Park District of Forest Park, accessed November 10, 2010, http://www.pdofp.org/softball/index.php; Monica Davey, "Gloveless Players Hold on to Softball Dreams," *New York Times*, September 17, 2009, accessed November 10, 2010, http://www.nytimes.com/2009/09/18/us/18softball.html.

7. The Baltimore Blues

The Colts and Civic Identity

DANIEL A. NATHAN

When I was a teenager, my grandfather gave me a discarded Baltimore street sign. He was born, raised, and lived in Baltimore his entire life. Over the years he had several jobs, including working for the city as a purchasing agent; maybe a fellow city employee gave him the street sign. Scratched and chipped, it's a 24" × 18" piece of painted steel. The background is royal blue and the lettering and border are white; it reads "Colts Trail." In between the two words is a simple, old-school white football helmet with a blue horseshoe on it. At the bottom of the sign is an arrow, pointing the way. I don't know where the city hung this sign, but I'm confident that many people observed it, because in Baltimore the Colts were a cherished civic institution, endowed with deep, lasting local meaning.

"Perhaps nowhere in America, save for Green Bay," journalist Thom Loverro writes, "did a football team mean more to a community than the Colts did to Baltimore. This team was the NFL's version of the Brooklyn Dodgers, a beloved team that during its heyday, with great players like Johnny Unitas and John Mackey, defined the city of Baltimore. When [team owner] Robert Irsay took the team to Indianapolis, he tore out a piece of the fabric of the city that could not be dismissed as merely a sports team."[1] Is this assessment romantic and hyperbolic? Perhaps. After all, other communities, large and small, can claim similarly deep emotional connections to "their" teams. Nonetheless, through the Colts, many Baltimoreans, like my grandfather and his friends and their children, constructed a preferred vision of themselves and their community's civic identity, one that continues to resonate.

Baltimore is a blue-collar, working-class town, perhaps best known for its row houses with white marble steps and painted window screens, its harbor and Chesapeake Bay crabs, its postindustrial decline and quirky charm. An interesting if unglamorous city, it is "forever in the lee of Washington and New York," notes sports commentator and native son Frank Deford.[2] Founded in 1729, Baltimore has a long, complicated history—think Francis Scott Key's "Star-Spangled Banner" and the 1968 riots that left much of the city smoldering—and an eclectic mix of neighborhoods and people.

Unfortunately, Baltimore has long been in decline, plagued by unemployment, poverty, crime, violence (much of it drug related), a crumbling infrastructure, and troubled public schools. Large parts of Baltimore are literally abandoned. It's a "town with too much past and too little present," quipped sportswriter (and disgruntled former Baltimorean) Mark Kram, back in 1966.[3] "A hard town by the sea" is how Randy Newman described the place in a 1977 song. David Simon's Baltimore, from *Homicide: A Year on the Killing Streets* (1991) to *The Corner* (1997) to the HBO series *The Wire* (2002–2008), suggests that things went from bad to worse over the next thirty-plus years.

In truth, there are multiple Baltimores, real and imagined. Even the imagined versions of the city are remarkably varied. John Waters's Baltimore is as campy, quirky, and irreverent as David Simon's is dark, gritty, and dysfunctional. There is also Barry Levinson's Baltimore: *Diner* (1982), *Tin Men* (1987), *Avalon* (1990), *Homicide: Life on the Street* (1993–1999), *Liberty Heights* (1999), and the ESPN documentary *The Band That Wouldn't Die* (2009). Collectively, Levinson's films constitute an appealing mix of social realism and sentimentality. Moreover, in Levinson's Baltimore, the Colts matter. In *Diner*, a coming-of-age story about former high school buddies becoming young adults, set in December 1959, days before the second consecutive NFL championship game between the Colts and the New York Giants, one character insists that his fiancée pass a Colts trivia test before he will marry her.[4] "When I was growing up in Baltimore," Levinson explains, "the Colts were not just a team that played in the city. It was part of the city."[5]

Levinson is right. For many years, from the late 1950s until 1984, many Baltimoreans derived a great deal of pride from its professional football team, which won four NFL championships, most famously the 1958 "sudden death" game against the New York Giants. The city and the Colts had a rich, seemingly symbiotic relationship. It was not an uncomplicated one, however, as the team's 1984 clandestine, middle-of-the-night departure for Indianapolis attests. A dozen years later, after much lobbying, disappointment, and patience, a new NFL team came to town, the Baltimore Ravens, the former Cleveland Browns. Although many people embraced the Ravens and the team won the Super Bowl in 2001, in memory and lore the Colts still

loom large in Charm City. "In Baltimore, nothing is more missed, more distinctly gone, than the Colts," intones columnist Dan Rodricks, narrating a
documentary about Maryland sports history. "Nothing is more unforgiven
than their departure and yet nothing is more affectionately remembered,
more unforgettable, than those distant glory days when all the uniforms
were blue and white, and all those Sunday afternoons golden."[6]

The Top of the World

For many Baltimoreans, December 28, 1958, was one of those golden afternoons, perhaps the most golden of them all. In New York City, where the
Colts played the Giants at Yankee Stadium for the NFL championship, the
afternoon sky was sunny and, for a time, the weather was unseasonably
mild. Later, as darkness fell, it turned freezing cold. This did not dampen
the spirits of the fifteen thousand devoted Colts fans who made the two-
hundred-mile trek to see their team play in its first championship game.[7]
Why, one might ask, would so many Baltimoreans travel so far to watch a
football game in late December?

Unlike the well-established Giants, one of the NFL's original franchises,
the Colts were a relatively new team, landing in Baltimore in 1953 after a
brief, unsuccessful stint in Dallas (where they were called the Texans).[8]
On the field, the Colts were hapless during their first few years, yet en-
deared themselves to many Baltimoreans, who identified with the team's
struggles and its players. In addition to playing football, a number of the
Colts also held other jobs to help pay their bills. Some were dockworkers
and mechanics, some worked as insurance agents and liquor salesmen.[9] As
a rookie, quarterback John Unitas worked at Bethlehem Steel.[10] The next
year, during the off-season, he was a salesman for a container company.[11]

The Colts were also accessible. According to journalist Tom Callahan, "The
players lived next door to the fans, literally. There wasn't a financial gulf, a
cultural gulf, or any other kind of gulf, between them. Except for a dozen
Sundays a year, the Colts were occupied in the usual and normal pursuits
of happiness."[12] One Baltimorean remembers, "The players lived in the area.
You would see them in the offseason and they were approachable. They were
just like us."[13] At the same time, William Gildea notes in his memoir, *When
the Colts Belonged to Baltimore* (1994), in the mid-twentieth century, "the
Colts were Baltimore's first major-league team, and to many Baltimoreans
they bestowed big-league status on the city. Players were co-opted by civic
pride, made to feel as if they had come home, were part of a family."[14] The
team's owner, businessman Carroll Rosenbloom, himself a Baltimorean,

promoted this by encouraging his players to live in the city, to be accessible to fans, and to be active members of the community.[15] For all of these reasons, the Colts quickly became "part of the city's fabric," emblematic of its blue-collar work ethic and sensibility.[16] It was what journalist Michael Olesker calls "the perfect match of town and team."[17]

On that memorable December 28 afternoon, the Colts were "a young team of castoffs from a small city that had never participated in a national championship in any sport," writes Mark Bowden in *The Best Game Ever: Giants vs. Colts, 1958, and the Birth of the Modern NFL* (2008).[18] The Giants, led by linebacker Sam Huff and the top-ranked defense in football, had home-field advantage. The Colts, led by quarterback John Unitas and the league's best offense, were well-rested and healthy. Seven weeks earlier, the Giants beat the Colts in the regular season, 24–21. There were good reasons for high expectations, perhaps especially for Colts fans. In retrospect, Barry Levinson observes:

> From a Baltimore perspective, of a kid in Baltimore, it was a game and it was more than a game. Baltimore at that time, with the economic changes that were beginning to happen in the '50s, was a fairly depressed area. On the train it was the place you had to stop between New York and Washington. We had no real identity. And all of a sudden we get to be in a championship game with the New York team, the Giants. It was like the top of the world.[19]

"From a Baltimore perspective," things would only get better.

With more than sixty-four thousand people in attendance and an estimated forty-five million more watching on television, a device on the verge of becoming ubiquitous and increasingly influential, the Colts capitalized on three Giant fumbles and took a 14–3 halftime lead.[20] The Colts' first touchdown was a two-yard run by fullback Alan Ameche. The second was a fifteen-yard pass to the sure-handed wide receiver Raymond Berry, Unitas's favorite target. (He caught a record twelve passes that afternoon, for 178 yards and a touchdown.)[21]

Over the years, this game has taken on mythic dimensions. It is often hailed for catapulting the NFL into the national consciousness and for signifying, as sportswriter Michael MacCambridge puts it, that "pro football had arrived as a viable alternative to baseball, not merely as the most popular sport, but the one that best defined America."[22] In truth, except for two extraordinary Unitas-led scoring drives late in the contest, it was generally a sloppy, if unusually dramatic game.[23] "It had structure and pace that the best novelists would envy," critic Jonathan Yardley remarks.[24] Still, both teams

John Unitas of the Baltimore Colts versus the New York Giants,
December 28, 1958, in "the greatest game ever played."
Courtesy of Getty Images.

made costly turnovers (seven, in all) and the poor field conditions adversely
affected play. Then again, the game is best remembered and historically
important for what happened late in the fourth quarter and in overtime.

In a surprising reversal, New York dominated most of the second half.
The Giants defense stiffened, most famously stopping the Colts from scoring late in the third quarter from the three-yard line, with first down and
goal to go. The Giants then scored two touchdowns: a one-yard run by Mel
Triplett and a fifteen-yard pass reception by Frank Gifford, to take a 17–14
lead, which they held for most of the fourth quarter. With 1:56 left in the
game, Baltimore took over on its own fourteen-yard line. In a masterful
display of time management, play selection, and execution, Unitas calmly
led the Colts downfield. With seven seconds on the clock, Steve Myhra,
an erratic placekicker who played linebacker for much of the day, booted a
twenty-yard field goal to send the game into the "sudden-death" overtime.
It was the first such game in NFL history (and remains the only championship game decided in overtime). Several of the players thought the game

was over, having ended in a tie. Instead, Tex Maule of *Sports Illustrated* reported: "The teams rested for three minutes, flipped a coin to see which would kick and which receive, and the Giants won and took the kickoff."[25] Unable to move the ball, New York punted. The Colts took over on their own twenty-yard line. With time no longer an issue, Unitas, Maule wrote, "mixing runs and passes carefully and throwing the ball wonderfully true under this pressure, moved them downfield surely.[26] On the drive's thirteenth play, fullback Ameche plunged into the end zone, head down, from the one-yard line to give the Colts a 23–17 victory and the city's first championship since 1896, when the Baltimore Orioles of "Wee Willie" Keeler fame won the National League pennant. The twenty-five-year-old Unitas was named the game's MVP. He also earned sports immortality.

Immediately after Ameche scored, "deliriously happy Colts fans," Arthur Daley of the *New York Times* observed, "a breed that knows no equal," lifted the fullback "to their shoulders and carried him down the gridiron."[27] Hundreds of Baltimore fans stormed the field, tearing down the goal posts. "The fanatics from Baltimore were parading up and down the field long after the combatants had dragged themselves to the clubhouses. The band played, drums boomed and miniature bombs were exploded," Daley reported. Almost simultaneously, the game was described in superlatives—and not just in Baltimore. Leaving the stadium, NFL commissioner Bert Bell said it was the "greatest game he had ever seen."[28] The next day, *New York Daily News* sportswriter Gene Ward predicted: "In years to come, when our children's children are listening to stories about football, they'll be told about the greatest game ever played—the one between the Giants and the Colts for the 1958 NFL championship."[29] Soon thereafter, Tex Maule's *Sports Illustrated* article was published: it was titled "The Best Football Game Ever Played." Time has not modified these claims. In fact, they have only deepened as NFL history has unfolded.[30]

The '58 championship game had (and has) tremendous local meaning in Baltimore. As one would expect, there was jubilation at the time, a massive outpouring of civic pride and excitement. Radio announcer Bob Wolff correctly predicted, "there will be hot time wherever Baltimore fans congregate tonight."[31] The Colts fans who were in New York to watch the game celebrated all the way home. "We just felt triumphant," William Gildea remembers, who was a teenager and at the game with his father. "Going home was an indescribable feeling. When we got back to Penn Station in Baltimore, I looked for the *Sun,* the Monday morning edition, because I wanted to verify what had happened."[32] Earlier, minutes after the game had concluded, fans back in Baltimore started heading to Friendship Airport to welcome the team, to express their elation.[33] Over the next few hours, thousands of people arrived at the airport. By the time the Colts landed, there were an estimated thirty-thousand fans waiting for them. "It was a mob," Alexander Gifford of the *Baltimore News-Post* wrote, "a happy bunch of semi-lunatics carrying signs, carrying babies, and some of them just carrying on."[34] Years later, Baltimore sportswriter John Steadman asserted: "What happened after the game in Baltimore, at the airport and away from it, was a combination of VJ Day and New Year's Eve."[35] Why? Because winning the 1958 NFL championship, said defensive lineman Art Donovan, was "the greatest thing that ever happened to the city."[36] Clearly it felt that way to many people, in part because it assuaged Baltimoreans' insecurities about being from (what many others perceived to be) a second-rate city.

The Colts' victory also vicariously legitimated the city and its citizens, gave them standing, the imprimatur of success, one that would endure for many years. December 28 "was the municipal love affair in its grandest hour," Michael Olesker declares.[37] Like a deep love and cherished memory, it has endured for years. My father, who watched the game on a small black-and-white TV with his father in a rented, semidetached house in a lower-middle-class neighborhood near Druid Hill Park, remembers it as an exciting, meaningful event. So Olesker is right to suggest that the game's "emotional impact on Baltimore lingers half a century later, when aging men still choke up when they hear the playing of the Colts fight song or see that picture of Ameche with his head down. It's not only a touchdown he's scoring; it's the birth of a generation finally feeling terrific about itself."[38] It is also, now, an expression of nostalgia, a yearning for a different (but not necessarily better) time and a kind of communal kinship.

Unitas

Winning the 1958 NFL championship was clearly a team effort, yet no one was more responsible for the Colts' win that day than John Unitas.

In Baltimore, Unitas has long been a valued cultural symbol and commodity, a local folk hero, something close to mythic, a source of civic identity and pride. A slight, 6'1" man with huge hands, a leader with a quiet, confident demeanor, Unitas played in Baltimore for seventeen years (1956–1972), set records, won championships (1958, '59, '68, '71), awards, approbation, love, and respect. When Unitas was unceremoniously traded to the San Diego Chargers in 1973, the *Baltimore Sun* editorialized, presciently, that his "17 years of football excitement and glory will be looked back upon enviously by fans not yet born."[39]

More important, though, Unitas embodied virtually everything that many Colts fans cherished and wanted to believe about themselves and their city. In the mid-to-late 1950s and well beyond, to most Baltimoreans, including many in the local media, Unitas was tough, dignified, clean cut, loyal, reliable, a professional, a white ethnic with blue-collar roots. On the field, he was shrewd and daring, in a matter-of-fact, workmanlike way, a winner without being a braggart, a fallible hero. He was, in a word, meaningful. But symbolic and cultural meaning is not found or fixed; it's always made, fluid, contested, negotiated. Moreover, there are multiple ways of making sense of Unitas as an expression of civic identity.

A laconic, retiring man, not easily discouraged, Unitas did not burst on the scene. To begin with an oft-told story: the Colts signed him as an undrafted free agent in 1956, after the Pittsburgh Steelers cut him the previous year before the season began. He didn't play much the first half of his rookie season and only got an opportunity to start after his predecessor as the Colts' starting quarterback, George Shaw, "the most promising young quarterback in the league," injured his knee.[40] Unitas, however, was prepared, calm under pressure, and earned the respect of his teammates and fans. Speaking for many, Barry Levinson asserts that when Unitas came to Baltimore in 1956, "he was a perfect fit for the city: a working-class guy, in a working-class town. And when he rose to legendary status, all of us were proud."[41]

For his part, though, Unitas, who "never regarded himself as anything other than an honest craftsman, a professional," was unsentimental about his football career.[42] Unitas once reflected:

I guess what I miss most is probably the camaraderie of the people that we had with us for 17 or 18 years. I was with these people on a day-in day-out basis for six months out of the year it's something that when it's not there, sure you miss that part of it. This football team was a family. You're all here for the same reason, and that's to win. But I don't miss getting hit.[43]

A clear-eyed antiromantic, permanently disabled because of football, Unitas developed meaningful relationships with people, but he never bought into saccharine narratives about sport or himself. "Football to him was no different than a plumber putting in a pipe," reflects Steve Sabol of NFL Films. "He was an honest workman doing an honest job. Everything was a shrug of the shoulders."[44] This is partly what Baltimoreans loved about him: the unpretentiousness, the resilience, the lack of self-importance even as he quietly competed with everything he had.

Soon after the 1958 championship game, a Unitas master narrative, which had been in the process of coalescing, fully emerged. It is something like a Cinderella story. The broad outlines are familiar. Unitas, the unwanted, stoop-shouldered quarterback who played semipro ball for $6 a game on Pittsburgh sandlots after being cut by the Steelers. His Horatio Alger–like rise from obscurity to success. The young quarterback's early struggles and dogged perseverance and unshakeable confidence. The emphasis on his unfashionable black high-tops, which became a trope.[45] The way his name signified his white ethnic roots. That for many people he was a blue-collar guy in a blue-collar town, an unaffected, physically unimposing Everyman type who valued and represented substance over style, a quiet, dignified hero who could be legitimately mentioned in the same breath with the legendary Joe DiMaggio. Tough, courageous, noble, the Unitas that emerges in this popular narrative is simultaneously an old-fashioned throwback and a man who redefined his position.

Local renditions of this master narrative have taken many forms, yet most do not deviate from it. It's found in heartfelt memoirs, thoughtful biographies, and scores of news stories. It's in front of M&T Bank Stadium, where the Baltimore Ravens play their home games, in the form of a thirteen-foot statue unveiled less than a month after Unitas died in 2002.[46] It's found in Baltimore's Sports Legends Museum at Camden Yards. Most important, perhaps, it's in the city's collective consciousness. In Levinson's *The Band That Wouldn't Die* a fan says, "for a brief shining moment, that team meant everything to this town." Soon thereafter in the film, Michael Gibbons, executive director of the Babe Ruth & Sports Legends Museums, explains: "It was almost religion. It was, every Sunday was like going to church for a lot of Baltimoreans, and I think that we really did come to worship at the altar of Johnny Unitas and I think that the further we got more involved, the further we went along with that, the more fanatic we became."[47] The "more fanatic we became" is another way of saying that the more Baltimoreans invested themselves emotionally and linked their identity with the Colts, the more it helped cultivate social solidarity. Unitas was at the center of this process.

In a 1999 HBO documentary about Unitas, one of his successors, former Colts' quarterback Marty Domres, reminisces: "John was the top personality in a town where steel workers and dock workers, people that worked in smelting pits, a blue-collar town, associated with somebody that wore high-tops and worked hard and had a brush-cut." After which, narrator Liev Schreiber adds, "Johnny Unitas was a Baltimore icon."[48] He still is, but the question is what does his iconicity signify? The argument here is that, through Unitas, Baltimoreans constructed and have maintained a preferred vision of themselves. All Baltimoreans? Of course not. But many, including one fan who wrote in a letter to the editor of the *Baltimore Sun* a few days after Unitas died: "He was one of us through and through. His gangly frame even made him look like one of us. His hunched shoulders and saddle-walk gait gave him a signature awkwardness that we all identified with. He took what God gave him and he gave us and our city an identity."[49] After Unitas's funeral, a woman who described herself as "just an ordinary Colts fan," reflected: "I sat out there on many a cold day. Today is very sad. He was Baltimore."[50]

These claims can seem sentimental and hyperbolic. One Baltimore journalist, Kevin Van Valkenburg, asserts that it's a cliché to depict Unitas "as the simple man who represented something much larger than himself, the blue-collar idealist who did his job without complaint; the Golden Arm with the golden crew cut; the rare athlete who made an awkward shuffle and unorthodox throwing motion feel, especially in retrospect, like a work of both art and grace."[51] Yes, we can make too much of athletic icons, endow them with too much meaning and cultural significance. The ability to throw a football far and accurately under duress shouldn't automatically be equated with dignity and heroism. We should always be wary of mythologizing athletes (or anyone, for that matter), past or present.

At the same time, for many people in Baltimore John Unitas was and remains a vibrant symbol and personifies their community's idealized civic identity and spirit. This phenomenon should be taken seriously, as it suggests something about local culture and the desire for communal belonging. In this instance, when people remember and glorify Unitas as Baltimore's favorite son, they are reifying a specific version of masculinity and perhaps implicitly bemoaning a lost racial order, for in Unitas's heyday Baltimore was segregated, even though the Colts were not. Yet they are also actively engaged in celebrating someone they think and feel represents their core values, their better selves.

Under Cover of Darkness

Nothing lasts forever, though. By the late 1960s, Colts' coach Weeb Ewbank was long gone, his replacement, Don Shula, left after seven successful seasons to coach the Miami Dolphins, and the team's best players had either retired (Donovan, Gino Marchetti, Berry, Lenny Moore, Jim Parker) or were in decline (Unitas). Likewise, Baltimore had undergone significant changes, economically and demographically, which only intensified in the 1970s. The city's postwar economic boom was over and thousands of well-paying manufacturing and other blue-collar jobs were lost. In addition to suburbanization, the steady migration of African Americans to the city and subsequent white flight dramatically changed Baltimore's racial composition. In 1950, less than 25 percent of the city's population was African American and the schools were segregated. Twenty years later, that percentage had doubled, and after *Brown v. Board of Education* in 1954 the schools were integrated.[52] Unquestionably, Baltimore in the 1960s and 1970s was a more economically depressed, a more racially complicated and contentious, and a more culturally fragmented place than it had been. To make matters worse, then came Irsay.

A successful Chicago heating and air-conditioning contractor, Robert Irsay became the Colts owner in 1972 when he purchased the Los Angeles Rams and then traded franchises with Carroll Rosenbloom. Rosenbloom hatched this plan, which enabled him to own the team he wanted and to avoid a significant tax bill.[53] Many people in Baltimore cite this moment as the beginning of the end for the Baltimore Colts.[54] In a 1986 *Sports Illustrated* profile on Irsay, E. M. Swift wrote, "One of the great dynasties in professional sports, dismantled by one man. Destroyed, not by luck or circumstance, but by what numerous people cite as incompetence."[55] Compared with many other assessments, this one is judicious. Over the years, Irsay (who died in 1997) was described as "blustery" and an "egomaniacal carpetbagger."[56] He was called "pugnacious, devious, and emotional."[57] One of his former players, quarterback Bert Jones, once said: "He lied and he cheated and he was rude and he was crude."[58] Jones added: "He doesn't have any morals. It's a sad state for the NFL to be associated with him." Not to put too fine a point on it, Irsay was called "an uncultured, self-conscious eccentric," "a meddler clearly out of his depth," and a "buffoon."[59] Frank Deford gets the last word on this subject: "A man who could screw up professional football in Baltimore would foul the water at Lourdes or flatten the beer in Munich."[60]

The machinations that led to the team's departure in 1984 are complicated. Basically, Irsay was concerned about falling attendance and wanted the city to refurbish Memorial Stadium and to provide him with a low-interest loan. He was also temperamental and less than honest with Baltimoreans about his plans, but his "decision to move the Colts to Indianapolis had multiple motives," explains political scientist Charles C. Euchner. "Certainly the desire for increased profits played a major role. However, Irsay's disagreeable, quixotic personality was another factor. Irsay had worn out his welcome with both the sports fans and political leaders of Maryland. He recognized this and sought refuge and enlarged profits in the Midwest."[61] The manner in which he did so, however, was startling, and provoked "criticism throughout the country," not just in Baltimore, where many people were understandably upset.[62]

After prolonged and contentious negotiations with Baltimore and Maryland officials, during which time he was also fielding offers to relocate his team to Phoenix and Indianapolis, Irsay was legitimately concerned that Maryland lawmakers would pass legislation to seize the Colts via eminent domain. This process enables the government "to take private property for a public use, without the owner's consent, if the owner is compensated for the full value of the property."[63] That is close to what happened. On March 28, 1984, Maryland Governor Harry Hughes signed an eminent domain bill to block the Colts from leaving the city; soon thereafter, Baltimore officials wired Irsay a $40 million offer to purchase the team (for the purpose of selling it to local investors); such an offer is normally a prelude to an eminent domain action.[64]

So that snowy evening the Colts hurriedly prepared to leave town. "The scene was surrealistic," writes former Baltimore broadcaster Ted Patterson, "like something from a movie."[65] Irsay had the team's equipment, furniture, and records loaded into a fleet of Mayflower moving trucks, which were "on the road to Indianapolis within a matter of hours. Startled Maryland officials, who had been negotiating with Irsay on the evening of the move, awoke to find the city and state without a professional football franchise."[66]

The day the Colts left Baltimore was traumatic for some people. "Some felt anguish, some felt used, and some could only mutter assessments so guttural that they would burn a hole through this paper if they were printed," wrote a *Baltimore Sun* reporter named David Simon.[67] For others, it was a relief, a sad but predictable end to an ongoing melodrama, which some felt the local media stoked. Many others felt no sense of abandonment or heartbreak. Life went on. "No, there's no moratorium on crime today," a city police lieutenant told Simon. "The criminal community is apparently still involved in a debate as to what direction their protest should take regarding the Colts."[68] Art Donovan, a former Colt defensive lineman, a World War II veteran, and one of the team's most colorful characters, put the move in perspective: "The team was really lousy and there were [only] 16,000 people in Memorial Stadium. Some people said it was a tragedy, but that's no tragedy. Children dying of cancer is a tragedy."[69] Obviously he's right. John Ziemann and other Colts fans understand that. In Barry Levinson's *The Band That Wouldn't Die,* Ziemann observes: "When the team left, it was hard. The sun came up the next day. Nobody died. Commerce in Baltimore was moving. But a big part of our heart was taken away. A big part of us was trucked out to Indianapolis."[70] In Indianapolis, as one would expect, many people—politicians, journalists, business leaders, and football fans—were ecstatic. "I'm sorry Baltimore hearts are broken," said

Indianapolis Mayor William Hudnut, who was not actually apologetic, "but I'm glad Indianapolis can rejoice."[71]

Back in Baltimore, some people likened the Colts' middle-of-the-night move to a messy divorce or even a death in the family.[72] In his *Baltimore Sun* column the day after the Colts left town, Michael Olesker lamented: "Something precious and irreplaceable has died. Not just a football team, but a symbiotic relationship between a team and a town that transcended athletics and even, once, transcended money."[73] Speaking of money, it was reported that two Colts fans were so upset that they "filed a $30 million lawsuit seeking damages for the pain and suffering caused by the team's departure."[74] One fan reminisced: "It was devastating. A tradition had snuck out overnight. The only feeling I can compare it to—I was only a little kid then, but I remember it—was the Kennedy assassination."[75] Perhaps this is a hyperbolic claim. But even if it is, it affirms what William Gildea claimed about the Colts leaving town: that many people were "left overwhelmingly empty. If the Colts could be taken away, Baltimoreans realized absolutely nothing was forever. Irsay's night flight had to signal the same clear message to anyone in America who ever loved a team."[76] A few years later, John Steadman mused: "There is still a feeling of loss. To look out there and see a team [the Indianapolis Colts] that meant so much to Baltimore for so long, that personified us in such a profound way, that's why I have so much bitterness in my heart. This community breathed life into the Colts."[77] Irsay had not just relocated a pro football team, contends Ted Patterson, he had transformed "a way of life," one that bound Baltimoreans all over the city to one another, one that was transgenerational: "He had taken a tradition, one of the proud legacies of the National Football League. About all he couldn't take, something that Indianapolis could never steal, were the memories."[78] Memories, of course, are not forever, they are clearly fading.

The Baltimore Colts were neither the first nor the last professional sports franchise to relocate. The list is long and includes the Boston (and Milwaukee) Braves and the Brooklyn Dodgers; the Minneapolis Lakers and the New Orleans Jazz; the Cleveland (and Los Angeles) Rams and the Chicago (and St. Louis) Cardinals, among others. The mayor of Indianapolis understood this when he asked: "Where did the Colts come from? Texas. Where did the Orioles come from? St. Louis. Franchises move around. It's just as moral now as it was then."[79] The morality of franchise relocation is not the issue. Sports teams are businesses, commercial endeavors. Market logic drives their pursuit for ever-greater revenue and greener pastures. What is intriguing, however, and the Baltimore Colts are an especially vivid example of this, are the ways in which local teams and iconic athletes represent their communities, how they help people make meaning and craft collective identities. What some have called "gloppy sentimentality" for sports teams can be a powerful, long-lasting epoxy, as the enduring melancholy in Baltimore about the Colts suggests.[80] Yet that melancholy is generational: "Teens or younger associate the old Colts with black-and-white television. Generation Xers remember the bitter end but not the glory days. Boomers and especially older ones are least likely to forgive or forget."[81] Eventually, the Baltimore Colt blues will fade away and along with them will go one facet of the city's former identity.

Notes

1. Thom Loverro, *Home of the Game: The Story of Camden Yards* (Dallas: Taylor Publishing, 1999), 12.

2. Frank Deford, "'The Colts Were Ours. . . . They Were One With The City,'" *Sports Illustrated,* April 9, 1984, 13.

3. Mark Kram, "A Wink At A Homely Girl," *Sports Illustrated,* October 10, 1966, 95.

4. Michael MacCambridge writes that *Diner* "evoked the central role that the Colts played in the psyche of the city of Baltimore." Not everyone is so generous. "Everybody in America thought this [the film's football quiz scene] quite hilarious," contends Baltimore journalist Michael Olesker. "Except people in Baltimore, for whom the premise made perfect sense. Who would marry a woman who didn't love the Colts?" Michael MacCambridge, *America's Game: The Epic Story of How Pro Football Captured a Nation* (New York: Random House, 2004), 350; Michael Olesker, *The Colts' Baltimore: A City and Its Love Affair in the 1950s* (Baltimore: Johns Hopkins University Press, 2008), 143.

5. Barry Levinson, "Personal Statement," accessed May 21, 2010, http://30for30.espn.com/film/the-band-that-wouldnt-die.html.

6. *Gone but Not Forgotten II,* videocassette, produced by Dan Rodricks, Marilyn M. Phillips, and Jonathan F. Slade (Owings Mills, Md.: Maryland Public Television, 1994).

7. MacCambridge, *America's Game,* 110.

8. David Harris, *The League: The Rise and Decline of the NFL* (New York: Bantam Books, 1986), 48. The Colts' early history is complicated. The first incarnation of the Colts arrived in Baltimore in 1947. The team was in the All-America Football Conference (AAFC), had previously been the Miami Seahawks, and joined the NFL, but folded in 1950. Harris explains: "The following year a syndicate started a new NFL team in Dallas, the Texans, but gave the franchise back to the League halfway through the 1952 season, unable to bear ever-mounting financial losses. [NFL Commissioner Bert] Bell's solution was to take the Texans franchise, transplant it to Baltimore as the reborn Colts, and this time do it right."

9. Mark Bowden, *The Best Game Ever: Giants vs. Colts, 1958, and the Birth of the Modern NFL* (New York: Atlantic Monthly Press, 2008), 112–13.

10. William Gildea, *When the Colts Belonged to Baltimore: A Father and a Son, A Team and a Time* (New York: Ticknor & Fields, 1994), 210.

11. "A Persevering Passer," *New York Times,* December 29, 1958, 25.

12. Tom Callahan, *Johnny U: The Life and Times of Johnny Unitas* (New York: Crown Publishers, 2006), 94.

13. Quoted in Jason La Canfora, "For Some Longtime Residents, Seeing The Shoe on Another Foot Is Still Difficult to Grasp," *Washington Post,* January 13, 2007, E4.

14. Gildea, *When the Colts Belonged to Baltimore,* 5.

15. Olesker, *The Colts' Baltimore,* 99.

16. Gildea, *When the Colts Belonged to Baltimore,* 50.

17. Olesker, *The Colts' Baltimore,* 44.

18. Bowden, *The Best Game Ever,* 8. Also see Dave Klein, *The Game of Their Lives: The 1958 NFL Championship* (Lanham, Md.: Taylor Trade, [1976] 2008); John F. Steadman, *The Greatest Football Game Ever Played: When the Baltimore Colts and New York Giants Faced Sudden Death* (Baltimore: Press Box, 1988); Lou Sahadi, *One Sunday in December: The 1958 NFL Championship Game and How It Changed Professional Football* (Guilford, Conn.: Lyons Press, 2008); and Frank Gifford, with Peter Richmond, *The Glory Game: How the 1958 NFL Championship Changed Football Forever* (New York: Harper, 2008).

19. Quoted in *The Greatest Game Ever Played.*

20. Bowden, *The Best Game Ever,* 2, 8.

21. Ibid., 203.

22. MacCambridge, *America's Game,* 112, 113.

23. John Steadman reports: "Most of the Colts are in agreement that the game was not the pure classic it has been made out to be but they aren't about to refute their given place in history." Steadman, *The Greatest Football Game Ever Played,* 82.

24. Jonathan Yardley, "A truly communal, live, national event—and one to remember," *Washington Post,* June 8, 2008, BW15.

25. Tex Maule, "The Best Football Game Ever Played," *Sports Illustrated,* January 5, 1959, 60.

26. Ibid., 60.

27. Arthur Daley, "Sports of The Times: Overtime at the Stadium," *New York Times,* December 29, 1958, 25.

28. Quoted in Steadman, *The Greatest Football Game Ever Played,* 45.

29. Ibid., 50.

30. A historical consensus has emerged. It asserts, in effect, that the 1958 championship game had a profound impact on the NFL (especially financially) and the course of American sport history. "The high drama of the first sudden death game in the history of the league," asserts writer Lou Sahadi, "ushered professional football into the television era as a bona fide sport that was embraced by millions of new fans across the country." Like Sahadi, writing fifty years after the game, sportswriter Steve Wulf claims that it was "a watershed for the NFL and the history of televised sports." In the documentary *The Greatest Game Ever Played: The Baltimore Colts vs. New York Giants* (2008), ESPN broadcaster Chris Berman declared the game "would forever change how America looked at football." Sahadi, *One Sunday in December,* xvi; Steve Wulf, "The End Came in Sudden Death," *Wall Street Journal,* June 9, 2008, 15; *The Greatest Game Ever Played: The Baltimore Colts vs. New York Giants,* DVD, produced by Marc Kinderman (New York: NFL Productions, 2008).

31. *The Greatest Game Ever Played.*

32. Ibid.

33. Steadman, *The Greatest Football Game Ever Played*, 70.

34. Alexander Gifford, "Fans 'Conquer' Airport," *Baltimore News-Post*, December 29, 1958, 1.

35. Steadman, *The Greatest Football Game Ever Played*, 76.

36. *The Greatest Game Ever Played*.

37. Olesker, *The Colts' Baltimore*, 215.

38. Ibid., 198.

39. "Sold to San Diego," *Baltimore Evening Sun*, January 24, 1973, A24.

40. Bowden, *The Best Game Ever*, 41, 71.

41. Levinson, "Personal Statement."

42. George Weigel, "Johnny U by Tom Callahan," *Commentary*, January 2007, accessed May 21, 2010, http://www.commentarymagazine.com/viewarticle.cfm/johnny-u-by-tom-callahan-10822?page=all.

43. *Gone but Not Forgotten II.*

44. Quoted in Callahan, *Johnny U*, 243.

45. See Dick Schaap, "Johnny Unitas: Sunday's Best," in ESPN *SportsCentury*, ed. Michael MacCambridge (New York: ESPN-Hyperion Books, 1999), 155.

46. Ken Murray, "Unitas statue unveiled at ceremony honoring Colts Hall of Fame players," *Baltimore Sun*, October 21, 2002, D10.

47. *The Band That Wouldn't Die.*

48. *Unitas,* videocassette, produced by Ross Greenburg (1999).

49. Terry Woods, "Letter to the Editor," *Baltimore Sun*, September 15, 2002, D4.

50. Quoted in William Gildea, "In Baltimore, No. 19 Receives A No. 1 Salute," *Washington Post*, September 18, 2002, D8.

51. Kevin Van Valkenburg, "Missing Unitas," *Baltimore Sun*, September 16, 2007, accessed June 21, 2012, http://articles.baltimoresun.com/2007-09-16/sports/bal-kvv-missing-john-unitas-020512_1_john-constantine-unitas-steelers-fans-friend.

52. W. Edward Orser, "Flight to the Suburbs: Suburbanization and Racial Change on Baltimore's West Side," in *The Baltimore Book: New Visions of Local History*, ed. Elizabeth Fee, Linda Shopes, and Linda Zeidman (Philadelphia: Temple University Press, 1991), 204.

53. MacCambridge, *America's Game*, 296.

54. Deford, "The Colts Were Ours," 13.

55. Swift, "Now You See Him, Now You Don't," 84. The Irsay who emerges in Swift's article is either a serial liar or someone with little knowledge of his own biography.

56. Pete Axthelm, "The Colts: A Cause for Anger," *Newsweek*, April 9, 1984, 105; Deford, "The Colts Were Ours," 13.

57. James Edward Miller, *The Baseball Business: Pursuing Pennants and Profits in Baltimore* (Chapel Hill: University of North Carolina Press, 1990), 204.

58. Quoted in Swift, "Now You See Him, Now You Don't," 87.

59. MacCambridge, *America's Game*, 297, 397.

60. Deford, "The Colts Were Ours," 13. For an alternative view of Irsay, see Dave Overpeck, "The other side of Robert Irsay," *Indianapolis Star*, March 31, 1984, 25.

61. James Edward Miller, *The Baseball Business: Pursuing Pennants and Profits in Baltimore* (Chapel Hill: University of North Carolina Press, 1990), 293.

62. Harris, *The League*, 606.

63. Charles C. Euchner, *Playing the Field: Why Sports Teams Move and Cities Fight to Keep Them* (Baltimore: Johns Hopkins University Press, 1993), 92.

64. J. S. Bainbridge Jr., "Eminent domain bill signed; city may sue," *Baltimore Sun,* March 30, 1984, A1.

65. Ted Patterson, *Football in Baltimore: History and Memorabilia* (Baltimore: Johns Hopkins University Press, 2000), 229–30.

66. Miller, *The Baseball Business*, 295–96.

67. David Simon, "Some Marylanders anguished, some irate," *Baltimore Sun,* March 30, 1984, A15.

68. Ibid.

69. Quoted in La Canfora, "For Some Longtime Residents, Seeing The Shoe on Another Foot Is Still Difficult to Grasp," E4.

70. *The Band That Wouldn't Die*.

71. Quoted in Bart Barnes, "Colts Slip Out of Baltimore and Into Indianapolis," *Washington Post*, March 30, 1984, F1.

72. Gildea, *When the Colts Belonged to Baltimore*, 295.

73. Michael Olesker, "Loyalty is nothing, money all," *Baltimore Sun,* March 30, 1984, A1.

74. Engelberg, ". . . but in Baltimore, It Leaves a Void in the Hearts of the Fans," 22.

75. Frank Ahrens, "In NFL-Starved Baltimore, Long Drought Ends Today," *Washington Post,* September 1, 1996, A1.

76. Gildea, *When the Colts Belonged to Baltimore*, 269.

77. Quoted in Brady, "Baltimore bracing for Colts," 1C.

78. Patterson, *Football in Baltimore,* 230.

79. Quoted in Jane Leavy, "Colts' 20-Year Lease Approved Formally By Indianapolis," *Washington Post,* April 1, 1984, 76.

80. Euchner, *Playing the Field,* ix.

81. Erik Brady, "Baltimore bracing for Colts: Emotions run high for first visit since move," *USA TODAY,* November 27, 1998, 1C.

8. The Voice of Los Angeles

ELLIOTT J. GORN AND
ALLISON LAUTERBACH

This chapter combines history and memoir. The authors are both historians and both grew up in Los Angeles as Dodgers fans. Gorn followed the team in the late 1950s and 1960s. Lauterbach became a fan a generation later. With the realization that the voice of Dodgers announcer Vin Scully was their common tie to Los Angeles, they decided to write about his importance to the city.

"A good evening to you wherever you may be." The familiar voice almost sings out of the radio, embracing listeners with the warmth of a soft Los Angeles evening. For more than sixty years, the same greeting has welcomed Dodgers fans to pull up a chair and listen to a baseball game. The man behind those words, Vin Scully, is more than just a well-loved sportscaster. He is the voice of L.A.

Born in 1927, Vincent Edward Scully grew up in the Bronx listening to sportscasters on the radio, a career that was barely as old as he was. He took up broadcasting while a student at Fordham University. After graduation, he briefly worked for WTOP in Washington, D.C., announcing news, weather, music, and occasionally filling in on the sports desk.[1]

Scully's professional breakthrough came on November 12, 1949, when he was just twenty-two-years old, thanks to Brooklyn Dodgers' announcer Red Barber. When Barber needed someone to call the University of Maryland–Boston University football game at Fenway Park for CBS Sports Radio, Barber remembered the red-headed kid he had met months before.

Scully assumed that he would have a press box from which to do the play-by-play, so he left his coat in the hotel room. But on that frigid November

New England night, he was relegated to the roof with nothing but a table and a microphone. Scully never complained. Barber heard the story later and was impressed with the rookie's professionalism. When Ernie Harwell left the Dodgers' broadcasting team two months later, Barber once again thought of Scully.[2]

"I had a feeling for years," Barber later wrote in his autobiography, "it was like a woman who has never had a child. I guess I had never gotten over my early ambition to teach. I always had the dream of taking an untutored kid who showed some promise and of putting him on the air for what he was, a neophyte learning the trade. Scully was a perfect choice." Barber went on to note, though, "Whatever made him the fine broadcaster he is, he had when he started."[3]

Scully joined the Dodgers at spring training in Vero Beach, Florida, in March 1950. More than sixty years later, he is still with the team, the longest tenured announcer in American sports history. When Scully began his career with the Dodgers, sportscasters had been doing regular live coverage for scarcely twenty-five years. Scully, in other words, has been at it for well over two-thirds of sports radio's existence.

Over the course of his six-decade career, Scully has worked in three home stadiums, for five Dodgers owners, during twelve U.S. presidencies, and under eight Major League Baseball commissioners. Dodger Stadium, opened in 1962, is now the third-oldest Major League ballpark (behind Fenway Park and Wrigley Field), and Scully has announced fifty seasons from it. Already a member of the Baseball Hall of Fame, the Radio Hall of Fame, and the American Sportscasters Association Hall of Fame, he is a four-time national sportscaster of the year, an Emmy Award winner, has a star on the Hollywood Walk of Fame, and was elected the American Sportscasters Association's "Top Sportscaster of all time."[4]

While he is the last to flaunt his celebrity status, Scully understands the great platform afforded to him. "Our job is to help people escape, to help them forget their troubles," he once explained.[5] He frequently reminds listeners that they are doing just that. In the fall of 2008, when the California hillsides were once again ablaze, he told fans that baseball was but a child's game. And like he did throughout Korea, Vietnam, the first and second Gulf Wars, and after the World Trade Center towers crumbled, Scully always made it clear that the game was a healthy, even necessary diversion from the real business of life, but a diversion nonetheless.

With a strong sense of perspective—of history—Scully emphasizes to listeners that baseball is a special little world, fascinating to be sure, but not to be overvalued. For example, during an otherwise unremarkable game against the San Diego Padres on June 6, 2010, Scully reminded the audience of life beyond the baseball diamond. Never straying from the task at hand, calling the game, Scully went on to tell the story of D-Day: "Oh yeah, you could just sum it up and say, 'oh sure, Allied Forces invaded Normandy.' There is so much more—as Troy Glaus checks in, Ely's pitch, fastball inside, ball one. First of all, D-Day, the 'D' in front of Day doesn't mean anything. It just meant the day of a military operation—the 1–0 pitch on the way, outside—and it used to be D-Day for any military operation but as the years have gone by when you say 'D-Day,' they're talking about *this* day in 1944. The 2–0 pitch fouled away . . ."[6]

This is one of the reasons Scully is so successful. Because he eschews hype and bluster, we come to trust him. Scully treats his listeners like adults who understand that the game is a fair-weather pleasure, a moment of grace in a hard world. He doesn't lie to us with apocalyptic intimations of sports' importance. He never exaggerates, either factually or emotionally. The game is enough, the game is the thing, the game unfolds like a nice leisurely story, told by a man who sees it all and speaks it in the cadences of summer.

More than anything, Scully is a storyteller. There is the story of each at bat, merging into the larger narrative of the game, the statistics (Scully's legendary pregame preparation assures that the right statistics are always at hand) that give the still longer view of the season, one of the hundred seasons that preceded it. Scully's flow of words is the flow of baseball history, the fan's history, and against that backdrop—the tale of the player who spent seventeen years in the minor leagues before his call-up, or of the one whose grandmother raised him and watched him pitch a perfect game, or of the players from the far corners of America and the globe, now on the field with the game on the line—he embeds each day's new stories.

Above all—magically, mysteriously—Scully's voice creates a bond of intimacy and community between himself and the fans. Maybe all sports broadcasting strives to accomplish this merging of the personal with the communal, and maybe other broadcasters pull it off sometimes, but Scully has done it for generations.

That closeness became especially visible in the early 1960s. We think of how wired we all are today, but before smart-phones and iPods, there were transistor radios. In Los Angeles, one of the most striking things about these portable sets, beginning just a few years after the Dodgers came to town, was how many fans brought them to the ballpark. "The transistor radio was probably the greatest single break that I had in Southern California," Scully once said. "It enabled me to talk more to the fans—and to elicit a response."[7]

But it wasn't just the number of fans who listened; any home radio could do that. When the Dodgers built their new stadium at Chavez Ravine and put together a contending team, the club also secured a loyal fan base. Thousands of fans brought their radios to every Dodgers game. Scully's voice literally echoed throughout the ballpark in the 1960s through the 1980s. Enough fans still bring radios that you often get his running commentary of the live action on the field. This is a metaphor for Scully's place in Los Angeles—the individual radios merging their sound into one big voice, pervading the ballpark, pervading the city.

Angelenos' sense of civic identity resonates with Scully's voice, because some of their most powerful memories are associated with that sound. Scully himself has said, "One of the nicest parts of my job is to have someone come up to me and say, 'When I hear your voice, I think of nights in the backyard with my mom and dad.' It's a wonderful feeling to be a bridge to the past and to unite generations." Always humble, he's quick to add, "The sport of baseball does that, and I am just a part of it."[8]

It is all about baseball, of course, but in Los Angeles, fans know the game through *his* eyes, *his* word-pictures, *his* voice, and it is the voice of intimacy. When Scully described the anniversary of D-Day above, he began, "I don't want this to be an intrusion, but I think we've been friends long enough, you'll understand . . ." And we do. That is why a 2010 *Los Angeles Times* poll found that Scully was tied with former mayor Tom Bradley as the city's most admired citizen of all time.[9]

Many die-hard fans still bring Scully to the games. The rest of us tune-in on TV, in the car, and, increasingly for displaced Dodgers fans, online. With the advent of satellite radio, Vin has developed even more of a following. "One of the things we hear from our listeners is how much they love being able to hear Vin Scully," notes David Butler, director of corporate affairs for XM Radio. "Many of them are people who may have seen him on TV or who are baseball fans who have heard about the legend of Vin Scully but had never had the luxury to hear him call a game on the radio."[10] For Los Angelenos spread across the world, online broadcasts offer the ultimate connection back home, whether they are on a military base in the Middle East, in an easy chair in New York, or in a college library in the heartland. Distance need not separate Dodgers fans from the team or city they love. Vin welcomes them back to both. He is attuned to how scattered his audience is, but he also knows that his voice brings them all together. That is his most important role.

Maybe most striking, in a city that routinely destroys all sense of tradition and history, that embraces each postmodern moment as distinct from the last, Scully is all about continuity. For half a century, Los Angelenos have always been able to count on four things: smog, traffic, seventy-degree winters, and Vin Scully. We mark time and the big moments by memories of his broadcasts. Fifty years isn't a long time in the course of human history, but for a town like Los Angeles, it represents the deep past. Not just longevity, but Scully's devotion to baseball, made manifest in his formidable knowledge of the game, matters here, too. He has occasionally announced other sports during his career, but not often. Angelenos' loyalty to Scully was reinforced by his loyalty to baseball.

The children of immigrants from eastern cities, of dust bowl refugees in the 1930s, and of midwesterners whose opportunities on the land closed down as farms consolidated, must have heard him as a voice from home. But others too—African Americans who came from the South in search of equality, jobs, and schools for their children in the 1940s and '50s; Asian immigrants and their descendants for whom midcentury California began to fulfill earlier promises; Mexican American kids whose parents sought fresh opportunities for their families—all had some familiarity with baseball, but came to think of it as quintessentially American. Scully's easy presentation of the game was tied up with the promise of California life.

Even in the ultimate polyglot city, Scully's voice crosses neighborhood boundaries. In East L.A., Gil Reyes, who trained tennis star Andre Agassi, learned English over the radio: "I had a little transistor. KABC every night. Vin Scully was my English teacher."[11] Writing in the *Los Angeles Times,* columnist Hector Tobar lists "appreciate Vin Scully" as one of his ten keys to being a "true Angeleno," and Tobar adds "drop Scully's name into a conversation, and it will instantly identify you as a real Angeleno."[12] Another Dodgers fan who calls himself "Roberto" named his website VinScullyismyHomeBoy.com.[13] A Chinese American blogger, who once taught a constitutional law class at a juvenile detention facility, recalled: "During one of my classes, a Mexican student quipped that though there is tension between blacks and Mexicans on Los Angeles' streets, the one person both groups would unite to defend would be 'the Dodgers announcer.' Scully has such unquestioned respect among people of all races because it is unquestionably evident he respects everyone."[14]

Los Angeles was the first American city to have Major League Baseball games announced in Spanish. Jaime Jarrin, himself a Hall-of-Fame announcer and a fifty-year veteran of L.A. Dodgers broadcasts, has a wide following among Spanish speakers, not just in Southern California but in Mexico too. Still, the children of immigrants—the kids we grew up with and now their kids—listen to Scully.[15] Without wishing to dismiss the nostalgia many people have for the Brooklyn Dodgers, the Los Angeles version of the team meant at least as much to the civic identity of the booming new megalopolis as it did in Brooklyn. Every tear shed by a Brooklyn fan watered Angelenos' sense of their town as a big, wide-open place, no mere stepchild to the East Coast. Suddenly, when the team came to L.A. in 1958, it was a major league city. This was not just a metaphor—we were becoming major league in every way, and for half a century, Vince Scully's voice reminded us that America's best was moving west.

* * *

Elliott recalls: One of my earliest childhood memories is of being at the old Coliseum for a Dodgers game in 1958, the team's first year in L.A. I don't recall who the Dodgers played or if we won, I just remember being there. And I remember that a year later, in October 1959 when I was eight years old, I must have been listening to the game at school—it seems amazing that they allowed me to—because my third grade teacher, Mrs. Friedman, let me announce to the class that the Dodgers had just won game six of the Series, making them World Champions. Even then I knew, because I read the backs of my baseball cards, and because our neighbor was from Brooklyn, that that Dodgers came to us with a glorious past. Living gods—Hodges, Snyder, Furillo, Podres—strode the field.

Hearing Scully's voice is also among my earliest L.A. memories. In the late '50s, I'd fall asleep with the Dodgers game coming lightly over the radio. Even as a kid, it was impossible not to recognize how good Scully was because the Dodgers had two broadcasters, Scully and Jerry Doggett, the latter perfectly competent at calling the games, but even to a nine-year-old's ear, Doggett was workmanlike, nothing special. The idea always was to stay awake through his innings to get to Scully's.

Maybe it was the radio still murmuring as I slept that indelibly planted Scully's voice in my brain. Radio was everything back in the Dodgers' first couple of decades in L.A. The team owner, Walter O'Malley, was convinced that television would kill attendance at the games, so he only broadcast nine games a year on TV, those three, three-game sets they played each season up in San Francisco against the Giants at Candlestick Park, where sometimes the fog was so thick you thought there was something wrong with your television.

It is amazing how powerful the memories are, not so much for the details, which are few, but for the emotions: Winning discount tickets for good grades (a promotion the Dodgers ran year after year in cooperation with the L.A. schools), going to beautiful new Dodger Stadium, which opened in 1962, with my brother and my father, hearing that same voice in the ballpark that I heard at home, and realizing that it was because of the thousands of fans who brought transistor radios to the game. Often in the evening I would go over to my friend Gary White's house, and there in his living room, Mrs. White stood ironing the next day's clothing for the family, always with Vinny's voice pouring out of the radio. He was with me also on many weekend afternoons as I did gardening jobs around the neighborhood. Those were the years of Sandy Koufax and Don Drysdale, of Maury Wills and Tommie Davis. Town and team were in love, and Vinny was the matchmaker.

Most vividly, I remember my father and I pacing the living room, listening to the 9th inning of Koufax's perfect game against the Chicago Cubs in 1965. What made it so memorable was less the game itself than how Scully spoke, never fast or overheated, but relaxed and conversational, yet building tension all the way. This is how he announced the early moments of the 9th inning in what is now an iconic broadcast (note to reader—you have to *hear* this; it is all about sound, so read it aloud):

> ... Here's the strike one pitch to Krug, fastball, swung on and missed, strike two. And you can almost taste the pressure now. Koufax lifted his cap, ran his fingers through his black hair, then pulled the cap back down, fussing at the bill. Krug must feel it too as he backs out, heaves a sigh, took off his helmet, put it back on, and steps back up to the plate. Tracewski is over to his right to fill up the middle, Kennedy is deep to guard the line. The strike two pitch on the way, fastball, outside, ball one. Krug started to go after it and held up. . . . One and two the count to Chris Krug. It is 9:41 P.M. on September the 9th. The 1–2 pitch on the way, curve ball, tapped foul, off to the left and out of play. . . . There are twenty-nine thousand people in the ballpark and a million butterflies. . . . Koufax into his windup and the 1–2 pitch, fastball, fouled back and out of play. . . . And it begins to get tough to be a teammate and sit in the dugout and have to watch. Sandy, back of the rubber, now toes it, all the boys in the bullpen straining to get a better look as they look through the wire fence in left field. . . . One and two the count to Chris Krug. Koufax, feet together, now to his windup and the 1–2 pitch, fastball outside, ball two. A lot of people in the ballpark now are starting to see the pitches with their hearts. . . . Two and two, the count to Chris Krug. Sandy reading signs, into his windup, 2–2 pitch, *fastball got him swinging.* . . . Sandy Koufax has struck out twelve. He is two outs away from a perfect game . . . [16]

I left Los Angeles in 1969, but I carried on as a Dodgers fan for twenty more years. I'd listen to games or go to Dodger Stadium on trips home to visit my family. I was back in California in 1988, living up in the Bay Area for a year, and there in October were my Dodgers, seemingly overmatched in the World Series by the Oakland Athletics, a team with some fine pitching and a couple of scary hitters, Mark McGwire and Jose Canseco. With great good fortune, Scully was doing the national broadcast that year. So there I am, lying on the floor of my dingy little Palo Alto apartment, watching game one on a twelve-inch black and white TV. I had little hope. The Dodgers' lineup was truly mediocre, especially with the heart-and-soul of this team, outfielder Kirk Gibson, hobbled by a hamstring pull in one leg and a torn up knee in the other. Scully had announced before the game began that Gibson would not see action that night. Orel Hershiser led a very tough L.A. pitching staff, but he didn't start the first game, and Tim Belcher, who did, gave up a grand slam in the second inning to Canseco. Somehow, though, the Dodgers hung in.

Bottom of the 9th, 4–3 A's, and one of the toughest closers in the game, Dennis Eckersley—the Most Valuable Player of the just-completed American League Championship Series—on the mound. Eckersley got two quick outs, and Dodger Stadium grew deathly quiet. But then outfielder Mike Davis worked the count for a walk. The pitcher was due up next, and no one was on deck. To everyone's amazement, Gibson—who had spent the whole game in the training room but had suited up and come to the dugout for the ninth—grabbed a bat and limped to the plate. He fouled off two, and you could see him wince as he tried to drive the ball with his legs. But he stayed alive, fouled off three more pitches and took three balls for a full count. Eckersley's ninth pitch to Gibson was a slider, maybe a little further inside than he wanted, and Gibson reached out and flicked it toward right, much harder than it first appeared.

"High fly ball into right field . . . she is . . . gone!" And then Scully didn't say a word for half a minute as the crowd went wild and Gibson gingerly jogged around the base paths. Scully only broke his silence as Gibson hobbled across home plate into the arms of his teammates: "In a year that has been so improbable, the impossible has happened." There was no grandiosity in his tone but humor, the humor of recognizing that life sometimes plays a little trick then chuckles at our surprise. Scully capped it all with this benediction: "You know, I said it once before a few days ago, that Kirk Gibson was not the Most Valuable Player, that the Most Valuable Player for the Dodgers was Tinkerbell. But tonight, I think Tinkerbell backed off for Kirk Gibson."[17]

One last thing about that moment. When Gibson hit the homer, after a moment of blinking incredulity, I was screaming along with those fans in Dodger Stadium. Screaming until I realized that the apartment building where I lived had gone dead quiet. Of course. I was just across the Bay from Oakland. My enthusiasm in that neighborhood was not appreciated.

I never moved back to Los Angeles, and I've since switched my allegiance to other teams. I tried being a Cincinnati Reds fan when I lived there in the early 1990s, but it never took. Something about that bland town and soulless Riverfront Stadium kept those good and exciting Reds teams from capturing my imagination. Then I became a Cubs fan, an addiction to failure that I still fight. I love Chicago, but whatever it is that goes on in that yuppie hell known as Wrigley Field, it isn't baseball.

I often go back to L.A. because my daughter lives there. There is nothing like hearing Vinny still calling games. I'm not a big fan of Southern California, but his voice somehow captures what is best about the place, the ease and flow of outdoor living, the beauty of mountains and desert and ocean. There is grace in Scully's cadences, just as there is grace in that mellow landscape in the twilight glow.

*   *   *

Allison recalls: My love of the Dodgers and Vin Scully is not a fleeting affection. I am, in fact, a fourth-generation Dodgers fan. My great-grandfather, Max, loved "Dem Bums" when they still played at Ebbets Field in Brooklyn. He stayed loyal when the team moved west, introducing my grandmother to Dodger Blue. After her, my uncle, and finally my little brother and myself, took up the Dodgers legacy. While the Dodgers have changed stadiums and uniforms, lineups and locales, two things have remained constant: Vin Scully and my family's loyalty to the team. Though I never met my great-grandfather, he knew, as I know, the sound of Vin's voice.

So it is against the backdrop of his broadcasts that my family knows Los Angeles. My aunt was literally born to the sound of his voice. A doctor who brought his addiction to the game into the delivery room caught her. My grandmother, of course, didn't mind.

My grandmother would later introduce me to Vinny, too. As a four-year-old, I stood in her kitchen, braiding challah for Shabbat dinner, Scully's voice ever-present in the background. Long before I understood baseball, I knew the sound of his broadcasts, the soundtrack of my childhood. While my grandmother passed away over sixteen years ago, when I hear Vin call a game, I'm instantly transported back to her yellow kitchen. With his help each season, my love of my grandmother and of baseball renews itself over and over again. Years later, sitting in the library reading for my Ph.D. exams, I was still listening to Vinny. The online archive of games kept a constant stream of his trademark anecdotes and stories streaming to my ears.

Although Scully has helped me mark several key milestones in my life, his broadcasts often serve as events in and of themselves. You remember where you were when Kennedy was shot, when the World Trade Center towers fell, or, if you're my mother, when Diana and Charles got married. Baseball fans have their own memorable moments: when Buckner missed the ball, when Larsen was perfect, when Gibson went yard (all of which Scully announced). Vin's 1965 play-by-play of Sandy Koufax's fourth no-hitter and only perfect game is one of those moments. You remember hearing that kind of extemporaneous poetry.

I was eleven in 1994. In the car on the way home from a Red Sox game at Fenway Park, my uncle and I got to talking about Dodgers baseball. Though he had moved to Boston years before, my uncle remained a loyal Dodgers fan, even naming his golden retriever after the team. The conversation inevitably turned to Vin Scully. In the days before Internet broadcasts, my uncle had no way of listening to games on a regular basis. When I asked how he coped, he quickly popped in a cassette tape.

"Three times in his sensational career has Sandy Koufax walked out to the mound to pitch a fateful ninth where he turned in a no-hitter. But tonight, September the ninth, nineteen hundred and sixty-five, he made the toughest walk of his career, I'm sure, because through eight innings he has pitched a perfect game . . ."

And so Scully and Koufax together began the ninth inning. As the Boston skyline passed by, my uncle and I traveled in time, transported back to the Chavez Ravine, the timeless broadcast echoing in the night air.

Even though I knew how the game turned out, I listened with bated breath. "Two and two to Harvey Kuenn, one strike away. Sandy into his windup, here's the pitch: Swung on and *missed,* a perfect game!"

Then the best broadcaster in sports did what only he could do: he went silent. For thirty-eight seconds, all we heard was the roar of the crowd. Vin let the audience tell the story.

Almost thirty years after that broadcast, my uncle and I were united around the radio. A moment my uncle had first shared with his mother, my grandmother, we had made our own.

Koufax's perfect performance was matched by Scully's call. That play-by-play is iconic in Los Angeles, and some even consider it a work of baseball literature. As sportswriter Dave Sheinin once observed, "To hear Scully call the ninth inning . . . is to make a baseball writer contemplate a career as a roofer. Off the top of his head, without the benefit of a delete button or an editor, Scully composed one of the most gorgeous pieces of baseball literature you will ever encounter."[18]

While several other broadcasts stand out, I remember best those I shared with my family. As a kindergartener, I got to stay up past my bedtime to watch the first game of the 1988 World Series against the Oakland A's. By the ninth inning, Vin was in charge of the television play-by-play. I sat on the couch next to my father and listened to Scully tell us that Kirk Gibson, the 1988 National League MVP plagued by leg problems, was nowhere to be found. Gibson, it turns out, was watching the broadcast from somewhere in the Dodgers' clubhouse while he underwent physical therapy. Legend has it that Vin's observation about Gibby motivated the ailing player to get in the game.

We all watched as Gibby wobbled to the plate. Once he was in the batter's box, Vin, as nobody else could, noted how he was "shaking his left leg, making it quiver, like a horse trying to get rid of a troublesome fly." The count got to three balls, two strikes. And then it happened. Gibson launched a long fly ball just over the right field wall, then he limped around the bases, pumping his fist. While I was screaming, Vin was silent, once again letting the crowd tell the story. And then, perfectly, "In a year that has been so improbable . . . the impossible has happened!" It is impossible for Dodgers fans and Angelenos to recall the home run without also hearing Vin's voice, it is played so often in Los Angeles. And I couldn't not tell it again in these pages.

Twenty-one years later, I sat in the nosebleed seats with my little brother on opening day 2009. My brother clutched his transistor radio (my gift to him for his recent birthday) as we watched the pregame festivities. The Dodgers honored Scully's sixtieth season with the team by asking him to throw out the first pitch (that day we all learned that he is a southpaw). After the ceremonial toss, Scully addressed the fans. "I have needed you a lot more than you have needed me," he told them. I'm confident that all fifty-six thousand fans disagreed with his assessment. And then, like he does before every broadcast, he almost sang the words, "It's time for Dodgers baseball."

The 2011 season was Vin's sixty-second with the Dodgers. For the past few years, he has signed a series of one-year contracts, each time renewing fan loyalties to the Dodgers. Before the 2010 season, however, we got a major scare. That March, one night during spring training, headlines flashed across the Internet announcing that Scully had fallen and hit his head. The news couldn't come fast enough as the City of Angels collectively held its breath. He was, to all of our relief, okay.

The incident was a reminder of the octogenarian's mortality. With each one-year contract, we count our blessings that we get to experience another

Scully season, but for how much longer remains unclear. And when he does finally retire, it seems likely that many fans will cut their ties to the team. People move on, find other passions, look to other sports. Scully keeps fans coming back to the Dodgers, at least as much as the other way around. More, much more, without quite realizing it, his voice has become one of those markers of place. Like the sign up in the hills that reads "Hollywood," like the first glimpse of the ocean as you approach Pacific Coast Highway, the timbre and rhythm of Scully's words say, "Welcome to Los Angeles."

* * *

If you grew up in Los Angeles then moved away, especially a generation or two ago, you had to get used to people looking at you and saying, "Huh? L.A.? No one grows up there, they just move there." One friend actually loved watching others react when he told them he was a fifth generation Angeleno (he lives in Virginia now).

Why is that? L.A. has been America's second-largest city for decades, and yet there is something inauthentic about it in our imaginations, as if having roots there was impossible. Of course Hollywood has everything to do with this. Anywhere else in America, the word "industry" conjures images of factories, of hot, cacophonous mills where men pour steel or pound cars together, of women sweating their lives away in textile mills and garment shops, of immigrants and minorities doing the work that the native-born shun, of blue-collar workers either exploited by their bosses or defiantly organized into powerful unions.

But in Los Angeles today, "the industry" means just one thing: the film and entertainment business, whose productions are mere light and sound, fleeting, weightless, insubstantial. We were wrong. It turns out that all of those mines and mills and factories were chimerical. Commercials, television shows, movies, reality TV, the whole image-driven world: That is what's real, that is what lasts. U.S. Steel: Gone. GM: On life support. Pixar: Thriving.

Los Angeles has always seemed to be in the grip of centrifugal forces. Sleepy towns wake up as booming suburbs, whole nations of immigrants pour in, new freeways slither over dry riverbeds. With Angelenos spending so much time in their cars, with new exurbs impossibly far from downtown, with so many immigrants busy becoming new Americans, it makes perfect sense that one of the things holding the town together is a voice on the radio. For more than sixty years Scully's has been *the* voice of L.A. And for those of us who no longer live there, what could be better than flying into LAX, renting a car, heading out the 405 freeway, scanning the radio band,

and up pops Vinny, still where he's been all these decades, welcoming us back to Dodgers baseball.

Even though we can't imagine the Dodgers without him, he has never ever been a homer like the late Harry Carey, so full of a hypocrite's devotion that he could love both the Cubs *and* the Cardinals. Nor was there ever in Scully's delivery even a trace of that horrible apocalyptic tone we've come to associate with the likes of Bob Costas or Marv Albert, as if they were announcing a Soviet invasion of western Europe. No, Scully is perfect for the Southland, because his voice resonates with that easy, flowing ideal of Southern California life.

Scully's persona comes through not in the cheap, overheated, and patronizing tones so common to sports announcing. On the contrary, it's his devotion to his craft—to getting the story right, giving us key statistics, filling in with the back-stories, building drama with his poetic rhythms—that tells us he is L.A.'s own. We love him because, in a city filled with outrageous self-promotion and continual self-regard, here is the real deal—an oasis of understatement, of substance, of art. All elegance and ease and seeming effortlessness, perhaps he is best thought of as a performance artist, without a hint of the pretentiousness that phrase sometimes conjures.

One last thing. Scully has done it in a town dedicated to being forever young. Los Angeles is all about youth, appearances, pleasing surfaces. The town is a living denial of age, of generational continuity. And yet there is Vinny, his shock of red hair now feathered with white, doing his job for more than six decades, offering the city nothing *but* continuity across generations and ethnic groups and neighborhoods. His are among the better angels of Los Angeles's nature.

Notes

1. See http://officialvinscully.com/biography.php.

2. Red Barber and Robert W. Creamer, *Rhubarb in the Catbird Seat* (Lincoln: University of Nebraska Press, 1997), 261.

3. Barber and Creamer, *Rhubarb in the Catbird Seat,* 261.

4. Curt Smith, *Pull Up a Chair: The Vin Scully Story* (Dulles, Va.: Potomac Books, 2010), xiv.

5. Claire Smith, "Dodgers' Deaths Bring Out the Best," *New York Times,* July 7, 1993, B9.

6. June 6, 2010, about fifty-seven minutes into the broadcast.

7. David Brown, "Answer Man: Vin Scully talks candy, Dodgers and 'Bewitched,'" Yahoo! Sports, September 16, 2010, accessed April 6, 2011, http://sports.yahoo.com/mlb/blog/big_league_stew/post/Answer-Man-Vin-Scully-talks-candy-Dodgers-and-?urn=mlb-270225.

8. Quoted in Michael Connelly, "Conversation With My Hero Broadcaster Vin Scully," *Parade Magazine,* October 18, 2009.

9. Steve Lopez, "From water czar to Zorro: Your votes for most admirable Angeleno," *Los Angeles Times,* January 15, 2010, accessed March 31, 2010, http://latimesblogs .latimes.com/lanow/2010/01/best-of-los-angeles.html.

10. Dave Sheinin, "A Legendary Career That Speaks for Itself," *Washington Post,* July 5, 2005, accessed April 6, 2011, http://www.washingtonpost.com/wp-dyn/content/ article/2005/07/04/AR2005070400935_2.html.

11. Quoted in Andre Agassi, *Open: An Autobiography* (New York: Vintage Books, 2010), 138.

12. Hector Tobar, "Some guidelines on how to be a true Angeleno," *Los Angeles Times,* May 27, 2011, accessed July 1, 2011 http://articles.latimes.com/2011/may/27/local/ la-me-tobar-20110527.

13. See http://www.vinscullyismyhomeboy.com/.

14. See http://www.humanevents.com/article.php?id=42698.

15. Jaime Jarrin is discussed in Samuel O. Regalado's *Viva Baseball: Latin Major Leaguers and their Special Hunger* (Urbana: University of Illinois Press, 1998), 176–82; Jarrin was interviewed on National Public Radio and spoke of Vin Scully mentoring him; see http://www.npr.org/templates/story/story.php?storyId=106415915.

16. Jane Leavy, *Sandy Koufax: A Lefty's Legacy* (New York: HarperCollins Publishers, 2002), 214–16; National Public Radio, "Recorded History: Vin Scully Calls a Koufax Milestone," April 23, 2007, accessed April 6, 2011, http://www.npr.org/templates/story/ story.php?storyId=9752592.

17. See http://www.dailymotion.com/video/xd2fhk_1988-world-series-game-1 -bottom-of_sport.

18. Sheinin, "A Legendary Career That Speaks for Itself."

9. We Believe

The Anatomy of Red Sox Nation

AMY BASS

Tessie, "Nuff Ced" McGreevey shouted/We're not here
    to mess around
Boston, you know we love you madly/Hear the crowd
    roar to your sound
Don't blame us if we ever doubt you/You know we couldn't
    live without you
Tessie, you are the only only only
The Rooters gave the other team a dreadful fright/Boston's
    tenth man could not be wrong
Up from "Third Base" to Huntington/They'd sing another
    victory song
—"Tessie" (2004), by the Dropkick Murphys

America does not have a national team. Though the Olympics often generate a national cheering section, in general, root-root-rooting for the home team is regionalized in the United States. Yet some teams are more nationally prominent than others. The Dallas Cowboys enjoyed a national reign that began in the 1960s. The Pittsburgh Pirates turned their 1979 World Series run into a phenomenon to the tune of Sister Sledge's "We are Family." And the New Orleans Saints' post-Katrina success made everyone shout "Who dat? Who dat? Who dat say they gonna beat dem Saints?" with some modicum of style.

For Red Sox fans, the definition of home has always been blurry. Although the professionalization and commercialization of sport in the twentieth century has allowed fans to "watch" sports without leaving home, Red Sox fans have always been part of a diasporic New England community more imagined than real, but maintaining what *Yankee* magazine dubs "an identity so strong that no matter where you were, if you said 'I'm a New Englander,' people would have a sense of who you were."[1] Even in its most parochial eras, the Red Sox have reached far beyond Fenway Park, rendering "Boston" as home for people in Maine, Vermont, New Hampshire, Rhode Island, parts of Connecticut, and the rest of Massachusetts.

This reach broadened in the wake of the 2004 championship season, when the team surpassed the New York Yankees as Major League Baseball's most profitable road attraction.[2] With the creation of Red Sox Nation, the team became a national phenomenon, enjoying a community that is rooted to whatever space it occupies at any given moment.

Red Sox fans, once angst-ridden, now enjoy a space in which the newly evolved championship ethos ensures that they are a Nation of Everywhere. They often outnumber those fans of the team they are visiting, drawing anyone with (real or imagined) New England roots to regain senses of community and self. For some, it is a necessity of access: the ongoing "sold out" streak of ticket sales at Fenway has made a trip to see a game one of planes, trains, and automobiles. How, then, does this vast community—its forty-thousand-member fan club represents all fifty states and some fifteen countries—maintain its connections? How did Red Sox Nation grow to this extent, both in terms of its organic roots and the marketing response of Red Sox management? How does this team maintain its identity when its fans are from places so remarkably different?

History's Team

Like all nations, Red Sox Nation is crafted to determine who belongs and who does not based upon an "ideological geography," a phrase coined by historian Matthew Jacobson.[3] According to *Boston Globe* sportswriter Dan Shaughnessy, "Those who can't stomach the self-pity of Red Sox Nation tend to be people who've come here from other shores. . . . The outsiders, they'll never know. But the natives, they understand."[4] For Red Sox fans, as with others before them, the idea of "home" easily translates into a language of national identity. Pittsburgh football fans refer to Steeler Nation, and the St. Louis Cardinals—a team whose regional pull in the Midwest rivals or equals Boston's in the Northeast—has a fansite that refers to its own diaspora.[5] High school teams, too, often inform visitors that they are now in a "nation," such as "Welcome to Arlington [Texas] High School! Home of the Colts! How sweet it is to be in Colts country!" Perhaps most famously, the Permian Panthers, first made famous by H. G. Bissinger's book *Friday Night Lights* (1990), reside in the imagined "Mojoland," rather than Odessa, Texas.[6]

The very suggestion of a home team implies the importance of the *idea* of the local, if not its *actuality,* in sports competition. Sports teams contribute to a community's definition, expressing pride, identity, and meaning alongside shared rituals and styles that reinforce belonging. This works well with Benedict Anderson's oft-revered and oft-critiqued notion of the nation as an "imagined community." The nation "is *imagined* because the members of even the smallest nation will never know most of their fellow-members, meet them, or even hear of them, yet in the minds of each lives the image of their communion."[7] This argument does not diminish the importance of national construction; rather, it differentiates perceptions of national belonging from feelings of communal belonging: instead of engaging in day-to-day interactions that solidify national identities, it is "the style in which they are imagined" that gives these bodies strength.[8] Further, when removed from its modernist foundations, this construction of nation can become an even more useful tool. For Boston fans, the home team is invented as a nation that relies upon a "diasporic imagination." According to Jacobson, such a construction "refers precisely to this realm of ideologies and engagement of minds: both the shared currency of cultural imagery, and the mindset of the individual as he or she navigates the inner geography."[9]

The most powerful underlying factor for the Red Sox is franchise history. "The Red Sox are different because of history," observes Shaughnessy. "They have a longer history than almost any professional sports team, and it is a bizarre lineage, stocked with great stars but cluttered with tarnished silver medals and chronic underachievement."[10] Indeed, few fans understand the importance of history more clearly than Red Sox devotees, who reinvented themselves and their sense of place in the twenty-first century by re-creating what it means to cheer for a home team. Take Fenway Park itself: in 1999, then–Red Sox president John Harrington proposed replacing the storied field with a more profit-bearing replica, a plan that fans battled. When John Henry and Larry Lucchino took the team's reins in 2002, they chose another path: update rather than replace, and do so by emphasizing, rather than eliminating, the "historical elements," a move that solidified Fenway, the league's smallest venue, as baseball's largest revenue-generating stadium.[11]

Scholars Michael T. Friedman and Michael Silk note that Harrington "underrated the value of authenticity and was willing to discard it, believing that consumers would readily embrace a different narrative of heritage abstracted from its original space."[12] But in the wake of the SAVE FENWAY PARK campaign, he changed his plans. As a result, Fenway remains the spiritual center for Red Sox Nation, "a term which in and of itself raises numerous questions with regard to categories of inclusion and exclusion, belonging, and inequality within and across the local, national and trans-national expressions of 'nation.'"[13]

For fans, that connection creates a demand for an imagined historical authenticity rather than Harrington's proposed nostalgia. The editors of *Red Sox Century: The Definitive History of Baseball's Most Storied Franchise* (2000) describe the team as "a gift to any historian, for in their dramatic history one also finds the story of baseball in the twentieth century."[14] Yet for most of that century, and then some, the team's existence relied on tales of its failure to win a World Series, producing mythologies from the Curse of the Bambino to the return of Tessie. After the Red Sox dominated the American League from 1912 through 1918, the championship drought that followed, as well as the furious rivalry with the Yankees, created a subcul-ture based on the torment of *not* winning. Red Sox fans created a symbolic culture beyond hats, tying together a disparate geographical region with the imagined identity that came from the burden of being a Red Sox fan and, perhaps in a more codified manner, the burden of *not* being a Yankee fan: Red Sox fans defined themselves by what they were not—champions. "It's bad enough we haven't won since 1918," says one fan. "It's worse that they've won *twenty-six times* since then. Much worse. It's New York. Goddamned New York."[15] The end result, Red Sox pitching great Dennis Eckersley once said, is "the ultimate manic-depressive fan base."[16]

A Nation Born

Before 2004, the 1967 season—the Impossible Dream—in which the team won the pennant for the first time since 1946, solidified the Red Sox as, ac-cording to team chronicler Howard Bryant, "an institution that represented all of New England."[17] But the heartbreaking 1970s followed: the Red Sox lost the 1975 World Series in seven games and the pennant in 1978 (on the last day of the season . . . at Fenway . . . against the Yankees . . . because of Bucky $%*&! Dent). The 1980s followed suit: individual Red Sox such as Wade Boggs and Roger Clemens experienced some success, but the team was overrun by painful failure, exemplified during the bottom of the tenth inning of game six of the 1986 World Series, when a ground ball rolled through first baseman Bill Buckner's legs, allowing the Mets to take the game and eventually the series.[18] What seemed to be an unbelievable turn of events shook *New York Times* sportswriter George Vecsey. After Buckner's gaffe, Vecsey rewrote the column he started before the game, which was to be about victory after years of disappointment: "I kind of gargled in the back of my throat and then proceeded to rewrite that column totally backwards, and totally turned around what my lead had been."[19] After the Mets won the title, Vecsey continued his historical theme. "All the ghosts and demons and curses of the past 68 years continued to haunt the Boston Red Sox last night," he explained. Harry Frazee sold Babe Ruth "to the lowly Yankees to finance one of his Broadway shows, and for 68 years it has never been the same."[20] For Vecsey—and soon legions of others—such a loss could not be explained rationally; the Curse of the Bambino had taken hold.

The birth of Red Sox Nation was based on ethereal belief, rather than the statistics that drive most baseball fanatics, making Red Sox fans resemble a religious faithful. Psychologist Daniel L. Wann explains, "The similarities between sport fandom and organized religion are striking. Consider the vocabulary associated with both: faith, devotion, worship, ritual, dedication, sacrifice, commitment, spirit, prayer, suffering, festival, and celebration."[21] For film critic Rand Richards Cooper, such devotion suits the bill perfectly. "Red Sox suffering is a cathedral of loss and pain," he wrote in *Commonweal* magazine. "It is holy. The Red Sox remind us that life is a trial; that it raises hopes only to crush them cruelly; that it ends badly."[22] It is not a stretch to imagine a stadium as a cathedral or players as gods. Religion, according to Wann, creates a transformative effect on its followers, as does sport for its spectators, existing as a "cultural anesthesia" designed to reroute daily anxieties and serve as an "opiate."[23]

Boston's belief system swims decidedly against this notion. To be a Red Sox fan is to accept a yoke of devotion. It is based on understanding why the team fails, rather than support the team's abilities or goals. And it is legitimated at the highest of national levels. In 1999, as the Red Sox battled the Yankees in the American League Championship Series (ALCS), Congressman Ed Markey (Massachusetts 7th District) brought the Curse of the Bambino to the House floor, pronouncing it on par with the Curse of Macbeth, King Tut's tomb, and Yahweh.[24]

Red Sox fans are not the only ones to believe in curses, of course; baseball fans are a superstitious lot, and fans of the Chicago Cubs, the Cleveland Indians, the Detroit Tigers, and the Philadelphia Phillies have all manufactured tales that explain their team's woes. But with the exception of the Cubs, none have reached the scale of the Curse of the Bambino, which since its creation has been both the living document necessary for the founding of the Nation and has re-created the team as a viable industry, creating new stability to its community. Philosopher Étienne Balibar argues that "in the history of every modern nation . . . there is never more than one single founding revolutionary event."[25] But for Red Sox fans, there were two: Vecsey's reimagining of the Curse and the actual coining of "Red Sox Nation" by Nathan Cobb in the *Boston Globe* in a story about how the 1986 World Series bifurcated parts of New England. Cobb wrote that the series was not between two teams but two cities, particularly in southwestern Connecticut, where "Boston and New York baseball fans are New England's Hatfields and McCoys." The border of "Red Sox Nation," according to Cobb, was somewhere "near Hartford, roughly parallel to the Connecticut River."[26]

And with that simple turn of phrase, a nation emerged.

Looking back, Cobb claims he did not know he created the term until he read Shaughnessy's *Reversing the Curse* (2005). Indeed, most credit Shaughnessy with it, just as many credit him with popularizing the theory of the Curse, if not originating it.[27] Vecsey only hesitantly takes ownership: "I kind of thought I invented it, but it never meant anything to me. . . . It was just a device. . . . Call it collective wisdom, whatever you want."[28] A week before Vecsey's column, Gene Sunnen, then president of the Society for American Baseball Research, had referred to "the curse of Harry Frazee" as a reason "the Sox haven't won a Series since 1918."[29]

Though Vecsey laid the foundations, Shaughnessy melded the two off-spring of that fateful World Series—"Red Sox Nation" and "the Curse of the Bambino"—to define a new kind of Boston fan. Shaughnessy's books, including *The Curse of the Bambino* (1990) and *At Fenway: Dispatches From Red Sox Nation* (1997), hit home for many. "Sox fans," writes Glenn Stout, "still reeling from the loss to the Mets, devoured The Curse of the Bambino like so much Prozac."[30] Rather than get at more structural explanations—like racism and cronyism—for past failures, "the Red Sox faithful accepted a soothing fairy tale that assured them that all was right with their world."[31]

The franchise, too, had a hand in its creation. The front office—almost two decades after Cobb's story about Connecticut—officially took hold of Red Sox Nation, acquiring the Web site from the fans that were smart enough to purchase the domain, and creating a multileveled membership club. Not everyone ponies up, and it is likely the majority of those who consider themselves citizens of Red Sox Nation lack card-carrying status (it's a good thing they're not Arizona Diamondbacks fans). But management's capitalization on the Nation solidified both an understanding of the team's history of failure and an optimistic conviction that a new century would bring with it a new slate, as "Breaking the Curse" became part of the team's official mission statement.[32]

Cowboy Up

Before the front office legitimated the declaration of nationhood, however, a group of self-described hirsute "idiots" forged this new slate during the 2003 season with a rallying cry of "Cowboy Up," uniting the legions of fans that had come together in the name of the curse while exorcising ghosts of the past. The team members that took the Red Sox into the twenty-first century appeared, at least superficially, to be almost disrespectful of the club's history. Still, the season ended with familiar heartbreak: on October 17, 2003, just past midnight, in the eleventh inning of game seven of the ALCS, Yankee third baseman Aaron Boone hit an unexpected home run, giving New York its thirty-ninth pennant and sending the Red Sox home. Again.

However, the important part of the 2003 season is not how it ended, but how it looked. Led by teammates Kevin Millar, who is credited with instilling the "cowboy up" mantra, and Johnny Damon, who proclaimed that the team was comprised of "idiots" who did not understand nor believe in any curse, the Red Sox took on a swagger not seen since 1967, if ever. Damon, for one, restylized what a player should even look like with his long locks and unshaven face, and supported Millar's Wild West attitude. "It's no bull," wrote Joseph P. Kahn in the *Boston Globe*, "Red Sox fans are talking a new brand of talk, pardner, as their team gallops toward a playoff berth." Millar, a Texan, first used "cowboy up" after a loss to the Oakland A's, when a sportswriter questioned how strong the team really was. "I want to see somebody cowboy up and stand behind this team and quit worrying about all the negative stuff," he said. It took hold. Pitcher Mike Timlin, also from Texas, made T-shirts that read "The Time is Now . . . So Cowboy Up," and Fenway began playing Ryan Reynolds' country hit "Cowboy Up" before games. "A cowboy is just like your tough guy, the guy that falls off the horse, broken arms and all that kind of stuff," said Millar. "This team has that kind of makeup . . . a bunch of guys that go out and basically cowboy up."[33]

In addition to "Cowboy Up," the team also got itself a new soundtrack. In addition to Neil Diamond's "Sweet Caroline," which has been official eighth inning fare since Henry and Lucchino took over,[34] local darlings the Dropkick Murphys added "Tessie" to the Red Sox Nation anthem roster, ensuring that team history had come full circle. The song, about a parrot in the 1902 Broadway musical *The Silver Slipper,* had been the anthem of the Royal Rooters, ardent fans of the Boston Americans (renamed the Red Sox in 1907) led by Michael "Nuf Ced" McGreevy, owner of the 3rd Base Saloon, a local hotspot for prominent politicians, including Mayor "Honey Fitz" Fitzgerald (John F. Kennedy's grandfather), sportswriters, and working-class fans, the majority of whom were Irish or of Irish descent. On game days, McGreevy's Rooters marched from the Third Base to Huntington Avenue Grounds (the home field before Fenway was built in 1912), where they had reserved seats on the third base line, close enough to hurl verbal assaults and sing to the visitors, often, according to many sportswriters, affecting the game's outcome. When Boston faced off against Pittsburgh in the first World Series in 1903, the Rooters' never-ending renditions of "Tessie" apparently drove the Pirates to distraction. The Rooters disbanded in 1918, after the team won its last World Series of the twentieth century.

For the Dropkick Murphys, an "Irish-punk" band whose mission is to "tap into the working-class and sports fan culture that permeates Boston and the New England area," the new song describes how the original version secured the 1903 title.[35] The band wrote it in 2004 at the request of Red Sox management. According to the band's drummer, Matt Kelly:

> The Red Sox pitched it to us. Dr. Charles Steinberg, who was involved with the Red Sox organization, was also a bit of a baseball historian. And I guess he had been talking with Jeff Horrigan, the sports writer, about how the song "Tessie" was the unofficial anthem of the Royal Rooters. . . . So we deconstructed the whole tune . . . and then Jeff Horrigan and Ken (Casey), our bass player and fearless leader, got together and re-wrote the lyrics to have to do with the Sox and the Royal Rooters themselves. We recorded it, and it just took off. That was in the 2004 season, which was a very lucky thing for us, because that was, of course, the year that broke the curse. When "Tessie" stopped being sung in 1918, that was the last year that the Sox had won the World Series, and it came back in 2004. . . . And wow, we were somehow involved. Responsible? No. But involved? Yes.[36]

The Dropkick Murphys were not alone in considering the new "Tessie" to be an important part of Boston's success: since its debut, the song, along with Three Dog Night's "Joy to the World" and the Standells's "Dirty Water," is played after every home victory. One of the critical aspects of what the song revived was the working-class ethos—or at least the perception of such—of Red Sox fans (and a particularly white ethnic immigrant ethos, at that) in the midst of the team's reinvention that began in 2002. John Henry was a lifelong baseball fan (he grew up watching the St. Louis Cardinals), a multimillionaire financier, and someone intent on breaking the Curse. He wanted to change what it looked and felt like to be a Red Sox fan, confronting, according to Lucchino, the team's "undeniable legacy of racial intolerance."[37] For Howard Bryant, Henry and Lucchino's efforts seemed to be genuine: "This ownership group is the first in Red Sox history that has pledged to take this problem on head-on because they realize it's not only race, it's economics."[38]

Few people besides Bryant have directly connected the team's racist history—it was the last major league franchise to integrate—to its largely Irish, working-class fan base, but the new management recognized the need to integrate these new beginnings with the team's older (and less offensive) traditions, playing upon the modern fan's imagined identity of being part of a white ethnic immigrant history. Though the Red Sox were a high-profile team long before the likes of Ben Affleck and company made their loyalties known, the club did not have the glamour of, say, the Los Angeles Lakers. The trick was to bring the good parts of the old into the fold with the new. The Dropkick Murphy's ensured a benign way to maintain the team's white ethnic roots via the history of the Rooters, offering a new—profitable—angle, nationhood, alongside an unfamiliar label: champions.

The 2004 season, whether reaping the whirlwind of "Cowboy Up" or under the ghostly influence of McGreevy, did more than produce the team's first World Series championship in eighty-six years: it ended the Curse of the Bambino. After going down three games to none in the ALCS against the Yankees, the Red Sox launched arguably the greatest comeback in sports history, with game six proving to be the most dramatic as pitcher Curt Schilling, coming off ankle surgery, threw seven innings in an increasingly bloodied sock. No team had ever recovered from such a deficit in the postseason, and the Red Sox went on to beat St. Louis in four straight for the title. "Swing and a ground ball, stabbed by [pitcher Keith] Foulke," radio announcer Joe Castiglione said. "He has it. He underhands to first. And the Boston Red Sox are the World Champions. For the first time in 86 years, the Red Sox have won baseball's world championship. Can you believe it?"[39]

Fans could, as belief was never a problem for members of the Red Sox Nation, marked by the signs of "WE BELIEVE" that they held, posted, and wore. Fans believed in the Curse. Fans believed in the Nation. And fans believed that the team would win. After Foulke tossed the ball to first baseman Doug Mientkiewicz, the fan base, as well as its sense of community, was no longer characterized by a history of anguish. But for Red Sox Nation, what replaced it? What is it composed of when it is no longer a community focused on overturning a "curse" that encompassed its history for almost a century?

From Cursed to First

For some, it meant closure. Stories in the days that followed the win included descriptions of people leaving copies of the *Boston Globe* declaring "YES!!!" on the front page and "FINALLY!" on the sports page on the graves of their parents and grandparents. For one blogger, it meant the end. On December 25, 2004, Edward Cossette—who once compared the impact of Buckner's bobble on New England to that of Pickett's Charge on the South—ended his online musings about his team, which he had started when he left Massachusetts for Virginia so that he could continue to ask people "How 'bout them Red Sox?" "This blog," he wrote, "is what gives me a feeling of connection to the other citizens of Red Sox Nation."[40] For *Boston Globe* sports columnist Bob Ryan, it was a moment when fans should not overthink the meaning of success:

> There were enough of you out there subscribing to the somewhat convoluted theory that the worst thing that could happen would be for the Red Sox to win the World Series, for that would shatter the woe-is-me mystique that has become so endemic to the experience of Red Sox fandom. By winning it all, the Red Sox would become just another team, not a romantically star-crossed aggregation. I always thought that was nonsense, an absurd reach on the part of pseudo-intellectuals who can spoil the fun with ludicrous over-analysis.[41]

Writer Scott Stossel, in response to Ryan, went so far as to ask what he knew to be a "heretical" question: "Wouldn't it have been better if the Red Sox had lost the World Series last year?" A long-time Boston fan, Stossel contended that fans "lost something" with the team's victory. Any team could win a World Series, he argued, including relative newcomers such as Arizona and Florida, teams with barely *any* history outside their championship seasons. To be a team that did not win, "and not just not winning, but flamboyantly, spectacularly, transcendently not winning," was, according to Stossel, a far more extraordinary feat. "Even the benighted Cubs," he wrote, "who have not won for longer than the Red Sox have not won, haven't not won with such dramatic flair as the Sox, who seemed to find ever-more outlandish ways to not win despite having victory in hand." This history of not winning was what made Boston fans special. "As masters of the perennial near-miss, members of Red Sox Nation may have been eternal losers—but in our predestination for failure, we had something special, a Calvinist sense that we were, in our humility and accursedness, somehow distinct from all those arrogant New Yorkers, or lazy Los Angelenos, or mild Minnesotans," Stossel wrote. "Now that we've won, we've taken a step toward becoming more like everyone else."[42]

Shaughnessy agreed, finding that after the World Series win, there was an immediate understanding that Red Sox Nation was no longer an organic entity. By the time the Red Sox captured another title, in 2007, the magic-markered "WE BELIEVE" signs had transformed into professional marketed paraphernalia, Web sites, and a "valuable membership program which offers various discounts, privileges and opportunities."[43]

The franchise was not alone in making nationhood more official. In 2008, Ken Casey of the Dropkick Murphys went in with Peter Nash, producer of a documentary about the Royal Rooters, to open a twenty-first-century version of the 3rd Base Saloon in Boston, which included a museum collection dedicated to Boston's baseball history.[44] NESN, which televises the team's games, decided to make sure that citizens were able to intermarry, creating the reality show *Sox Appeal*, which features a series of blind dates that take place at Fenway, with the suitor choosing his/her mate by the seventh-inning stretch.[45]

Yet the subculture of old-school fans found new ways to carve out identity and avoid being seen as a late-coming poseur, including a Facebook page for "People who were actually Red Sox Fans before 2004." Others eschewed any belief in the Curse, including Mike Vaccaro, author of *Emperors and Idiots: The Hundred-Year Rivalry between the Yankees and the Red Sox, from the Very Beginning to the End of the Curse* (2005): "You want to call it 'the curse of the Bambino,' the way so many poets, documentary producers, and radio call-in show hosts did? You are taking a simpleton's approach to what afflicted Boston's baseball fans for all those many years. And you risk really, *really* pissing off the ward heelers of Red Sox Nation."[46]

Home Away From Home

Attending games became one way "authentic" fans defined themselves. As the team's popularity grew, so did the franchise's success, on and off the field. Until the Impossible Dream season, Fenway had drawn fewer than a million people annually. But with the increased on-field success of the twenty-first century, alongside Henry's careful management and community efforts, Fenway has boasted of a sold-out streak since May 15, 2003.[47] Many attribute the streak to the increase of postvictory "bandwagon fans" (although it began early in the "Cowboy Up" era). But the scarcity of tickets has created an avenue for diehards to express devotion in a similar fashion as the traveling Royal Rooters had almost a century before: the road.

In 2007, the Red Sox surpassed the Yankees as the largest road draw in the major leagues, averaging 39,136 fans per stop. According to *USA Today,* "the fan base known as Red Sox Nation has grown into its name."[48] Boston management insisted this growth was organic. "The rise of Red Sox Nation has little to do with a marketing strategy," said Sam Kennedy, the team's vice president of sales and marketing, of Boston's road attendance. "We'd be foolish to say we had anything to do with Red Sox Nation."[49] Yet the franchise augmented the number of games fans saw on the road, something necessitated by the limited availability of Fenway tickets, with the creation of Red Sox Destinations, which organizes trips—all of which also sell out—to stadiums from Philadelphia to Toronto to Baltimore to Seattle.[50] Yet these trips, including those created by independent travel agencies, cannot account for the number of fans at away games. Many sportswriters marvel over how Red Sox fans often outnumber those cheering the home team. "Some fans are newcomers, having latched on to the team of the moment," writes Paul White in *USA Today.* "Others are die-hards who have found it easier to see their beloved Sox away from Boston because it's often difficult and expensive to get tickets to games in Boston's tiny Fenway Park . . . [but] wherever the Sox play, their fans arrive by plane, bus and car."[51]

The *Boston Globe* explains that "Boston fans are packing distant stadiums so often and in such numbers that they've turned the Red Sox into the de facto home team in [some] places."[52] Baltimore, although farther from Boston than New York, is a popular destination, as it is easier to get a ticket and is reachable by car or train. Interleague play has made the Washington Nationals another Red Sox fan destination. When Boston played in Nationals Park in 2009, a *Washington Post* blogger seemed stunned by the "Red Sox Invasion," guessing that visitors comprised 65 to 80 percent of those attending and that "there were sections where it was awful hard to find Nats gear."[53]

Red Sox fans are not shy about boarding an airplane, either, regularly filling seats in Seattle, San Diego, and Tampa. "I remember the first time [the Red Sox] came to San Diego for interleague games," says Kennedy. "I'm not exaggerating when I say the stadium was half Red Sox fans."[54] In Florida, Tampa Bay fans are often "outnumbered and outshouted" by Boston fans, according to the *Globe,* with the ranks including road trippers and "expatriate New Englanders."[55] From 2004 to the middle of the 2007 season, Tampa Bay saw its attendance go from 16,300 for an average home game to 25,700 when Boston was in town. One fan, Mike Walsh, who works as a food vendor at Fenway, flew to Florida to attend all three games of the regular season series. "Tickets are so cheap here," he said. "If you can find people to stay with, you can turn it into a family vacation."[56]

The travel industry paid attention to fans like Walsh. Southwest Airlines announced in February 2009 that it would initiate service from Logan International Airport so that fans would no longer have to travel to Rhode Island or Hartford to catch a cheap flight to a game.[57] The airline's announcement countered that of rival Jet Blue, the "Official Airline of the Boston Red Sox," which launched its relationship with the team earlier that year by hawking a nine-hour sale that started at 9 o'clock in the morning with one-way fares for nine dollars to other American League cities in honor of Ted Williams, who wore the number nine.[58]

Not everyone needs to hop a plane when duty calls. In Santa Monica, fans head to Sonny McLean's Irish Pub, "your Boston sports headquarters!"[59] Denver lays claim to no less than four Red Sox bars.[60] For Denver attorney Chris Yvars, who grew up in Massachusetts and graduated Boston College, the Pour House is his choice to "go drink a bunch of pitchers, and yell along with a lot of other Sox fans, and stomp around to 'Tessie.'"[61] During the 2007 World Series, the bar had no qualms about continuing to offer a free shot of whiskey for each Boston home run, even if it meant sealing the fate of the hometown Rockies.[62]

For the Red Sox faithful, the notion of "home" is interpreted in many ways, whether by those who travel with the team or by those who create makeshift homes in bars and restaurants committed to making the team accessible. Red Sox Nation exists wherever the team takes up space. It is an identity that speaks to the fan base that supports it and the communities in which it resides. The Red Sox fan wears the hat not merely to signify that he or she watches the game but to showcase where he or she is from, and what that might mean, especially as the historic 2004 season recedes into the past. "New Englanders still love the Red Sox but will never think of them in quite the same way," argues Shaughnessy. "The 'unique sense of community and passion' is inalterably changed."[63] Über-fan Steve Silva of BostonDirtDogs.com colorfully agrees: "You have these assholes who are walking around and e-mailing me with this FROM CURSED TO FIRST crap shirts, and a Web site. Give me an effin' *break!*"[64]

While Boston's 2010 season, marked by a disabled list that likely could have won the World Series, and falling television ratings, might have dampened the spirits of Fenway, the winter acquisitions, in which the team spent somewhere around $300 million in less than forty-eight hours to acquire first baseman Adrian Gonzalez and outfielder Carl Crawford, indicate that Red Sox Nation has little worry about its future as a championship team.

Far from Fenway, The Pour House Pub is one of several Red Sox bars in Denver, Colorado. Pictured are Pour House proprietors Storm and Jeff Ireland, with a homemade cutout of Jonathan Papelbon, celebrating the Red Sox's 2007 World Series victory against the Colorado Rockies. Courtesy of Shelly Waters.

But it might need to fear that it has transformed into an empire, abandoning the practices that brought it success—and devotion—to and from its citizenry.

Postscript: November 30, 2011

The Red Sox officially announced the hiring of Bobby Valentine today, and it appears that he will not manage a Red Sox empire, as I somewhat foolishly predicted last May when I put this piece (or so I thought) to bed. How could I have been so confident? Do I practice the historical amnesia I preach against? (And did they really just hire Valentine?) To say that the Red Sox experienced a catastrophic collapse—losing twenty of twenty-seven games in September and a nine-game lead over Tampa Bay for the Wild Card—is to ignore everything else about them. Walter Benjamin's caution that "the 'state of emergency' in which we live is not the exception but the rule" serves us well, because what happened on the last day of the 2011 regular season was—for so many—all too familiar.[65] Fans witnessed a historic night in baseball, to be sure, as the nation and the Nation watched two games, one in Florida and one in Baltimore, to determine who—Tampa or Boston—would make the postseason. Come midnight, it was Crawford's former team, the Rays, who were the chosen ones, despite the fact that the Red Sox had a one-run lead over the Orioles going into the ninth, and were one out away when "sure thing" reliever Jonathan Papelbon surrendered three straight hits and Crawford could not get under Robert Andino's line drive, and despite the fact that Tampa, down by seven runs, needed twelve innings to put away—wait for it—the Yankees.

Did I mention the one-hour, twenty-six-minute rain delay in Baltimore during the seventh inning, which allowed Boston to actually watch from the dugout the Rays rally?

Boston's decline in September was unfathomable only to those who had forgotten. And the aftermath was bloody: manager Terry Francona and general manager Theo Epstein—who had led the team and its fans to the light in 2004 and 2007—were fired amid rumors of beer and fried chicken in the clubhouse, Francona's marital problems, and one unfounded claim that the beloved manager had a pain-killer addiction. Had the Curse never gone away or had it come back? Was it the Yankees again or the Yankees still?

Perhaps for Red Sox Nation, it doesn't matter, because it is, as Benjamin warns, just a new version of an old normal. And with it, perhaps, comes the return of that sense of community that some had feared was gone with the championship seasons of the twenty-first century.

Do we still believe?

Notes

1. Mel Allen, "Looking Back, Looking Ahead," *Yankee*, September/October, 2010, 12.

2. "Nation Building: Red Sox Are MLB's Top Road Attraction," *Sports Business Daily*, August 23, 2007.

3. Jacobson uses "ideological geographies" to describe connections that immigrants maintain to their homeland. Matthew Frye Jacobson, *Special Sorrows: The Diasporic Imagination of Irish, Polish, and Jewish Immigrants in the United States* (Cambridge, Mass.: Harvard University Press, 1995), 2.

4. Dan Shaughnessy, *At Fenway: Dispatches from Red Sox Nation* (New York: Crown Publishers, 1996), 46.

5. See www.steelernation.com and www.cardsdiaspora.com.

6. See http://www.aisd.net/ahs/ and http://www.mojoland.net/.

7. Benedict Anderson, *Imagined Communities: Reflections on the Rise and Spread of Nationalism* (London: Verso, [1983] 2006), 6.

8. Ibid.

9. Jacobson, *Special Sorrows*, 7.

10. Dan Shaughnessy, *The Curse of the Bambino* (New York: Penguin Group, 1990), 16.

11. Michael T. Friedman and Michael L. Silk, "Expressing Fenway: managing and marketing heritage within the global sports marketplace," *International Journal of Sport Management and Marketing* 1, nos. 1/2 (2005): 38–39, 44.

12. Ibid., 46.

13. Ibid., 49.

14. Glenn Stout and Richard A. Johnson, *Red Sox Century: The Definitive History of Baseball's Most Storied Franchise* (New York: Houghton Mifflin, 2000), xvii.

15. Tony Zannotti quoted in Mike Vaccaro, *Emperors and Idiots: The Hundred-Year Rivalry between the Yankees and the Red Sox, from the Very Beginning to the End of the Curse* (New York: Doubleday, 2005), 26.

16. Quoted in Kathryn Shattuck, "Reality TV Melds Baseball And That Other Pastime," *New York Times,* July 31, 2007, E4.

17. Howard Bryant, *Shut Out: A Story of Race and Baseball in Boston* (Boston: Beacon Press, 2002), 25.

18. The string of events that put Buckner—who was dealing with knee problems and was usually replaced late in games by defense expert Dave Stapleton—in that position, alongside a horrific pitching performance by Calvin Schiraldi and a wild pitch by reliever Bob Stanley, make blaming Buckner simply ignorant.

19. Vescey quoted in Glenn Stout, "Nothing but the Truth: The Untold History of the 'Curse,'" *Elysian Fields Quarterly* 22, no. 4 (2004), accessed December 16, 2010, http://www.efqreview.com/NewFiles/v22n4/onhistoricalground.html.

20. George Vescey, "Babe Ruth Curse Strikes Again," *New York Times,* October 28, 1986, D33.

21. Quoted in Nigel Barber, "Is Sport a Religion?" *Psychology Today,* November 11, 2009, accessed December 16, 2010, http://www.psychologytoday.com/blog/the-human-beast/200911/is-sport-religion. Also see Daniel L. Wann, Merrill J. Melnick, Gordon W. Russell, and Dale G. Pease, *Sport Fans: The Psychology and Social Impact of Spectators* (New York: Routledge, 2001).

22. Rand Richards Cooper quoted in Scott Stossel, "The faithful," *Boston Globe,* August 22, 2004, F1.

23. Quoted in Barber, "Is Sport a Religion?"

24. Shaughnessy, *Reversing the Curse,* 8–9.

25. Étienne Balibar, "The Nation Form: History and Ideology," in *Race, Nation, Class: Ambiguous Identities,* ed. Étienne Balibar and Immanuel Wallerstein (London: Verso, 1988), 87.

26. Nathan Cobb, "Baseball Border War," *Boston Globe,* October 20, 1986, 8.

27. Cobb, "Sox fan's words led to the birth of a nation," *Boston Globe,* September 26, 2005, B7.

28. Vescey quoted in Stout, "Nothing but the Truth."

29. Gene Sunnen quoted in Ibid.

30. Ibid.

31. Ibid.

32. Shaughnessy, *Reversing the Curse*, 9.

33. Joseph P. Kahn, "Rallying cry spurs Sox to finish ride," *Boston Globe*, September 24, 2003, D1.

34. Quoted in Stephanie Vosk, "Another mystery of the Diamond, explained at last," *Boston Globe*, May 29, 2005, 1.

35. See http://www.dropkickmurphys.com/about.

36. Interview with Matt Kelly, July 8, 2010, accessed March 11, 2011, http://www .songfacts.com/blog/interviews/dropkick_murphys/.

37. Lucchino quoted in "The Boston Red Sox and Racism," National Public Radio, October 11, 2002, accessed December 16, 2010, http://www.npr.org/programs/ morning/features/2002/oct/redsox/.

38. Bryant quoted in "The Boston Red Sox and Racism."

39. See http://www.boston.com/sports/baseball/redsox/articles/2004/10/31/ commemorative/.

40. Edward Cossette, "Bambino's Curse," http://www.bambinoscurse.com/bio/.

41. Bob Ryan, "That nice taste in your mouth? It's gravy," *Boston Globe*, August 24, 2005.

42. Scott Stossel, "The tragedy of '04," *Boston Globe*, August 28, 2005, accessed December 16, 2010, http://www.boston.com/sports/baseball/redsox/articles/2005/08/28/ the_tragedy_of_04/.

43. "Red Sox Nation president and vice president announce five point plan," April 6, 2008, accessed March 11, 2011, http://boston.redsox.mlb.com/news/press_releases/ press_release.jsp?ymd=20080406&content_id=2497990&vkey=pr_bos&fext=.jsp&c _id=bos. In 2010, the packages of citizenship ranged in price from $140.00 to $250.00.

44. See http://www.mcgreevysboston.com/history.html.

45. Shattuck, "Reality TV Melds Baseball," E1.

46. Vaccaro, *Emperors and Idiots*, 131.

47. Lenny Megliola, "Red Sox sellout streak about Fenway Park, too," *Patriot Ledger*, July 20, 2010, accessed December 16, 2010, http://www.patriotledger.com/sports/pros/ x550418979/Red-Sox-sellout-streak-about-Fenway-Park-too.

48. Paul White, "Red Sox Nation new king of the road," *USA Today*, August 23, 2007.

49. Quoted in "Nation Building: Red Sox Are MLB's Top Road Attraction."

50. See http://mlb.mlb.com/bos/ticketing/destinations.jsp.

51. White, "Red Sox Nation new king of the road."

52. Bryan Marquard, "Faraway faithful," *Boston Globe*, August 23, 2007, accessed March 11, 2011, http://www.boston.com/sports/baseball/redsox/articles/2007/08/23/ faraway_faithful/.

53. Dan Steinberg "What the Red Sox Invasion Looked Like," *Washington Post*, June 24, 2009, accessed December 16, 2010, http://voices.washingtonpost.com/ dcsportsbog/2009/06/what_the_red_sox_invasion_look.html.

54. Quoted in White, "Red Sox Nation new king of the road."

55. Marquard, "Faraway faithful."

56. Quoted in ibid.

57. Dan Lamothe, "The Red Sox road show just got a whole lot bigger," February 18, 2009, accessed December 16, 2010, http://blog.masslive.com/redsoxmonster/2009/02/the_red_sox_road_show_just_got.html.

58. Nicole C. Wong, "JetBlue makes pitch to Sox fans," *Boston Globe*, December 19, 2008.

59. See http://www.sonnymcleans.com/.

60. Carol Beggy and Mark Shanahan, "Fans of Rockies Roll On," *Boston Globe*, October 29, 2007.

61. Interview with author, November 29, 2010.

62. Daniel Barbarisi, "Red Sox nation migrates west," *Providence Journal*, October 27, 2007, accessed December 16, 2010, http://www.projo.com/redsox/content/SOX_IN_DENVER_10-27-07_0V7LoK5_v15.3228d57.html.

63. Shaughnessy, *Reversing the Curse*, 238.

64. Quoted in Vaccaro, *Emperors and Idiots*, 132.

65. Walter Benjamin, "Theses on the Philosophy of History" in *Illuminations*, ed. Hannah Arendt (New York: Harcourt Brace Jovanovich, 1968), 257.

10. American Brigadoon

Joe Paterno's Happy Valley

DAVID W. ZANG

Never have I had a piece become outdated so quickly. Since news of Joe Paterno's firing on November 9, 2011, in the wake of the most horrific scandal in American sport history, the temptation has been to retouch this original version, completed in May 2011. I have resisted because it is more provocative and instructive to read sentences like: "Joe has done far more good for the game and for Penn State than he can possibly undo in his fading years." I was wrong about that and a few other things. It turns out the values associated with Penn State were just as unsustainable and illusory there as elsewhere. My apprehension about the statue being premature seems prescient, however, and the riots that took place after the coach's dismissal seem to confirm a great deal of what I wrote about defending our voluntary associations to the death rather than entertain the possibility that we've lived a foolish life (and I've been wondering these past few days whether my father would have been one of JoePa's supporters—I'd like to think not). It is easy to stick by my contention that Paterno's exit trumpets the end of Happy Valley as Brigadoon, and we all learned that losing his football lifeline indeed foretold the end of Joe Paterno's life.

D.Z., January 4, 2013

"Too many conflicting emotional interests are involved
for life ever to be wholly acceptable, and possibly it is the
work of the storyteller to rearrange things so that they
conform to this end. In any case, in talking about the
past, we lie with every breath we draw."
—William Maxwell, *So Long, See You Tomorrow* (1980)

"God has given you one face, and you make *yourself* another."
—Shakespeare, *Hamlet*

It's October, and as I've done on nearly every autumn Saturday for four
decades, I've settled in front of a television. As a panoramic shot captures
a gorgeous landscape of distant mountains and rolling foothills, ESPN's
announcers reveal that "we are live from Happy Valley." Scanning the more
than one hundred thousand spectators in Penn State's Beaver Stadium, a
camera comes to rest on a manic student who is gesticulating wildly, as
contemporary fans tend to do when they realize their three seconds of fame
have arrived. This one is wearing a full-headed rubber mask that caricatures
the bulbous nose and black pompadour of Penn State football coach Joe
Paterno, and I can think of only one thing—well, two, really: first, I want
one of those masks, and, second, if my father had lived to see it, he would
not only have owned one, he'd have actually worn it.

And who could blame him? My father didn't like himself all that much,
but he was happy around Penn State football, specifically Penn State football under Joe Paterno. Raised near the State College campus, my dad grew
up playing tackle football with his brothers in the shadows of the school's
sheep barns. My grandfather was an itinerant preacher, and his travels
took my dad in his teens to the suburbs of Philadelphia. He remained there
until the mid-1970s when, nearly fifty, he decided to chuck his pension
and twenty-seven years of seniority at a local chemical plant to return to
Happy Valley. He bought a rundown biker bar at the top of Mt. Nittany and
operated it as a restaurant for more than twenty years. (One night in the
1980s, Joe Pa stopped in for dinner. The staff did not think—bother—to
summon my father from his home fifty paces across the parking lot.) All
the while his love for the area expanded severalfold, revolving around and
boosted by Nittany Lion football.

Maybe I'm just guessing at some of this, but I think his passion for Penn
State—and that of many others—grew from an illusion that Happy Valley,
particularly and uniquely under Paterno, was as much a mindset as a place.
I know, I know, you could argue the same about any number of campus

locales, Tuscaloosa being just a mental way station for those in search of the lost, mythic South, for example. But even there, fans are acutely aware of being Alabamans (or, in other areas, substitute Nebraskans, Iowans, Ohioans, Kansans, and on and on) in a way that Penn State fans are not connected, for the most part, to a sense of being Pennsylvanians. Indeed, many natives hate Penn State; Philadelphians and Pittsburghers, in particular, are anchored to different realities and identities. That's not to say that there aren't shiploads of alums and fans in those metropolitan areas, but when I envision the prototypical Penn State fan, he is from a geographical band that begins around Johnstown, runs northeast through Scranton, and stops in Allentown near the Jersey line. Life in those areas, though transforming from the days when they supported coal and steel industries, is still decidedly slower and more loyal to the state's blue-collar ethos.

Deeply invested in tradition, these Penn State fans draw their sense of community from the shared belief that Happy Valley is not only a mythic place but a singularly righteous one as well. Further, they are adamant that the righteousness is deserved, springing as it did from the success that Paterno seemed to fashion from values outdated and unsustainable elsewhere. In short, many, myself included, see Happy Valley as a fantastical American Brigadoon that will vanish forever when Paterno is gone. There. I've said it. Now stop rolling your eyes at the pompous academic and listen up.

The State College, Pennsylvania, area acquired the "Happy Valley" nickname because of its seeming immunity to the economic misery of the Great Depression. In the decades thereafter, most industry—other than Penn State—largely withered away. Still, because the university grew into a prominent research institution (on the back, some believe, of Paterno's football successes), many inhabitants are confident that the area remains recession-proof. Years ago *Psychology Today* declared it one of the least stressful places in America to live, and one publication or another in the decades since has trumpeted its livability. Penn State's enrollment has grown to nearly forty-five thousand and the campus, large enough that when I taught there in 1980 I had to jog briskly to get to classes on time, is truly monstrous. The town has spread a bit, but it still feels quaint, even charming by some measures. The Tavern (Paterno's favorite), the Corner Room Restaurant, and the Rathskeller have scarcely changed in more than sixty years, and there is nothing chichi about the businesses or the town's aspirations. Still, to travelers not in the mood for shopping for 150,000 different articles stamped with "Penn State" or its stylized mountain lion's head logo, and resistant to the nonstop efforts of travel agents to pump up the place, the area can seem a bit anachronistic—which is just how the mythmakers like it.

Paterno came to State College as an assistant coach in 1950. Four years later, *Brigadoon* debuted in American movie theaters. It was the tale of an enchanted village that appeared once every hundred years; by covenant, if anyone left, the village would disappear forever. Though set in Scotland, it served as a metaphor for threatened ways of life everywhere, one more twist on the notion of not being able to go home again. In short, Brigadoon was more about time than space; more precisely, it is about the inextricable linkage of the two. Lose contact with one or the other and you risk losing both. Passing years or abandoned spaces lead to irretrievable loss, a surety underscored in Brigadoon when one of the show's leads asks: "Why do people have to lose things to find out what they really mean?" Paterno's wife Sue alluded to the same sense of paradise lost while addressing a Homecoming crowd a few years back: "Welcome back to the home where your heart was," she told alums, "and always will be."[1]

Like Brigadoon, the lore of State College began with physical inaccessibility. The town is isolated in the center of the state, so for the better part of the twentieth century visiting teams had to make their way first to Harrisburg, from which point, according to a New York sportswriter, "you swung the final ninety miles through the trees."[2] Paterno's legendary first assessment: "it was a cemetery."[3] It was a perfect place, in another words, for Paterno to conduct, shortly after becoming head coach in 1966, what he called the "Grand Experiment," a slippery concept alluding to the possibility that Penn State could become virtually the first football program in American history to reconcile the gap that existed between intercollegiate ideals and the reality of how college sport was conducted. It meant that he would—in the face of ramped-up expectations, new money from television, ascending influence from wire service polls, and a generation of students poised to blot out the traditions and values of all preceding generations—hold Penn State to a character-based standard. It was a giant gamble, because the standard he had in mind was pretty much passé by the mid-50s and had never gained a foothold in the actual behavior of college football players.

Identified pejoratively by young athletes today as "old-school," Paterno's experiment was to fulfill the tenets of sport's character-building ideology, or as *Philadelphia Inquirer* sportswriter and astute Paterno chronicler Frank Fitzpatrick wrote: "He seemed single-handedly to be defending loyalty, simplicity, and virtue against the disturbing forces that were just beginning to shake sports and the wider world."[4] And it worked, owing to two time-honored truisms: "location, location, location" and "timing is everything."

Paterno had the privacy (which many claim grew into unseemly secrecy across the years) and the timely blossoming of his team's on-field success to make the experiment look like reality. So assured did the program and its backers become over the next two decades that Paterno was able to define his standards in language that seemed to belittle every win-at-all-costs coach (basically nearly everyone else): "What really matters is reaching a level of internal excellence. It does not matter whether one is thought of as being successful, that is, a winner. It does not matter, simply because too often we make the serious mistake of equating excellence with success, and they are not the same thing."[5] Try taking that and a 1–9 record to your athletic director and see what it gets you.

Penn State had frightening success. Within two years of his hiring, Paterno posted back-to-back perfect seasons. He rolled into the early '90s with so much weight and public confidence behind him that people began to think that he was, as his actions hinted, really more than a winning football coach. In the shadows of the ever-expanding battleship of a stadium (original capacity: 46,284; now: 107,282), Paterno gave generously: millions to endow faculty positions, to the Mt. Nittany Medical Center, and to the main campus library that now bears his name.[6] Bill Lyons of the *Philadelphia Inquirer* wrote: "Even though he is enormously successful at it, from the perspective of meaningful contributions to society, the least important thing Joe Paterno does is coach football."[7] The clincher, according to Fitzpatrick, had come in 1972 when Paterno's rejection of the New England Patriots' lucrative overtures lent him unquestionable moral authority. All well and good, and nary a cynic ever suggested that the coach's generosity was not both valuable and sincere. But what did all this goodness add up to in terms of community?

This is the point where I hoped to have a few words from Paterno himself. I sent him correspondence requesting a brief meeting, but I guess, as John Updike observed, the gods really don't answer letters. Just as well. It would have been unfair to ask Joe what I was going to ask him. I wanted to ask him how he managed to create something beyond Bear Bryant's Alabama or Woody Hayes's Ohio State, but more than that, I wanted to find out how much of it he thought was real and how much was public relations hocus pocus. Anyway, there is no way he could have answered honestly and maintained any sense of humility and, who knows, maybe he's never really thought about any of this stuff anyway. Lord knows, there is already enough horrific academic theory and jargon floating around to turn any normal person off, much less a busy emperor. One professor, for example, has posited that Joe's white shirt and dark tie suggest status and power and that the plain Penn State uniforms symbolize values like hard work and teamwork.[8] Well, when Joe wakes up on game day how many choices of clothes do you really think he has? Do you think he asks his wife, "Now where did I put that outfit that summons perceptions of low self-esteem and social timidity?"

If clothing and apparent symbols like a mascot in a "fuzzy costume" that "suggests the fun and lightheartedness associated with the collegiate ideal" are too facile—if not nonsensical—as contributions to Penn State's exceptionalism, they have nonetheless become part of the accepted landscape surrounding the school's sports.[9] Let me try something every bit as ordinary, but, I think, less nonsensical and more persuasive: there are two keys to our membership in voluntary associations (and, if you ask me, to all human behavior). The first is that we all need to spend some time being someone other than who we are (or think we are); and second, nobody wants to think they've lived a foolish life.[10] The first creates a grounding for the communities we choose to belong to; the second compels us to defend those communities to the death.

The post–World War II proliferation of self-help books urging us to find ourselves and then be true to what we find is powerful testament to the fact that we are more than a tad afraid of what we think is there. Every time I hear former defensive end Michael Strahan say, "I love me some me," I think, "probably not so much." If self-esteem were as attainable as pop culture hints, self-help gurus wouldn't have to keep clubbing us over the head with the claim that it was within our reach.

Like religion, community is the hope that something bigger than us can save us from ourselves. To indulge in community is to refute isolation. Being alone can be a fearful condition because most of us are not comfortable with ourselves. A writer whose name eludes me ventured (I'm paraphrasing) that the worst place to be is alone with yourself driving on a rainy night, because, with nothing for company but the slapping of windshield wipers, that is when you are most inescapably who you are. Philosophers, of course, have always known this (except for the windshield wiper part), and in the once-upon-a-time of the Middle Ages, all segments of society knew it. The festivals in which "the world turned upside down" allowed peasants and rich lords alike to don masks and invert the social order for a day here and there.

Two aspects of modern life still offer vestiges of this possibility. There are the several secular celebrations like Halloween and Mardi Gras in which we indulge in the fantasy of becoming something other than what we are, and there are sports. Sports lend themselves readily to the medieval conceit; in fact, contests that allowed the common class to publicly exhibit the veiled threat of their physical prowess were often part of the festival celebrations.

In sport, the power of the crowd creates both the possibilities for doing the right thing and for the less-noble results of a mob mentality. The character-building ideology sides with the first, holding that we are something different—better—when connected to uniforms. We subsume ourselves in team, work hard when we don't have to, and make believe that the lowest of us can, on any given day, rise to the top of the heap. The uniforms themselves make for fine masks; Michael Vick, dogslayer, for instance, costumed in pads and helmet masquerades as a role model and leader. My father had a fondness for costumes and public occasions when he could holler out loud without penalty. Feeling always outstripped by his brothers, my father desperately sought the esteem bestowed by an official association with sports. In a photograph of his second grade class, he is the one wearing a full baseball uniform.

In our time, even the facsimile of a uniform can be enough to claim membership in a community. I was at an outlet mall recently and saw a twenty-something wearing a T-shirt emblazoned "Abercrombie Track." Because I know that the trendy clothier has lots of money invested in ad campaigns featuring nearly nude models, but none in athletics per se, this at first struck me as odd and more than a bit off-putting. On second thought, however, I realized that Abercrombie & Fitch has as much right as any other commercial entity, including, oh, say, a university, to tap into our need for artificial, virtual, and even nonexistent communities.

Though I'm guessing that strangers in Abercrombie Track shirts do not seek out one another, belonging to Abercrombie Nation is as telling as membership in Red Sox Nation. Both signal the post–World War II rise of atomism that has meant the loss of American communities—including civic clubs, bowling leagues, and faculty dining rooms, as detailed in Robert Putnam's *Bowling Alone* (2000)—that were once rooted in interwoven vectors of time and space.

In choosing our voluntary associations with one community and not another, we have been freed from the requirements of proximity. Once, we identified with whatever was at hand—if you got stuck with Al Davis, the Phillies, or Rice University, so be it. When those things were in opposition to what we thought ourselves to be, whether elitist, thuggish, or undeserving, we wore the mask anyway. In other words, we didn't so much turn the world upside down as have it flipped over on us. But now, bound as we are only by the axiom that no one wants to think they've lived a foolish life, victory has surpassed geography in claiming our allegiances. Little else explains the recent unattractive explosion of Red Sox Nation than the increasingly status-hungry need to be a winner. Has anyone heard from Pirate Nation?

While technology has made it easy to jump onto any bandwagon that rolls down the information highway, and while I would never claim that Penn State football could have grown in the absence of great win-loss success, for many the program's real appeal is that it combined the best of all worlds, that is, it won "the right way," an idea last articulated for public consideration in the dying days of Paterno's old stomping grounds, the Ivy League of the late 1940s and early '50s. There, it was claimed by its athletic directors, they could "hate enough to beat each other, but trust enough to schedule each other."[11] A Web site has adopted this same exclusive attitude as its banner: "We are not normal. We are legends. We are Penn State."[12]

Nearly alone in the world of big-time college football, Paterno's Penn State was an independent until the early 1990s, freed from conference dictates and so free to construct its own identity. With a schedule that critics derided for decades as too soft, Paterno was able to be selective in recruiting athletes that furthered his declarations about the possibility of truly joining the dichotomous aspects of sport and the academy, blending them together to make the term scholar-athlete something other than oxymoronic. When Heisman winner John Cappelletti's heroic support of his dying brother became the subject of a primetime television special in 1977, the nation began to think that maybe the air around central Pennsylvania was indeed rarified.

More remarkable, perhaps, than the insistence on principles out of step with the Woodstock generation—the same insistence that would drive a number of head coaches to the unemployment lines—was Penn State's ability to win big while quietly integrating a handful of black athletes. Elsewhere, coaches were heavily recruiting blacks, and, though they struggled to reconcile the differing sensibilities that mixed teams invited, there was tacit agreement, even in the Ivy League, that teams without African Americans would be settling at the bottom of conference standings.

Penn State, in no small part because of its geographic and cultural distance from black communities, was and remains a difficult sell to black recruits. The State College area, even in the twenty-first century, is 85 percent white and 3.7 percent black.[13] But Paterno has been able to continue a tradition begun with standout running back Lenny Moore and defensive lineman Roosevelt Grier in the 1950s, convincing a few quality black players to come to his Brigadoon and stay. In the '70s and '80s my father was nearly

Joe Paterno, in 1998, after winning his three hundredth career game,
was lionized by Penn State fans. Courtesy of Penn State University Archives,
The Pennsylvania State University Libraries.

as proud of this—noticeable in the cases, for example, of Lydell Mitchell,
Franco Harris, and Curt Warner—as he was about any other facet of the
program. Part of the nostalgia for Main Street America, particularly during
the Vietnam era, was that there once had been a time when blacks were
able to adapt to their second-class status and live happily in mainstream
white America.

Some might say that this is all fine when you talk about Penn State
in the '60s, '70s, and even the '80s, but the notion that Paterno and the
values of a pre-1960s America are still a part of Penn State is laughable in
2010. Some will say that this essay comes at least ten years too late, that
the throwback luster Penn State once had was wiped out when the new
millennium delivered a series of public arrests of football players involved
in campus altercations, embarrassing Big Ten losses by the truckload, and
a team that struggled to beat even the nonconference foes once brought
to Beaver Stadium for early season sacrifice to the Lions.

There is no doubt that losing seasons in 2000, 2001, 2003, and 2004
disenchanted older fans and positively alienated the younger generation,

which increasingly sees athletes as commodities (witness the rise of fantasy sport leagues), teams as entertainment troupes, and rules as impediments to become overcome in the name of victory. The crowd in Beaver Stadium has turned more demanding, and, at times, ugly. Paterno has drawn some boos, and in one of those losing seasons, I watched a young, untested quarterback leave the field at halftime to a scathing and obscene stream of vitriol from an entire section of fans seated near the players' tunnel to the locker room.

The spate of JoePa masks that flood Happy Valley in the fall became as much mockery as tribute. When Paterno righted the ship, however, in the last few years, the fan base reached renewed consensus that things were both okay and still distinctly unique in Happy Valley (because, remember, no one wants to believe they've lived a foolish life). In 2005, *Sports Illustrated* stamped its approval, calling game day in Happy Valley "the greatest show in college sports."[14] And when Paterno told the *Philadelphia Inquirer* on the cusp of a new season, "right now I have no plans whatsoever as far as whether I'm going to go another year, two years, five years, or what have you," the loyal agreed that he has earned the right to go at a time of his choosing.[15]

Still, it's impossible to argue that things are as they were before. If Brigadoon did not disappear, it certainly began a slow fade. Little by little, whenever Paterno and Penn State fall short, the community will be changed, settling for less of the old as they cede to the standards of the new. For the older crowd, it will be as if the Amish decided that the new way to get around would be on Harley Davidsons.

To a dwindling number, including me, the losses will be minor compared with the glimpses we've had of JoePa when he has let the mask slip. The unpleasant sight puts me much more in mind of *The Wizard of Oz* (1939) than *Brigadoon*. First, there was his nomination of George H. W. Bush at the 1988 Republican National Convention.[16] Though Paterno's politics are still tough to pin down, his journey from Sports World to the Real World betrayed the apolitical nature of all American dreamscapes, Brigadoon included. On a college campus, even tweed-and-pipe profs can nurture a secret love of football so long as the reactionary forces running it don't make an issue of politics.

More rankling still were the contradictions that Joe's behavior offered against his claims about internal excellence. In defeat, he often became whiny and petulant. In 2002, after a loss to the University of Iowa, Joe ran off the field in angry pursuit of a referee. The next day he failed to apologize, rationalizing that what we witnessed had been blown out of proportion by the press.[17] In an unsporting gesture to victory's importance, in 2004 Paterno repeatedly waved his arms on the sideline, exhorting the home crowd to make enough noise to drown out Purdue's ability to hear its own signals.[18]

Most disturbing of all, and in contrast to the lack of ego that Paterno often proclaims, was the 2006 placement outside Beaver Stadium of a seven-foot-tall bronze statue of the coach. To me, the statue smacks of the same lack of humility we see in Duke University's arrogantly named basketball floor, "Coach K Court." In both cases, the coach is the most powerful employee at the institution (and, at least in Paterno's instance, the highest paid). Would it be too much to ask them to simply say, "I'm flattered that you want to memorialize me. If you can't wait for me to die, could you at least hold off until I retire?"

Still, because I too don't wish to believe I've lived a foolish life, I've maintained my membership in the Penn State community, forgiving Paterno at every turn, choosing to remember his cheerful but innocuous greetings at 6:30 each morning, our paths momentarily crossing as I walked from the graduate building to Rec Hall. I forgive him, too, because focusing on his shortcomings is as much a collective failure as his—the willful ignoring of the care to be taken against idealizing any human being. In truth, Joe has done far more good for the game and for Penn State than he can possibly undo in his fading years. It is we, the media and fans, who created Happy Valley, and we who fear it to be a college version of Brigadoon. If Paterno or Penn State didn't take great pains to discourage our illusion, why would or should we expect them to? This coach is a man in search of victories, each one carrying him one more week, one more month, and one more season in a life of his own choosing and one that many of us envy. We should all be so lucky.

I forgive also because of a personal failing. To try to state outright my fondness for what Joe brought to my life would push me too close to a blubbery sentiment that would in turn expose me as being soft and vulnerable. In this, I am much like my father (at my sister's wedding, when my grandfather, the officiating preacher, asked who gives this girl's hand in marriage, my father intended to say, "Her mother and I do." What emerged instead was a great, ghastly sob that left most guests awkwardly stunned and myself thinking, "There but for the grace of God go I.")

What I most wanted to tell Coach Paterno if he'd granted me an interview, then, was how much he meant to my father's life. If he needed to wear a mask to do it, well, I would have needed one to address him on such intimate matters. It's what we all do now and then, isn't it?

When my father died in 1995 (in a hospital where a nurse inexplicably referred to him as "Mr. Zerbe" and just as inexplicably turned off the radio broadcast of a Penn State women's basketball playoff game, possibly the last sounds my father ever heard), the only item I wanted, other than family photos, was the Penn State jacket he wore to athletic events. With embroidered letters and logo it was—by necessity—slightly more tricked out than the famed plain jerseys. Some years later, having been unable to bring myself to wear it, I tossed it into a bag of clothing headed for the Salvation Army. I wish I had it back. Somewhere there is a man walking the streets of Baltimore wearing a piece of my life and one of the few tangible remembrances I had of my dad. He is also wearing a symbol of homage to an illusion extinct for sixty years outside Happy Valley.

Soon enough, all the tales will be nothing more than mythology. For Joe Paterno, Penn State football is not a passion; it is his life, and watch how quickly his physical presence follows when that lifeline slips out of his grasp. (Paterno has long believed this, and has commented before on Bear Bryant's passing just thirty-seven days after stepping down at Alabama. More than once, Paterno has said: "I don't want to die. Football keeps me alive.")[19] When time ignores his wishes, another piece of my father's world will be gone, and—just like the visitors to Brigadoon—I guess I'll have to begin to assess the meaning of that loss, though I think I already have a clue. When that part of my father is extinguished, it means that I'll be stripped of the grace of god and left with more of myself to search for and defend. Hand me the mask, please.

Notes

1. Quoted in Frank Fitzpatrick, *The Lion in Autumn: A Season With Joe Paterno and Penn State Football* (New York: Gotham Books, 2005), 207. A longtime *Philadelphia Inquirer* writer, Fitzpatrick is, in my opinion, the foremost authority on Paterno's personal and professional lives and their effect on Penn State football. Much of the background for this essay draws on his writings.

2. Quoted in Fitzpatrick, *The Lion in Autumn*, 33.

3. Frank Fitzpatrick, "State College Has Stepped Up Its Game," *Philadelphia Inquirer*, September 19, 2010, N1.

4. Fitzpatrick, *The Lion in Autumn*, 93.

5. This quote was attributed to Paterno on one of those fliers that circulates through athletic departments. I don't know, then, if he actually said it, but it sure sounded very close to similar preachings I've heard from him across the years.

6. Fitzpatrick, *The Lion in Autumn*, 29.

7. Quoted in the PDF at http://www.gopsusports.com/auto_pdf/p_hotos/s_chools/psu/sports/m-footbl/auto_pdf/head-coach-joepaterno#00, accessed October 4, 2010.

8. J. Douglas Toma, *Football U.: Spectator Sports in the Life of the American University* (Ann Arbor: University of Michigan Press, 2003), 52.

9. Toma, *Football U.,* 52.

10. For decades, I've believed this phrase was Tom Cottle's, from his wonderful book *Time's Children: Impressions of Youth* (1971). I combed every page of it, however, and was unable to come up with a citation. If it belongs to another author, I apologize for the misattribution.

11. Quoted in David W. Zang, *SportsWars: Athletes in the Age of Aquarius* (Fayetteville: University of Arkansas Press, 2000), 53.

12. See http://www.blackshoediaries.com/, accessed December 22, 2010.

13. See http://quickfacts.census.gov/qfd/states/42/4273808.html, accessed December 16, 2010.

14. See "Penn State football weekend tabbed 'Greatest Show in College Sports,'" http://live.psu.edu/story/14344, accessed December 22, 2010.

15. Quoted in Frank Fitzpatrick, "The Final Stand for Paterno?" *Philadelphia Inquirer,* September 3, 2010, A13.

16. Fitzpatrick, *The Lion in Autumn,* 199.

17. Joe Drape, "Penn State Does Little to Help Ailing Paterno," *New York Times,* September 29, 2002, I3; Fitzpatrick, *The Lion in Autumn,* 76.

18. Fitzpatrick, *The Lion in Autumn,* 180–81.

19. Quoted in Fitzpatrick, *The Lion in Autumn,* 276. Also see Kerry Eggers, "JoePa: Still doing it his way at Penn State," *Portland Tribune,* September 8, 2008.

11. Jayhawk Pride

MICHAEL EZRA

When the University of Kansas (KU) men's basketball team loses a game, it upsets me. I'm a big fan. It wasn't always this way, though. I used to loathe KU basketball. This is the story of someone whose personal evolution as an academic and human being was mirrored by his changing feelings toward his alma mater's most recognizable and cherished institution.

After living my first twenty-two years in New York, I matriculated to KU, which is located in Lawrence. I assumed that Kansas was a backwater unaccustomed to New Yorkers, and that its university would be the same. Wary, but also unprepared to do much besides attend graduate school, I knew I had little choice because KU was the only one that would have me. When I told people that I was going to get my Ph.D. in American studies at the University of Kansas, they usually laughed, sometimes made stupid *Wizard of Oz* references, and often gave me their unsolicited thoughts about what life there would be like, even though nobody I knew had ever been to Kansas or had any reliable perspective on living there. Many of their comments stoked my fears.

My misgivings vanished during a summertime visit to Lawrence, to be replaced by eight years of fondness for the place I proudly called home. I liked to show Lawrence off to out-of-town visitors, because I knew that they, too, would appreciate its charms. Lawrence had many cultural perks and it benefited from the good things a college town has to offer, like intellectual energy and school spirit. Victorian homes and tree-lined streets spun off from the university for miles in all directions, giving Lawrence a substantial area where you could feel the city's pulse. The pocket between KU and downtown, known as the student ghetto, was its nerve center. Packed with all kinds of characters, it was my favorite part of town.

What most New Yorkers failed to consider is that there are differences between Lawrence and the rest of the state. Kansans acknowledge these differences. Some say the state has two sections—the urban and suburban span radiating forty-five miles from Lawrence (which is located in the northeast) and the rural remainder of the state (known as "Western Kansas"). When it comes to cultural diversity, Lawrence is unique to the Sunflower State.

Despite its riches, Lawrence lacks scary volatility. Its Kansan characteristics—spaciousness, civility, friendliness, and affordability—check discontent. It's a cosmopolitan and easygoing place that provides residents from a broad range of income groups the opportunity to enjoy a low-pressure, interesting lifestyle. Lawrence is a nice place to walk and a stress-free place to drive. Things that are made into inconveniences in comparable locales are made simple in Lawrence. A parking ticket at an expired meter is a $3 fine. The town attaches envelopes to the citations and drop boxes to the meters, so you can just pay cash on the spot.

Some behavior that was normal in New York was problematic in Kansas, including Lawrence. One of the first days I was there, I was stopped behind two elderly folks at a traffic light that turned from red to green. I honked my horn because they didn't move. I passed them once we started driving, but ran into another red light after a half mile. When they pulled up in an adjacent lane, I waved and smiled. No hard feelings, right? They stared at me with rebuke. Their glare said it all: we don't honk the horn around here unless it's an emergency.

Despite the occasional cultural misstep, Lawrence was a place where things immediately fell into place for me. To my great financial advantage, the state and university granted me residency and in-state tuition, which they rarely did for students who hadn't lived there beforehand. I came to town knowing nobody, but within fifteen minutes of arriving found someone nice enough to help me move the bulkier contents of my U-Haul into a second-floor apartment. Getting my license at the DMV took about as much time as it does to eat at McDonald's. I found just about every consumer item I needed. I made good friends and had an active social life. I loved living there.

About thirty-five times a year, however, when KU men's basketball games were scheduled, I developed a temporary sense of displacement from Lawrence and its people. It troubled me that I found the whole KU basketball scene so annoying, and I never came up with reasonable justification for this attitude, but I really couldn't stand it. The problem was that no one else felt this way. Most people I associated with—at school, in town, at work—arranged their schedules around KU basketball games. KU men's basketball is Lawrence's and the university's lifeblood, fundamental to their character and identity. The KU Athletic Corporation is separately incorporated from the school, which retains oversight, so in effect the franchise belongs to both the city and the university. But if town-gown relations were ever to become strained, you could bet that both parties would still love the Jayhawks. It is the town's and the university's pride and joy, most successful venture, and most visible symbol.

It's hard to overstate KU basketball's significance to locals. Journalist David Halberstam writes, "Passion, bordering on madness, is very much encouraged" in Kansas and that "the passion and noise generated in Lawrence are without parallel, even in college basketball."[1] For outsiders, it can be difficult to grasp the relationship between the team and its fans. "If a guy grows up outside the Midwest," says current basketball coach Bill Self, "he doesn't truly understand the passion and mystique until he gets here as a student."[2] Even players from within the state don't always get it at first. Greg Dreiling, the Jayhawk center from Wichita, who later played in the NBA, admitted that before he got to KU he "didn't know who [KU coaching legend] Phog Allen was, to tell you the truth. But with [inventor of basketball James] Naismith bringing the game here and things like that, it gets into your subconscious. You feel like you've got the breeding or something."[3] Thomas Boswell of the *Washington Post* agrees: "To many who haven't lived near Kansas, it's hard to understand the depth of passion for KU basketball."[4]

Coaches understand that passion and its importance. In its long history the university has only employed eight head basketball coaches. Each has "developed an appreciation for the full history and tradition of basketball at the university," according to Roy Williams, who piloted the team between 1988 and 2003.[5] Bill Self adds, "One thing I have learned as a coach at the University of Kansas . . . is that Kansas basketball isn't a typical program. Instead it's a way of life."[6] Larry Brown, whose team won the 1988 NCAA national championship, comments: "When you're the coach at the University of Kansas, you realize who was there before you."[7] On game days, Williams would jog through the local cemetery where Allen and Naismith are buried and pat their tombstones for good luck.[8]

Coming to KU without understanding the school's basketball tradition is not a capital offense, but leaving KU without having come to appreciate the program's meaning is hard to explain and perhaps unforgivable. A player is unlikely to impact the program without buying into it, which is why KU coaches have players recite the university's beloved "Rock Chalk" chant before games. At KU, being coached doesn't just mean being taught

Kansas Jayhawk basketball fans in 2007 at Allen Fieldhouse.
Courtesy of *Lawrence Journal-World*.

basketball skills; it means being schooled about how to belong to a community. Writing about Rex Walters, who became a first-round NBA draft pick and a Division I coach, Williams claimed: "The simplest way to get me mad is with selfishness, lack of concentration, or lack of hustle. Rex showed up with all three. Rex may have been the only player I ever threw out of practice twice."[9] When Walters caught up with Williams years later, however, he told him, "Coach, I just want you to know that every success I've had is directly related to my time spent with you."[10] It wasn't that Walters needed to be shown how to become a basketball player; he needed to learn how to be mentored, and ultimately to mentor others, if he was to ever reach his potential as a human being. You could have said the same thing about me.

A successful Jayhawk should respect Kansas basketball's accomplishments, and he must also respect the mentoring tradition that is responsible for them. Though the basketball team's impact on the university and wider community is huge, it is not necessarily its overall won-loss record or many tournament victories or the number of NBA players it has produced that defines it. KU basketball does have a few peers. Through the end of the 2010–2011 college basketball season, there were three NCAA Division I programs that had reached the two thousand win plateau—the University of Kentucky (2,052–647), Kansas (2,038–799), and the University of North Carolina (2,033–729).[11] What stands out about KU basketball, though, is its hand in producing so many legendary coaches. KU is where a disproportionately influential number of the sport's all-time great mentors have been mentored.

The most-winning coaches in both Kentucky's and North Carolina's history—Adolph Rupp and Dean Smith—played at KU under the legendary Forrest "Phog" Allen, who Rupp said would "go down in history as the greatest basketball coach of all time."[12] Even Smith's father, who was a high school basketball coach, came to KU several times to learn at clinics conducted by Allen. Allen's Hall of Fame coaching protégés include Ralph Miller, Dutch Lonborg, and John Bunn. Allen also helped develop successful coaches like Dick Harp, Louis Menze, Ray Sermon, Andy McDonald, and Frosty Cox. In short, Phog Allen, it can be argued, had more impact on college basketball than anyone since, well, James Naismith.[13]

Naismith, of course, invented the game in 1891 at the YMCA Training School in Springfield, Massachusetts, and the Basketball Hall of Fame is named after him. He also made KU his home for more than forty years. Although Naismith takes a backseat to Allen in KU basketball lore, he greatly impacted the program's institutional culture. A decent, accomplished man, Naismith was never what one would call a basketball star. He wasn't a successful coach, didn't care about winning and losing, and only played the game twice. A critical eye, however, reveals the values he tried to imbue. For most of his life, Naismith refused to profit from the sport he invented and shared with the world; only in his later years did he receive some compensation for endorsing a model of basketball. His generous spirit, of putting the community before the individual, is fundamental to the mentoring tradition that guides the KU program. Naismith himself was a successful mentor. He was the one, for example, who influenced John McLendon, the Hall of Fame coach, who once said, "There's no question that my life would not have been anything near what it has become if I had not had Dr. Naismith as my adviser."[14]

Because I refused this tradition, I resented the ubiquity and unanimity of Jayhawk pride. I rooted against the team and hoped it would lose. When this happened and the fans became upset, it made me happy, even though almost everyone I cared about in Lawrence was a devoted follower. In 2000, Roy Williams was offered the chance to return to his home state to coach the University of North Carolina. Fans demanded to know what was happening, so Williams held a press conference that was important enough to be simulcast onto a JumboTron in front of sixteen thousand fans at KU's football stadium. I hoped Williams would leave because I wanted to enjoy the turmoil and heartbreak that would have come from his desertion. His opening statement, "I'm staying," and the joyous roar that ensued, made my heart sink. A few years later, Williams left KU to coach North Carolina. Fans were predictably enraged, but I had graduated by then and didn't much care.

I was never antisocial enough to vociferously reveal my feelings about KU basketball. Occasionally, when I was getting a haircut, I even pretended to care about the team's chances in whatever upcoming game the barber was chatting about. I'd rather have a good haircut and pretend I was a KU fan than make my feelings known and risk a bad one. But I couldn't go so far as to root for the team. A lot of people had a lot of good times during KU basketball games from 1994 to 2001, but I was not one of them.

I cannot explain my dislike for KU basketball as part of a larger problem I had with sports. I took an immediate rooting interest in the KU football team, especially its 1995 run that resulted in an end-of-the-year top-ten ranking. The area sports media was excellent; I listened to Sports Radio 810 WHB and read the *Kansas City Star*. While a KU student, I attended Kansas City Chiefs and Kansas City Royals games, World Wrestling Federation shows, professional boxing matches, and high school football games. I was in fantasy baseball, football, basketball, and hockey leagues. My Ph.D. dissertation was about Muhammad Ali. It would have made more sense for me to study KU basketball rather than try to ignore it.

I cannot explain my dislike for KU basketball as part of a larger problem I had with KU. Before nagging insecurities about my dissertation and the job market took center stage, the graduate school experience was pleasant enough. The campus was lovely and the university offered many opportunities. The classes were interesting. The university provided me a job at a fair wage and waived my tuition when I started teaching classes. KU did nothing to justify my bitterness toward its centerpiece.

I cannot explain my dislike for KU basketball as part of any larger malaise I was experiencing at the time. I had good friends at KU. I went to parties, restaurants, and movies. I exercised and played sports. I talked too loudly too often and had a bad temper, but I wasn't what you would refer to as disturbed, depressed, or an outcast. I fit the profile of someone who would love planning his social life around KU basketball games.

More subtle explanations don't hold water, either. KU basketball is a top-ranked program, but I don't gravitate toward the underdog. I want the New York Yankees to win as many World Series as they can. I have no tendency toward irrational sports-fan hatred, except for the Boston Red Sox. And I wasn't against the celebratory and anti-intellectual atmosphere that KU basketball games produced. I always treated Lawrence like a party town. For whatever reasons, though, I didn't enjoy the biggest party of all.

I've never figured out where my attitude toward KU basketball originated and what sustained it, although as I came to appreciate the significance of mentorship in my own life, my attitude toward the program softened and I became grateful for all its accomplishments.

* * *

I underrated KU as a place to go to school, just as I misjudged Lawrence as a place to live. I wanted to get a Ph.D. in American studies because I wanted to become a college professor. I was a student at KU between 1994 and 2001. I got a tenure-track job in 2003 and earned tenure in 2008. I look back with reverence at KU's Department of American Studies and its ability to prepare students like me to achieve their goals. Time lends perspective, so I have come to realize that the same things that are great about KU American studies are what people appreciate about KU basketball. During the 1990s the department was packed with bright, dedicated, and collegial faculty who gave students myriad opportunities to learn how to become scholars and teachers. That so many KU American studies alumni have found steady jobs in academia is testimony to their graduate school experiences.

In retrospect, it seems to me that the KU American Studies Department functioned like great teams do. The cooperation and complementary skills of the core faculty made the program into something more than the sum of its parts. They created a sense of community around teaching students, of preparing us for professional success. The program also attracted inter-disciplinary talent from around campus, which increased students' chances of finding mentors. I can name ten professors who helped me to become an academic. More so than anyone, though, Professor David Katzman con-tributed to my professional development and eventually to my appreciation of KU basketball.

I returned to Lawrence in 2010 to attend the retirement ceremony of my mentor and fellow New Yorker Katzman. During his speech, he shared with the audience a story he had told me when I first got to town sixteen years earlier. Shortly after he had arrived in Lawrence, a pipe in his house burst and his basement started filling with water. While his brother performed damage control, Katzman sped off to the nearest hardware store, sputter-ing as he crashed through the door: "A pipe ruptured . . . basement filling with water . . . need help now!" After a long pause, the storeowner asked,

"You're new to town, aren't you, have we ever met?" Only after making the proper introductions did Katzman get served. We don't honk the horn around here unless it's an emergency.

David reached out to me so many times while I was at KU that it was impossible to refuse his sage advice, like I did with so many others. When I would try to thank him for the things he did for me, he would usually just tell me to pass it on. My goal as a college professor is to repay that debt. Sean Malone, the most promising undergraduate I've had the privilege of working with, became a KU American studies graduate student in 2008.

When Sean was a senior, I had the chance to pass on to him something that David Katzman had given me. I came upon a summer fellowship opportunity in American history for undergraduates sponsored by the Gilder Lehrman Institute in New York City. I showed the announcement to Sean and he said he was interested. We sat down to work on his application. He wrote it and then I rewrote it, because sometimes a student just needs to see how it is done to learn how to do it. I know this from the time Katzman had told me about a NEH sport history seminar in Chicago, rewrote most of my application, and gave me the opportunity to enjoy the best summer of my life. In New York, Sean had a great time while getting one step closer to his professional goals. I could tell that Katzman was touched when I told him that story. With my academic spawn entering the program and my academic father leaving it, I remain a loyal fan of KU American studies and its tradition of mentorship.

*   *   *

On April 7, 2008, KU's men's basketball team rallied to win the NCAA tournament after being down by nine points with about two minutes remaining in the championship game. I watched the contest from my home in California and, to my surprise, got caught up in the euphoria of the comeback, rooting as hard as I ever have for the outcome of a sporting event. My joy lingered for weeks, stoked by dozens of communications with friends from my KU days.

I can't locate when my disposition toward KU basketball turned. The title game marked the moment these feelings became apparent, but I don't know exactly when the process began. In the years following my graduation, I maintained my disinterest in the team, although I noticed that when I saw a professional basketball game involving a KU alumnus, I would root for him. When I sat down to watch that title game, I didn't think I would care about the outcome. I watched the game out of a sense of obligation, but to what I didn't know.

That night, however, I realized that I had become a KU basketball fan. Once I left Lawrence, the whole I-don't-like-KU-basketball thing became irrelevant. Jayhawk fever doesn't matter outside Kansas, so there was no more reason to consider it. But that doesn't account for the principles that spurred my turnaround. A more complicated response rests with what happened after I graduated, particularly my becoming a professional academic, which put me in a position to understand the impact that the KU American Studies Department has had on my life. By the time of that championship game, I had completed two book manuscripts, chaired my department, taught ten different courses, and felt certain that I would receive tenure and be promoted. I developed not only as a scholar but as a teacher, colleague, and mentor, and I realized just how many times I invoked the lessons I had learned from my KU professors.

The joy I felt during the 2008 NCAA Finals can be attributed to the profound gratitude I have for KU American studies. Anyone planning to spend years of his/her life getting a Ph.D. in hopes of becoming tenured should know what a gamble the whole process is before he/she gets into it. The 2008 title game happened when, for the first time in years, I could see my future unfolding clearly, tenured and married. I've often made the mistake of pretending to go it alone in my life, but I knew by then that my well-being rested upon realizing my mentors' visions of community and teamwork and passing it on to others. Like at KU, I often fail to live up to its example, but watching KU's most famous team win the title seems an appropriate moment to mark my understanding of this principle.

I'm sure that David Katzman didn't mind when the University of Northern Iowa's upset of KU in the 2010 NCAA Tournament prevented his retirement proceedings from coinciding with March Madness. Katzman was one of the few people I was close with in Lawrence who was not a KU basketball fan. He would prefer that the team be called the Lawrence Jayhawks and that the KU Athletic Corporation pay its players. I think he sees the whole student-athlete narrative as hypocritical. During the 1983–1984 season, a failing grade in Katzman's U.S. history survey rendered KU point guard Cedric Hunter academically ineligible. A scandal ensued when Katzman blew the whistle by telling the local press that Larry Brown had lobbied him to change the grade. The incident was reported in *Sports Illustrated*, including Katzman's throwdown: "There are untenured faculty who might believe Larry Brown has the authority to influence them. He doesn't."[15] Katzman's family received threatening phone calls. Shots were fired at his home. We don't honk the horn around here unless it's an emergency.

Regardless, I was looking forward to a Jayhawk tournament run that would have resulted in its Sweet Sixteen game taking place the weekend I returned to Lawrence. It would have given me a second chance to enjoy KU basketball from the epicenter. KU basketball embodies to many people the spirit of community and teamwork that made KU American studies great. Rooting for it would have been an appropriate way to celebrate my mentor's career. Without Katzman's guidance, my evolution from graduate student to college professor would have been much more difficult. I trace my wanting to take part in KU basketball at this late date to my finally having the ability to give back to the profession what my mentors gave to me. One cannot truly embrace the spirit of community and teamwork unless one can contribute to them. Being a graduate student is about taking something away from the educational process. Being a professor is about putting something into the educational process. You take as a graduate student so you can give as a professor.

One way to understand KU's basketball scene and American Studies Department is as related phenomena influenced by shared values—community building, mentorship, reliance on teamwork, and the pursuit of excellence—that are reflections of Lawrence, Kansas. Lawrence reveres both intellectualism and athleticism. Ties to either generate cultural capital. Lawrence's free spirit comes from it being a safe but exciting place. Incivility is checked there because all kinds of people flourish. It's a place where community building, reliance on teamwork, and the pursuit of excellence bring positive results. Although what happened to Katzman when he failed Cedric Hunter proves that the spirit of these values can become perverted, in my estimation it was an exception to the rule. There is truly no need to honk the horn unless there is an emergency.

Like KU basketball, then, KU American studies was not just about teaching its disciples the skills necessary to go on to individual achievements, but more important, the ability to help others replicate those accomplishments. KU American studies was not just mentoring scholars; it mentored mentors. What is a college professor but a combination of scholar, teacher, and mentor? Successful graduate students, like successful basketball players, are the ones who are coachable. But you have to buy into the tradition for it to affect you.

My own case illustrates how sport, community, and identity can be interlinked. KU basketball is an inextricable part of life in Lawrence, drilled into the town's foundation. KU basketball symbolizes the values that gird the community and the institutions within it. To go against it without just cause is antisocial. It runs counter to the values of community building, teamwork, mentoring, and excellence. Thus for me, when I lived in Lawrence, it yielded misery. Booing KU basketball was akin to booing myself. Only when I was able to live up to those values as a college professor and family man could I understand and celebrate them. When I embrace KU basketball, I embrace the institutions that helped me get where I wanted to go and put me in a position to give to others what was so generously bestowed upon me as I desperately tried to scratch out a professional identity. I can best explain my unexpected about-face toward KU basketball as a result of what can happen when someone's past catches up to his present.

Sometimes we go wrong in life. We define success in unproductive ways and lose sight of how we got where we are. It took me a long time to realize that the revelry toward KU basketball was not about slam dunks, fast breaks, lopsided scores, and no-look passes. Although those things might be the most recognizable embodiments of the spirit that produced them, at their heart are values far more profound than what takes place on the court. Celebrations of KU basketball are celebrations of the very best things in life: serving others and making the world a better place. When students learn these ideas is the moment they start becoming their best selves. I feel fortunate that my KU American studies mentors convinced me to take this message to heart. "Rock Chalk, Jayhawk, KU."

Notes

1. David Halberstam, "The Passion, The Intensity, The History," in *Echoes of Kansas Basketball: The Greatest Stories Ever Told,* ed. Matt Fulks (Chicago: Triumph Books, 2006), 150.

2. Bill Self, foreword to Fulks, *Echoes of Kansas Basketball,* v.

3. Quoted in Malcolm Moran, "A Triumphant Heritage Rebounds with Jayhawks," in Fulks, *Echoes of Kansas Basketball,* 162.

4. Thomas Boswell, "Follow Your Heart—And History," in Fulks, *Echoes of Kansas Basketball,* 139.

5. Roy Williams, foreword to *James Naismith: The Man Who Invented Basketball,* by Rob Rains with Hellen Carpenter (Philadelphia: Temple University Press, 2009), vii.

6. Bill Self, foreword to *Game of My Life: Memorable Stories of Jayhawks Basketball,* by Steve Buckner (Champaign, Ill.: Sports Publishing, 2007), vii.

7. Jeff Bollig and Doug Vance, *What It Means to be a Jayhawk: Bill Self and Kansas's Greatest Jayhawks* (Chicago: Triumph Books, 2008), 182.

8. Roy Williams with Tim Crothers, *Hard Work: A Life On and Off the Court* (Chapel Hill, N.C.: Algonquin Books, 2009), 183.

9. Williams, *Hard Work,* 193.

10. Walters quoted in Williams, *Hard Work,* 251.

11. *NCAA Division I Men's Basketball Record Book,* 45, http://fs.ncaa.org/Docs/stats/m _basketball_RB/2011/D1.pdf., accessed November 29, 2011.

12. Adolph Rupp quoted in Blair Kerkhoff, *Phog Allen: The Father of Basketball Coaching* (Indianapolis: Masters Press, 1996), 204

13. Kerkhoff, *Phog Allen: The Father of Basketball Coaching,* 208.

14. McLendon quoted in Rains, *James Naismith,* 148.

15. Katzman quoted in Alexander Wolff, "Here Today, Here Tomorrow?" *Sports Illustrated,* February 13, 1984, 102.

12. Finding My Place

A Sports Odyssey

SUSAN CAHN

"Community, like the sacred, is an idea that becomes
reality because we believe in it, not vice versa."[1]
—Mary Catherine Bateson

When I was a young girl, I spent many hours by myself. At school I was socially adept enough to avoid complete outcast status—those unfortunates
we called "queers." A smart girl and good athlete, I managed to remain
interesting to the popular girls, but never became part of their cliques.
My tomboy persona simply didn't fit in with the girl culture at my school
and there were no alternative girl playmates in my neighborhood. In the
absence of friends, I experienced intense bouts of loneliness and sadness.
Yet even as my tomboyish love of sports contributed to my isolation, it
also helped solve it.

Sport provided me solace and joy—even a kind of magic, because I could
simultaneously be by myself and not alone. When I pitched tennis balls
against the front steps, imagining I was facing down major league batters,
I was both myself—the *me that felt most authentic*—and someone else, my
favorite baseball star in a fantasy of cheering teammates and fans. My
imaginary observers noticed what I wanted real people to see: my athleticism and competitive zeal, not my queer gender nonconformity. In this
mental gender geography, a girl like me could occupy space in professional
ballparks during a pre–Title IX era, the late 1960s and early 1970s, years
when it was taboo even to inquire about playing Little League.

But I was never fully alone; I played sports with the boys in my neighborhood. When I think of the relationship between community and sports,
this is what first comes to mind, although in retrospect my experience falls
short of most definitions of community. The boys I played with year after

year made up for the *absence* of the kind of idealized community promised by post–World War II suburban life and a Catholic parish near Chicago. I felt like I belonged to my family, but to no other entity. Our group—nine boys and me, spanning a six-year age range—played sports year-round on our front lawns and in back alleys. These boys were not my friends, but they were my playmates and, most important, they enabled my survival. We didn't talk gender; we talked sports. And I had talent, which upped my value. When playing, I wasn't a girl or a boy, just Sue the shortstop or half-back. But I also knew I wasn't truly one of the boys. During bad weather or long weekends, they played with toy soldiers or watched monster movies. None of this interested me, nor was I invited to participate in their male-bonding rituals.

Together, the physical space of one suburban block, tolerance bred by familiarity, and my supple imagination got me through elementary school and into high school, when my neighborhood crew scattered in different directions. I played three years of high school basketball but can't say that this provided me with a real community. By my early teens I had become too wary to take risks, too shy to explore social possibilities. I missed out on friendships because of my reluctance to become a multisport athlete and risk being known as a "girl jock," an epithet with lesbian overtones that may have hit too close to home. Not until college would I experience a genuine sense of community.

By 1976, much had changed. I had finished high school, met my first girlfriend, and headed west to California, where I announced to the world (but not my parents) that I too was "gay and proud." At the University of California, Santa Cruz, I became a women's studies major and joined the small Gay and Lesbian Student organization, pouring myself into the newly available world of feminist and lesbian studies. I finally met people like myself, or at least with similar interests, and began to make my first sustained friendships with women. Sports entered the picture haphazardly. I joined the school's basketball team, where the physical exertion, mental pleasure, and emotional release felt like coming home. But few teammates shared my lesbian or feminist identity.

My luck changed a year later when a friend steered me toward "a dyke softball team" in town. Anticipation mixed with apprehension, because I hadn't played softball in years. Moreover, I was about to enter the world of "town dykes" in a locale where the town/gown split often generated resentment. I showed up for practice and nervously introduced myself, then took my turn at batting and fielding drills. By the end of practice I realized that these "scary dykes" had welcomed me on their team. I was thrilled; for the first time ever I was going to play ball on a team with women, not boys, and lesbians no less. Before the season ended, I had found a community that became one of the mainstays of my existence in Santa Cruz and, some years later, in Minnesota where I attended graduate school.

This is the wonder of sports. I didn't set out to join a community but a team. Community grows from repetition, in this case practices, games, and postgame socializing at local bars over the course of a twelve-week season plus playoffs, tournament weekends, and travel time. Over the years I played on different teams with lesbian as well as straight and bi-sexual teammates. I now claimed the ball field, as well as the basketball court, as my own space. Importantly, this physical space was also a space to be physical. Here I was, doing things I did as a kid—running, batting, sliding, throwing, getting dirty—but with women. My physicality, whether athletic, sensual, or sexual, all figured into my lesbian identity. Having places to express my athleticism became important to my sense of living an integrated, full life. These locations also formed a social space in which women of all kinds gathered to play, some to compete seriously, others for a "girl's night out" with friends.

Because I'm certain that the majority of athletes on all the teams in all the leagues were heterosexual, how was this a lesbian community? Signifi-cantly, people did not refer to the sports scene as a "lesbian community" or any other kind of community. Rather we talked about teams, players, ball fields, and gyms. Ball fields and gyms were not places to meet lesbians ex-clusively, but they formed a place—physical, social, and mental—for queer women to find each other and become acquainted in a relatively safe space. Sports offered the chance to forge sustained relationships with athletes and fans, ranging from late-adolescence to middle age, over the course of, first, a season and then years. I met lesbians who in many ways resembled me. We liked sports, often shared a style of dress and self-presentation one might call "butchy," and frequently drove Toyotas (something I can't explain). Just as important, I met lesbians who *did not* resemble me. In college, the politically charged lesbian feminism I encountered created a community based on intense effort, constant self-reflection, and always a striving toward perfection. If that community was intensive, the sports community was extensive, with broad outlines and permeable boundar-ies. I met women of every age, class, and conceivable occupation: concrete layer, waitress, line worker at a microchip factory, electrician, computer programmer, and newly minted high school graduates, some of whom were going off to Ivy League colleges and others directly into the workforce.

Relationships rippled outward, as women who knew of jobs informed those who were looking. Others were encouraged to return to school or retrain for new work. Teammates became housemates, provided shelter to others during breakups, and offered (sometimes conflicting) advice. Eventually, one could gain access to most of what people found in other communities: drinking buddies, a used car for sale, a one-night stand or a long-term partner, illegal drugs, or a church to attend. The extensive nature of the community meant that it included not only friends and acquaintances but ex-friends and ex-girlfriends, because everyone remained in someone's network. Thus we knew people's feats and foibles on and off the field, as gossip spread through the social networks that form the finer filaments of community.

In *Finding the Movement: Sexuality, Contested Space, and Feminism* (2007), historian Anne Enke uses the word "movement" literally as well as figuratively, arguing that feminism grew out of movement into public spaces such as bookstores, ball fields, health clinics, coffee houses, and bars. She finds that the freedom and confidence gained by athletic movement and skill emboldened women already allied with feminist politics, *and* it spread feminist ideas to women athletes, many of them lesbians, who may not have embraced the women's movement initially but were enacting feminist principles through self-confident embodiment and sharing desirable skills.[2] In both California and Minnesota I experienced a sense of belonging among athletes who, through movement, formed a women's community that integrated my physical, personal, and political life.

Yet it is critical not to romanticize communities, whether tied to geographical locations or subjective identities. Gender studies scholar Miranda Joseph warns especially against the tendency to imagine community as a vestigial entity supplying caring, attentive relations that the harsh, impersonal culture of late-capitalism has eroded. Communities never stand outside the institutional hierarchies and pervasive inequalities of a surrounding society. Moreover, the sense of belonging derived from a community depends equally on creating boundaries of exclusion: the "them" that defines the "us."[3] In both queer and geographical communities, such boundaries are less often based on a physical line than on a symbolic one that demarcates community members from their requisite outsiders.

I learned this lesson the hard way upon moving to Buffalo, my current home. It was daunting to break into a lesbian community comprised primarily of Buffalo natives—seemingly lifelong friends who congregated only in bars or private homes. After some demoralizing years, I again found a pathway to lesbian community via sports, this time through an ongoing "women's" pickup game at a local community center. "Women" doubled as a term for people gendered female and code for lesbian; all were welcome. Anywhere from five to twenty players showed up on a given Saturday, ranging in skill from neophytes to former collegiate athletes. Alas, after seven years the group broke up when some players shifted to competitive league play and others moved away or withdrew. Because I had settled into a long-term relationship and established lasting friendships, the "break-up" did not leave me isolated. Yet I missed having a supportive place for sports that fulfilled my need for physicality and social connection.

And then, without looking for it, I found it in a completely new guise. My current weekly basketball game is not about seeking out others "like me." I found it when a work-friend invited me to join a small group who played Sundays on a driveway hoop. As our numbers grew we tried several locations until eventually ending up on Buffalo's east side at a community center known affectionately as "The Bob," short for The Bob Lanier Center; Lanier is a former NBA star from Buffalo. As soon as we moved to the Bob, the composition of our group changed from predominately white, middle-age men to a mixed group: white and black, men and women (two, my partner Tandy and me), and kids through retirees. Seeking only basketball, I stumbled into a new kind of rich, satisfying group experience. We do not have a common "identity"—racial, gender, professional, or political—nor do we share a culture that extends beyond the building. Rather, through "Basketball at the Bob," I have come to know and rely upon people whom I would probably not have met, beyond the briefest interaction, under any other circumstances.

This small community is, loosely speaking, geographically based in that it takes place in Buffalo and draws people from across the city. However, it's not representative of the "Buffalo community" because there is no such entity. Americans today rarely feel like they belong to something as amorphous as an entire city's "community." As historian Eric Avila explains, post–World War II "highway construction, urban renewal, and their cultural manifestations reversed the fundamentally *urban* process by which the city's classes and races came to 'know' each other by virtue of their mutual presence within public venues."[4] In addition, suburban expansion drained off much of the middle-class tax base that supported cities, assisted by real estate redlining, restrictive covenants, and blockbusting practices that cordoned off residential areas as "white" or "minority."[5] The decline of public transportation, in favor of solitary car travel, and the resegregation of leisure further reduced interaction among metropolitan residents. During and after the civil rights movement, urban recreation grew *increasingly* segregated as big amusement parks and swimming pools formed the site of bitter turf battles, leading to eventual closure or relocation.[6] As cities floundered, school systems suffered financially, encouraging people who could afford to do so to relocate to the suburbs for better-funded, less troubled schools. Once there, suburban residents are more likely to feel themselves to be "in community" and rally to protect "our children" and "our schools," usually from encroachment by poorer, urban students (evident in attempts to make countywide versus citywide school districts).[7]

Despite the legal prohibition of racial segregation, schools, neighborhoods, and recreational sites have become places where urbanites (or suburbanites) rarely encounter people of diverse backgrounds, cultures, and beliefs in a situation of relatively equal power (that is, not the janitor, boss, or bus aide). Sport is one activity where children, students, adult athletes, and fans might bridge racial and class divides, but even here, unequal funding and access create different ladders of opportunity. For example, suburban soccer or volleyball teams routinely beat urban ones because their school teams are better-funded and many kids also play in more competitive, expensive, elite youth leagues.

Buffalo is one of the poorest and most racially segregated cities in the nation. Its residents typically live in enclaves of people relatively similar to themselves, except for a few neighborhoods celebrated for their "diversity" (usually neighborhoods experiencing economic "transition" or immigrant relocation). Sports teams like the Buffalo Bills and the Sabers might momentarily draw people together, as cheers or groans simultaneously emanate from open windows across the city after a score or a loss. But these brief moments of shared sentiment do nothing to break down the powerful geographic and structural barriers that limit the possibilities for a truly diverse urban community with common interests, values, support systems, or even activities, especially considering that people typically watch or attend games with friends or family members, meeting other fans only briefly and casually.

What I enjoy about Basketball at the Bob is that it crosses most of the boundaries that living in Buffalo usually throws up to prevent relationships from forming beyond one's neighborhood or affinities of ethnicity, race, religion, politics, and sexuality. Though we do not refer to ourselves as a "community," the regular players confirm that the game is somehow special to them. For me, the diversity of players is significant, allowing me to interact on a regular and meaningful basis with people I would otherwise not get to know. I could categorize this difference as African American teenagers and young men as well as a range of white men not usually in my orbit—people I might meet in passing in stores or on the street, although even this rarely happens in Buffalo, where geography determines so much about where and how one lives. The enjoyment, however, derives precisely because it never feels like I'm interacting with a different urban "demographic." People have long ceased to represent a category and become simply, and marvelously, themselves.

Malik, who runs "The Bob," is a boxer who trains kids and young men for AAU boxing while assuming roles from janitor to event co-coordinator as he and his mother keep the community center alive. Carl is a thirty-one-year-old father, husband, full-time worker, and student who finished his bachelor's degree last year and is now in a masters of social work program, still working full time. Greg is a Gulf War veteran, works as a landscaper, and went to high school with Carl. Mike, David, and I are academics, joined by community college professor Don Lee, who teaches the building trades and turns construction work into community activism. Anthony, Cory, and Robert are brothers, avid ballplayers who attend three different high schools based on unique abilities. They brought Steph, a recent high school graduate who hopes to attend college soon. Tandy is a school administrator who, having never played sports growing up, is gaining athletic confidence as she learns the sport. Harry is a retired computer engineer who substitutes at Buffalo schools and also teaches tai chi. The list goes on, especially young men and kids as young as twelve who hear about the game through word of mouth. Adults pay five dollars, kids pay two.

What we share is not an identity or demographic trait but a set of values that makes this game the most friendly, humane "pickup" game I've ever found. Like any type of community linked to sport, it starts with a love of the game. We are adults and youth who not only love basketball but love *playing* it. We couldn't match up with the best pickup games in the city, yet we could hold our own with many of them. Still, we make room for different skill levels and physical needs. This is one of the ways we have built a certain culture, or ethos, that makes our game feel so worthwhile. For example, there is a "Don't hurt Tandy" rule, one that any newcomer learns by the second game. As a relative newcomer to sports, Tandy shies away from hard contact or rebounding in a crowd. So we try not to foul her, rifle hard passes her way, or expect that she put herself in harm's way for the good of the team. By contrast, I like contact, have the skills to compete, and don't mind taking a body hit. But acknowledging my lesser body mass and creaky aging joints, there is an unspoken rule against hard fouls that would end with a "take down." The same goes for the smaller kids and anyone over sixty.

Otherwise, gender-based differences are minimized. This means that the regulars quickly quash the kind of gender taunting I've encountered elsewhere. "Awww, you let a girl score on you?!"—loudly stated to shame my defender or goad him on to better performance. This ups the stakes, often causing my defender to play rougher or quit trying altogether so as not to lose face. I want my opponent to *lose* but not to lose face, his pride, or sense of manhood. The tone we set emphasizes we are all players, making gender relevant only when it comes to protecting vulnerable bodies.

Another aspect of our community ethos is the emotional balance that, as a group, we try to strike. People argue about fouls, calls, or the score; they complain about someone else's play; they might even get visibly and audibly angry: we are not exempt from the usual flare-ups and volubility of pick-up basketball. But we balance this with cheering for a good play, whether made by a teammate or an opponent. We laugh hard when a good fake or great move makes a defender look ridiculous, knowing it will be our turn sometime. Along with goodwill and humor, there is a surprising degree of politeness. One day when sitting out a game, twice I called "good shot" to a player I'd met only that Sunday, and both times he responded "thank you" as he sprinted downcourt on defense. On the other hand, if someone gets really angry and doesn't show his or her best self, this is acceptable, on one condition: an expectation that they get over it and return the next game or week in a friendly mood, absent grudges or paybacks. Like any community, we make room for imperfection and the full range of people's emotions. Yet we also expect a kind of cohesiveness that promotes social control. No one is asked to swallow his or her principles, but rather to diminish emotional intensity to minimize dissension and maintain a positive atmosphere. Humor, however, remains undiminished, as a wry comment, slapstick imitation, or comedic running commentary serves as a balm to wounded egos or bodies.

Basketball at the Bob functions as a community not only because of what happens on the court but off it. By now if someone who plays regularly misses a week or two, we want to know why: Is he traveling or she sick? Is everything all right? There are also ripple effects that extend beyond sports. We have shared information about career pursuits, educational choices, home remodeling, landscaping, and how to help support the chronically underfunded Bob Lanier Center. Together, the enjoyable on- and off-court atmosphere and sheer fun of the game make Sundays at The Bob meaningful for its regular participants.[8]

Is a valued experience the equivalent of a small community? Recognizing that the attributes I value may not be the same qualities appreciated by

others, I posed it as a question. The most frequent answers referenced the
good quality of the people and the game: good competition, friendly but
competitive atmosphere, or "the people, definitely the people." One person
referred to the beauty of the court itself (full-sized, polished wood floor),
another to the game "keeping him out of trouble," and others mentioned
the ability to improve their skills. For several parents who work full time the
game is a way to carve out a few hours of the week that is for themselves,
rather than about being a good parent, husband, or some other relation.
But the most common answer, expressed in various ways, involved a combination of the diversity of the people and a feeling of community.

These two factors don't always go together. As a lesbian who relies mostly
on women friends, my major interaction with men as *peers* (not colleagues,
students, bosses, or teachers) has always been basketball, where I've in-
teracted with African American men, and depending on my residence,
also Latinos, Vietnamese, Hmong, South Asians, and working-class men
unlikely to live in my neighborhood. This has led to degrees of familiarity
and sometimes contentment, or conversely to moments of hostility and
misogyny, but never community. Why? Possibly I'm seeking something
now that was not important to me before. More secure in my own identity
and frustrated by living in a city so divided and lacking in many ways, I'm
probably more interested in finding a new type of community. But I don't
think community resides under the surface, just waiting to be discovered.
Rather, we create community through repetition and imagination.

Week after week we occupy the same physical space and play games
by the same rules, allowing for repeated encounters with a core group of
people as well as newcomers or occasional players, all of whom come to
play the same game in an enjoyable atmosphere. And, I would argue, we
function like a community. We share a major life activity; share resources
beyond that activity; allow for the full range of human potential and emotions; have developed a value system; have an informal, unwritten system
of socialization into community norms; keep a lid on dissent that could
threaten the group; and experience a kind of pleasure that encourages
deeper investment in each other while creating bridges across the common
social divides of twenty-first-century urban life.[9]

Nonetheless, I want to be cautious in my claims of "community," raising
three possible points of contention. First, despite trying to be inclusive,
we are undoubtedly exclusionary and, thus, not an open community. Not
everyone comes back, although this could be for any number of reasons
(too early in the morning, demands of church or family, quality of game
not up to par). However, it would be naive to think that everyone who has

played necessarily likes the climate, the values, and the diverse group of people that have assembled over time to constitute the group's core. We've never asked anyone to leave, but people may have gotten the message that we do things a "certain way" (that is, have a culture), causing discomfort or alienation. But self-selection is at the heart of all community formation. If boundary setting is an ongoing process in communities, at least ours are not aimed at defining an exclusive "us" against an undesirable "them."

My second caution concerns my own motives. Am I sure this is not some shallow version of feel-good multiculturalism, because my relative privilege resulted in a job in which the majority of my colleagues, students, and even neighbors are white—and of similarly privileged backgrounds? I cannot swear that these sentiments are absent, but it seems to me that that Basketball at the Bob goes beyond self-satisfied liberalism because the setting allows for a different level of learning and solidarity. Two examples will suffice.

I regularly read the daily newspaper's crime reports, which consist of two or three shooting or homicide incidents per day, usually on the city's east and west sides, where poverty, drugs, and gangs co-reside. I've always been angered by a society where such violence occurs without an uproar, making the "casual" in casualty ring alarmingly true. Then one day Ty, an early regular, informed us that his teenage son had been shot multiple times, had undergone five surgeries, and remained in critical condition. He was registered at the hospital under a false name so the shooter couldn't finish the job. A card I sent (using the false name) came back stamped "nobody here with this name," creating an eerie sense of a young man full of life cut down in a hail of bullets, then disappearing in a vapor. Since then, the violence in Buffalo has become more visceral and painful to me. I wondered why I hadn't felt the same level of outrage every day when I read the newspaper, knowing the victim was always *someone's* son, brother, daughter, sister, or father.

Similarly, I've known for years how much more often people of color, especially young men, get pulled over by police. Sitting on the bleachers one day, hearing several young men trade stories of recent DWBs (stopped for "driving while black") and recite the many danger zones made unsafe by suburban police, I wanted to cry and laugh at the same time. Those "safe" white suburbs were anything but safe for men who, with a little income, might want to move out of the city to try suburbia for themselves. Moreover, I could only laugh at the idea that their "danger zones" were the mirror opposites of the many suburbanites afraid to drive into the city because of what my co-players—and DWB victims—had come to represent in a fearful, racist imagination. This kind of learning is not unique to Basketball at the Bob. I learn all the time from students, friends, and acquaintances whose lives differ substantially from my own. This is one of the pleasures of being a social creature. But at The Bob it enhances community by deepening connections and building solidarity around difference.

My third caution concerns the concept of community. How does a motley crew that congregates for a few hours a week in a dilapidated building to play a game constitute a community? Isn't this too small and infrequent a gathering to really impact people's lives? Well, impact comes in many shapes and sizes. We lack some of the usual indicators of community—a formal organization, an affiliation to some larger body like a religious faith, or a larger identity that unites us. I would venture, though, that in day-to-day life, my shared sports experience is exactly what most people get from other forms of community.

Basketball at the Bob is about familiarity, a sense of belonging, meaningful activity, and ties that bind. For me, it begins to fulfill a hopeful image of urban living. I live in the city to allow me to interact with large numbers of people who are visibly like and unlike me, with identities like and unlike mine (and anyway, once you know them, everyone becomes alike and different in ways that go beyond categorical markers), but who are all residents of a geographical and political entity named Buffalo. These are interactions that post–World War II capitalism, globalization, and insidious racism have made almost impossible to have on a regular basis. What we have at The Bob are the necessary pieces of any community: people with some commitment to each other; shared values and pastimes; passion; genuine goodwill along with room for imperfection and variation; a common space and a structure of repetition.

Finally, I want to address a contrasting vision of sport and community linked to sport spectatorship. This view maintains that widespread, deeply committed fandom around a local college or pro sports team can unify geographic communities in meaningful ways.[10] I'm curious about the difference it makes to play, versus watch, a sport together: Where does physicality fit in? At The Bob, we share space on Sundays with two small churches that rent rooms for their Sunday services. My guess is that most people would have no problem thinking of these as "faith-based communities." I imagine that if we rented space for a bridge club and met just as regularly, with the same positive feelings about the game and each other, it could also form the basis of community. Yet I also believe that the physicality of sport is crucial to our community. Playing ball involves physical pleasure, contact, and occasional pain—important means of connecting both to the self and others. Play is one of the deepest and, under the right circumstances, purest expressions of subjectivity; an athlete experiences a range of emotions in a chosen activity that is sensory and cerebral, individual and social. Most of all, sport is creative physical play, something many of us give up as we age. Playing Basketball at the Bob, I've bumped, touched, pushed, stepped on, accidentally hit, and made contact with dozens of other players, some of them week after week, until I know what their bodies feel like as well as look like. On any given Sunday, my sweat becomes intermingled with a number of others, so that when I leave the gym my sweat-soaked shirt and dripping-wet body is actually someone else's sweaty body and vice versa. Bodily fluids go a long way toward reducing distance and inviting closeness; so does the sheer pleasure of play, especially play in which body, mind, instinct, practiced skill, and spontaneity all become one and are shared with others.

From suburban Chicago to the West Coast, upper-Midwest, and western New York, sports have provided me a lifeline with multiple strands. Sports connected me to my "self," one that made intuitive and physical sense even when it made no cultural sense and led to social ostracism. Through play and imagination, sports helped stabilize a "core" self that would form the base of a more secure adult gender and sexual identity. Because I expressed my own subjectivity through sports, I searched for others like myself, illustrating the seemingly paradoxical definitions of identity as both "the fact of being who or what a person or thing is" and "a close similarity or affinity."[11] To realize myself, I had to see myself in others; yet in the process of finding a lesbian community through sports, I learned about all the differences that make a "lesbian community" at once rich, diverse, amorphous, divided, and—in truth—as much imagined as real.

To belong to a lesbian community is satisfying only so long as it is tangible and leads to relationships of value. For this reason, whether in Santa Cruz, Minnesota, or Buffalo, I learned that a community based on a shared identity still had everything to do with geographical location and social space. I also learned about the unreliability and sometimes hurtfulness of communities, a lesson that only partially prepared me for my experience in a Rust Belt city like Buffalo, where neither the economy nor the state and federal government has been kind across decades of decline. The community I found through Basketball at the Bob involves small numbers without any claim to shared neighborhood, faith, identity, or belief system. But even if we are small in numbers and the feeling of community is largely a product of mingled sweat and active imaginations, our ability to create a sense of community through basketball provides insights into the potential of combining bodies, passion, and values to redress some of the dissatisfactions and inequalities of contemporary urban life.

Notes

1. Mary Catherine Bateson, "Double Helix," in *Peripheral Visions: Learning Along the Way* (New York: Harper Collins, 1994), 42.

2. Anne Enke, *Finding the Movement: Sexuality, Contested Space, and Feminism* (Durham, N.C.: Duke University Press, 2007) 5, 4.

3. Miranda Joseph, *Against the Romance of Community* (Minneapolis: University of Minnesota Press, 2002). On sports communities, see Michael Messner, *It's All for the Kids: Gender, Families, and Youth Sports* (Berkeley: University of California Press, 2009).

4. Eric Avila, *Popular Culture in the Age of White Flight: Fear and Fantasy in Suburban Los Angeles* (Berkeley: University of California Press, 2004), 214.

5. Avila, *Popular Culture in the Age of White Flight,* 5.

6. Victoria Wolcott, "Race, Riots, and Recreation," book manuscript shared by the author.

7. See Thomas Sugrue, *The Origins of the Urban Crisis: Race and Inequality in Postwar Detroit* (Princeton, N.J.: Princeton University Press, 2005) and Matthew Lassiter, *The Silent Majority: Suburban Politics in the Sunbelt South* (Princeton, N.J.: Princeton University Press, 2007).

8. By regular, I don't mean the few who show up every week but the fifteen to twenty players who come in spurts, off and on throughout the year, or enough times to be on a name-to-name basis with a majority of players.

9. These two functions are what political scientist Robert Putnam, under his concept of social capital, would call bonding capital (deeper investment in bonds of similarity) and bridging capital (which creates ties of community between groups who do not share deep affinities). Robert Putnam, *Bowling Alone: The Collapse and Revival of American Community* (New York: Simon and Schuster, 2001).

10. Warren St. John, *Rammer Jammer Yellow Hammer: A Journey into the Heart of Fan Mania* (New York: Crown Publishers, 2004).

11. *New Oxford American Dictionary.*

13. A Philadelphia Nocturne

MIKE TANIER

By day, they are Philly sports fans: rabid hooligans, bellicose malcontents, central-casting slobbering-partisan stereotypes. They boo everyone from Phillies Hall of Famer Mike Schmidt to Santa Claus, beat up visiting fans that wear the wrong colors, and provide the national media with a lazy, go-to symbol of sports obsession turned violent. They are the barbarians who run onto the field to be tasered by security guards, who vomit like turkey vultures to dissuade arresting officers. They are an angry mob, torches and pitchforks always at the ready. Philly fans have a bad reputation, and some revel in living down to it.

By night, though, Philly fans become something else: something quieter, more contemplative, less predictable—something much more complex than the unruly mob of perpetually dissatisfied pessimists that are forever vilified by high-horse sports columnists. I have walked among these fans for four decades, seen their soft side, the night face they rarely show the world. This is the story of Philadelphia after sunset, of the fan life that on-field cameras cannot capture.

Evening

Broad Street is Philadelphia's pulmonary artery. It stretches from the warehouses and sports complexes to the south through ever-changing ethnic neighborhoods, loops around the city's impressive, impractical City Hall, then flows due north for miles, connecting university campuses and slums, abandoned warehouses and elegantly faded brownstones. In an effort to boost some barrier neighborhoods, parts of Broad Street were renamed

"Avenue of the Arts" in the mid 1990s. Near City Hall, the label stuck, and a theater district sprouted. Elsewhere, the "Avenue of the Arts" street signs hang with incongruous optimism over demilitarized intersections.

Broad Street is still "Avenue of the Arts" at the Blue Horizon's Girard Avenue corner, but the title is ironic in a part of town where survival is an art form. The theater district is more than a mile south, and Temple University's campus center lies several treacherous blocks to the north. Blight encroaches upon Broad Street quickly in this neighborhood; abandoned houses and vacant lots await every wrong turn. The Blue Horizon is a boxing landmark, Mecca for fight enthusiasts, and a favorite destination for suburbanites on ghetto safari.

Old timers will tell you that the Horizon has been sanitized for suburban visitors; it was once rougher, seedier, more authentic. It's hard to imagine what it was like before the slapdash gentrification. Security guards frisk patrons assertively. "Any knives?" one asks while pawing a wad of keys inside a pocket, sounding as if he hears at least ten "yeses" per fight night. Ringside seats are folding chairs, balcony seats are made of hard, mismatched teakwood. Concessions are hot dogs, chips, beer, water, and soda, served with minimal courtesy and dubious hygiene. The building is unapologetically un–air conditioned, and on a humid June evening sweat pours from patrons as they climb two flights of stairs to sit in an arena upper deck that looks and feels like a choir loft.

Philadelphia was once a boxing town. "Philly fighters" were the precursors of Philly sports teams: they were street-tough ruffians with a knack for losing championships, devastating punchers with personal problems or unsophisticated styles or just bad timing. Joe Frazier was the last and best of the old-guard Philly fighters, a sharecropper's son who came to Philadelphia to develop his craft so he could beat Muhammad Ali. Later, Bernard Hopkins rose from the city slums, learned to box in Graterford Prison, and became one of the greatest middleweights in history, fighting at the Blue Horizon on his way to the top. In between Frazier and Hopkins, boxing lost its mainstream appeal, overwhelmed by wall-to-wall television coverage of team sports on one side and the glitzy violence of Extreme Fighting and Mixed Martial Arts on the other. The Blue Horizon is a museum when it isn't hosting bouts, and even more so when it is.

The crowd is diverse in every way. There are black men of all ages, young toughs in T-shirts with gold chains, old men with white whiskers, collared shirts, and Panama hats who look like they haven't left their seats since Frazier's first fight. There are women in halter tops and women in burkas, septuagenarians and school-aged boys at ringside who fist-bump fighters as they pass. The suburbanites are there, too: doughy white men holding Bud Lite bottles to their heads to cool off; middle-aged couples, the wives prim and surprisingly chipper in one-hundred-degree heat. Everyone comes to experience something less sanitized than the contemporary sports experience. They come to watch men fight, and to sweat with them.

The boxing action is immediate and furious. A youngster named Keenan "Killa" Smith, all ribs and sinew, enters the ring for just his second professional fight, facing Alex Monte. The 125-pound featherweights charge each other like schoolyard bullies, then dance, weave, and deliver flurries. Big hits spray sweat across the ring and spawn cheers from the crowd. Between rounds, two ring girls with gelatinous thighs, high-heeled boots, and raspberry-frosted weaves strut through the square circle. Smith, a member of a local promotional group called Battlestrong Boxing, wins his three-round fight.

A ladies' match follows: Akima Stocks of Newark versus Olivia "The Great" Fonseca of North Philadelphia. Stocks is statuesque, athletic, and professional, with the body of a basketball forward. Fonseca is short, wide-hipped, and furious, a distaff old-school Philly Fighter with little time for the technical aspects of the sport. The bell rings, and Fonseca pounces, landing blow after wild, careening blow as Stock's priorities shift suddenly from footwork to self defense to survival. The bout is won in the first minute, though Stocks staggers through all four rounds. The crowd treats the novelty of female boxing no differently than any other match, cheering for good combinations, wincing at the nastiest blows, and howling for Fonseca, the Philly fighter.

Throughout the night, there is a girl standing just off ringside with a Kodachrome sundress and café au lait skin. She is almost pretty in the rare moments she isn't scowling. Blue Horizon regulars will tell you there's always a girl, a fighter's lover or sister or some other hanger-on, too lovely to be there but too hardened to be anywhere else. The girl is attached to the Battlestrong fighters, and her screams—a mix of corner-man strategy and desperate pleas—pierce the arena, adding life-or-death drama to each punch. TKOs are not an option for the girl, who demands blood even when her champions are clearly in control of the ring. "Think!" she shouts again and again, ironic advice for men (and women) trying to dodge blows to the face.

The headline fighter for the night is Farah Ennis, "The Silent Storm," slated to fight a gangly white soup can from Missouri with a 24–24 record. While the crowd waits for Ennis, a bunch of guys in Flyers jerseys climbs onto the fire escape with their cell phones. Six miles to the south, past the slums and orchestra halls and Italian-turned-Vietnamese neighborhoods, the Flyers are facing the Chicago Black Hawks in the Stanley Cup Finals.

So what are Flyers fans doing at a boxing match? "It's his bachelor party," one says, pointing to the groom-to-be. All of the men have grown scraggly good-luck beards, and they are thrilled to learn the Flyers hold a 3–1 first period lead. The Blue Horizon tickets were bought months in advance and are too expensive to give up. As for the wedding itself, it is two weeks away: there's no fear of a marriage-killing schedule conflict between the walk down the aisle and a Flyers parade down Broad Street.

Farah knocked out his soup can in less than a minute; the sweaty Missourian taking the quickest route he could to the mat. Maybe he wanted to see the Stanley Cup Finals as much as the bachelors did. Ennis began a march up the middleweight ranks that night. Perhaps he's the next-generation Philly fighter, heir to Hopkins and Frazier. No one sticks around to ponder the thought. The bachelors have hockey to watch and a groom to toast. The Kodachrome girl leaves with the Battlestrong entourage. Outside the Blue Horizon, an eighty-degree night in the city feels cool and refreshing.

Night

Philadelphia lies to itself. It pretends to be a blue-collar town. Stroll through Center City—Philadelphia has a Center City, not a downtown—and you'll find bistros and boutiques, tony taverns and antique galleries. But ask the lawyer sipping cabernet sauvignon at the al fresco café about sports, and he'll thump his chest and claim kinship to working-class heroes, from Chuck Bednarik to John Kruk to Dave "the Hammer" Schultz. The city's heart is trapped in the 1970s, a beer-and-shot aesthetic lurking beneath tailored suits and towering skyscrapers.

The neighborhood around 12th Avenue and Locust Street, just a few blocks from City Hall, is upscale, sophisticated, and diverse. It is nestled among university hospitals, business districts, gayborhoods, and South Street—once the place where all the hippies meet, now crassly commercial—historic homes and performance theaters. Instead of cheesesteak emporiums, there are bistros with menus featuring charcuterie, truffle oil, and castelveltrano olives, with sleek modernist dining rooms too sophisticated for television coverage of the Stanley Cup Finals.

As night falls deeper upon Locust Street, flickering light emanates from the porch of a corner townhouse. It's candlelight, plus the extrabright stroboscopic flash of sports on a high-definition television. In that prime nook of expensive urban real estate, a lone Flyers fan maintains an open-air hockey vigil, laptop by his side, play-by-play just loud enough to pierce the conversations of passers-by.

"What's the score, buddy?"

"Flyers are trailing the Hawks, 5–4."

Around the corner, the Caribou Café is far removed from the taproom where dad drank boilermakers and cursed at Dick Allen after a long shift at the shipyard. It's a French brasserie with Toulouse-Lautrec reproductions for décor and *truite aux amandes* on the menu. A tiny television above the bar delivers blurry Flyers images; a gay couple nuzzles beneath the set, glancing away from each other for periodic hockey updates.

Other Saturday night haunts, the Irish pub across the street and the crowded South Street bars, teem with orange and black–clad hockey fans. Those are the true Philly fans. Or are they? How many were there in February, when the Flyers were mediocre and the winter nights too foreboding for Center City revelry? For how many of the college-aged drinkers, their girlfriends in newly purchased pink Mike Richards sweaters, is "true fandom" a fashion, a masquerade to be tossed aside when the teams are weak and the social scene stagnant? Maybe the gay couple in the brasserie are true Philly fans. Certainly the Locust Street vigilant in his porch-front shrine is. Same with the Kodachrome girl with the razor attitude at the Blue Horizon. For fandom, even Philly fandom, is more than fury, face paint, and frustration.

"Hey guys, what's the score?"

"The Flyers just lost, six to five."

"Bummer."

"But did you hear about the Phillies? Roy Halladay pitched a perfect game."

Midnight

True hope's death demands silence. Real pain requires comfort. Pattison Avenue is eerily quiet, despite the presence of fifty thousand sports fans. It's midnight. The baseball playoffs are over; Ryan Howard struck out looking.

A week earlier, Pattison Avenue hummed with energy. The Phillies won game two of the National League Championship Series, beating the Giants on a three-run Jimmy Rollins double. Fans chattered and cheered leaving Citizens Bank Park.

Just a half-hour ago, the stadium rattled with nervous commotion as the Phillies mounted a late rally. After Howard's strikeout, there were no boos, no cries of despair, just the gasping midnight murmur of thousands of souls ripped back from our fantasy world into everyday life.

The area around Citizens Bank Park is a wasteland of warehouses, ugly and industrial. Before games, the acres of blacktop come alive, a vast concrete beach awash with tipsy tailgaters. After Howard's strikeout, the streets and lots are haunted by ghosts. Girls cling to droop-shouldered boyfriends and glide silently into the night. Old men whisper through gritted teeth. Brash young guys stumble to their cars in wide-eyed silence. Everyone has been stunned sober.

It's time for whiskey shots, and at a bar not far from the stadium, fans in Chase Utley jerseys and Halladay T-shirts toast their fate into the morning. Philly fans are notorious for their lingering anger, but the barstool crowd is too exhausted, or too pickled, to curse the darkness. They've been through it all before together. They drink Jack Daniels and Jameson; wives slip outside to smoke while barfly girls play the jukebox.

It's sad and subdued, but at least it's familiar.

The Wee Hours

City Line Avenue is choked with traffic for most of the day. It's one of the main arteries between Center City and the western suburbs, and it has attracted an urban sprawl of its own, a gnarled jumble of office buildings and shopping plazas that make the street a stop-and-go nightmare from the crack of dawn until long after sunset.

But by the time Big Daddy Graham starts his sports-talk radio show, City Line Avenue is empty. Traffic lights control the flow of imaginary cars. Parking lots are spooky concrete prairies. It is 2:00 A.M. in late January, Martin Luther King Day weekend. Philadelphia is as silent as a city can be. But sports talk never sleeps.

Graham is a broadcast legend in Philadelphia. He recorded novelty songs and comedy routines for rock-n-roll morning shows in the 1980s, then graduated to talk-show host, moving from station to station before landing on 610-WIP, the region's well-known twenty-four-hour sports talk provider. WIP is the station that bused a cabal of angry fans to New York in 1999 to boo the Eagles for drafting Donovan McNabb. The station inserted itself into the story of every failed sports hero of the last twenty years, from McNabb to Eric Lindross to Allen Iverson, exacerbating every bad situation, sensationalizing every minor scandal, often giving an around-the-clock voice to the angriest, most disillusioned fans, the ones America thinks typify the rest.

Graham is rarely involved in the king making and idol shattering. As overnight host, he's less tied to the scandal du jour. He rejects the notion that he's broadcasting to sports-obsessed insomniacs, angry loners still gritting their teeth at 3:00 A.M. about the latest loss. "I defend my listeners," he tells me during commercial breaks. "I hear from every type of person."

Graham's first caller is the owner of a chain of hoagie shops. He's tipsy, traveling home from a family party. "My daughter's driving," he assures Graham, whom he knows personally. The sandwich mogul talks a little bit about the 76ers, then about Motown music, then about sports again, a rambling back-and-forth that lasts about ten minutes and sometimes descends into private jokes between host and caller. The conversation is funny if unfocused, Graham guiding his caller back onto topic here and there. The hoagie tycoon sounds like a regular Joe, the antithesis of a seething sports lunatic. "That guy's a millionaire now," Graham says off-air.

Basketball is Graham's favorite sport, but the 76ers, who lost in overtime to the Minnesota Timberwolves earlier in the evening, are in the middle of a forgettable season. Few callers want to talk hoops. Graham riffs on 1960s music, his "snack of the night" (a sticky bun), his "babe of the night" (Sandra Bullock), and other tangents. When he does go to the phones, he allows funny or interesting callers extra time but quietly cuts off the dopes in mid-rant. One caller, lamenting the state of the local sports scene, claims that the Phillies are "just doing okay." The Phillies have won four division titles, a pennant, and a World Series in the last four seasons. They are the most successful Philly sports team of the last thirty-five years. "Okay? Okay? Are you kidding?" Graham exclaims, shutting the caller off with a toilet-flushing sound effect in midsentence.

Graham launches into extended soliloquies, even with callers waiting on line for more than twenty minutes, their names and topics blinking on a prompter next to his console. "I assume that people listen to my show to hear me," he explains. He works in a darkened studio, with just a producer and an intern, a soundboard, and a few computer terminals. A small television in the corner rebroadcasts the Sixers game. These are the horse latitudes of Philly sports: the dead of winter, no Eagles or Phillies, the Flyers early in hockey's endless season, the Sixers helpless. There's little to be riled about, nothing to cheer for.

At 4:00 A.M., Graham's late-night show becomes an early morning show. It's alarm clock time for nurses and warehouse workers, fisherman and businesspeople with hour-long commutes. Graham stops talking about tonight's Sixers game and starts talking about last night's Sixers game, flipping the calendar in his mind. Graham's listenership spikes and his

demographic shifts after four o'clock: in two hours, he will deliver a hefty
audience to WIP's noxiously popular morning show.

Just after the hour, a sound byte comes over the wire from Miami, where
the interminable pre–Super Bowl hype is in full throttle. Kyle Eckel, a nobody for the Saints who spent a half-season with the Eagles, praised the
leadership of his quarterback, Drew Brees. In the tradition of sports-talk
radio, there's more to his quote than meets the eye. There are tea leaves and
entrails to read in Eckel's comments. Praise of Brees's leadership . . . isn't
that a veiled attack on Donovan McNabb's leadership? Graham's producer
thinks so, and he comes on air to make his point.

Graham agrees reluctantly, and the game is afoot.

Magically, the phones light up. Callers want to talk about the ever-con-
troversial McNabb, the most polarizing player on the Philly sports scene
since the last "most polarizing player," heir to a love-hate legacy more than
five decades old. At the mere mention of his name, the snack-of-the-night
and babe-of-the-night give way to hardened sports talk. Some callers support McNabb. Some criticize him. A few astutely comment on what sounds
like a manufactured controversy. The burnt orange glow of dawn breaks
over the parking lots and into the window. Callers sound more caffeinated
than inebriated.

Graham seemed distracted off the air that night: arrived late and complained of serious back pain. A few weeks later, he announced that he had
throat cancer, and left the air for several months for chemotherapy. He
returned as ornery and unpredictable as ever, his show once again a mix of
trivia, oldies, and local color, four hours of shared civic experiences where
you would expect only sports-related grievances.

But as City Avenue fills with Tuesday traffic, and McNabb boosters and
bashers clash on the airwaves, Graham sounds healthy and energetic, encouraging the clever callers and cutting short the dull ones. It's morning
in Philadelphia. Time for sports.

Dawn

Bethlehem is sixty miles north of Philadelphia. Lehigh University is an engineering college on the outskirts of Bethlehem. To get from Philly to Lehigh,
you drive from city to suburbs to country, then back into a scruffy, mountain-
ous steel town. You drive on Expressways and Turnpikes, then dusty state
highways, then dark, twisty country lanes. If you are heading to Lehigh in
July, you only have one destination: Goodman Stadium. Eagles training camp.

A wrong turn in one direction leads to the gritty row homes of Bethlehem, which dangle for dear life from hillsides. A different detour leads to a county two-lane following endless cornfields to the horizon. A third wrong turn leads to the Lehigh Mountain Campus, fed by roads as rugged and secluded as a rough stretch of Appalachian Trail. There's only one correct route, marked by green arrows hung from trees and power lines, blazed by campers and SUVs with Eagles flags on their antennas.

The fan convoy already winds through the outskirts of campus at 7:30 A.M. To arrive this early, the Philadelphians leave before 6:30, maybe waking up before dawn to hear the tail end of Big Daddy Graham's show. In the stadium parking lot, fathers toss footballs to their sons, men of a certain age share coffee and donuts on the tailgates of trucks. There's no alcohol, at least no obvious alcohol, on a Monday morning before business hours. But there are babies in Eagles onesies, preschool girls in cheerleader costumes with pom-poms, old men in faded Ron Jaworski jerseys, and fetching twenty-something lovelies in brand-new pink Kevin Kolb jerseys. It's a party, one that moves slowly from the parking lot to the jogging track to the metal bleachers that line the enormous football training facility.

The bleachers are full long before the team leaves the clubhouse. One player, running back LeSean "Shady" McCoy, jogs out onto the field a half hour before the others to stretch. "Good morning, Shady," a woman yells from the corner of the bleachers. McCoy smiles and waves, then starts his warm-up.

Training camp is not a football game. It's not a pep rally or a "meet-the-players" carnival. Training camp offers little for cheerleading tykes or autograph-seeking fanatics. It's not interesting or fun. Allen Iverson can sum it up for us: "It's just practice, man. It's just practice. It's just practice."

Fans skip work, wake at dawn, dress children, pack snacks, and load their families into the minivan to watch practice. Most fans are hundreds of feet from the "action," wedged hip-to-hip in the hot sun to watch linebackers slap tackling dummies and running backs execute footwork drills. A few lucky fans earn field access, where they are shepherded between chalk-outlined boxes on the sidelines by team representatives. Behavior in the boxes is strictly, severely enforced: no Twitter, no umbrellas, no opponent's jerseys. One genius chose to wear a Redskins McNabb jersey into a field box, and was ordered to change or leave. He received national media attention, but he did not represent the fans. He acted alone.

Full-squad drills provide what passes for drama at training camp. The Eagles run real plays, with real blocking and tackling. During full-squad drills, the sidelines are just a few feet from the bleachers, so players and fans can share some rare, unscripted interaction.

"Leonard Weaver! You the man!"

The Eagles' fullback turns to acknowledge his admirer. "Thanks!"

"I remember the Giants game, man. You gave me goosebumps!"

Weaver turns to the crowd and raises an eyebrow. "I gave you *goose-bumps*?" A whole section roars with laughter.

Midday will come soon, and the Philly fans will be themselves again. They will drive home from Lehigh, listening to WIP and anticipating the evening Phillies game. If the Phillies do badly or the Eagles make some preseason blunder, they will boo and curse. One or two will even make fools of themselves. It will happen in broad daylight, and everyone will see it.

These are the real Philly fans. They are sandwich-shop millionaires and boxing fanatics; gay lovers in French brasseries and downtown sophisticates who prefer their hockey by candlelight; bachelors who toast bride, groom, boxing, and Flyers; fathers who swaddle infants in Eagles blankets and drive two hours to watch practice; old men who need one more shot in the saloon before they accept the end of the season. They boo lustily, but I have seen their night face: the face of real passion for sports, real affection for sports heroes. The real Philly fan accepts loss, frustration, disappointment, and the malicious profiling of a nation that doesn't understand him (or her). But he is at peace. At least it is familiar.

14. The Cult of Micky Ward in Massachusetts

CARLO ROTELLA

The retired boxer Micky Ward and the movie star Mark Wahlberg, escorted by publicists from Paramount Pictures, were sitting at a round table in a conference room in the Four Seasons hotel in Boston. It was early December 2010; *The Fighter,* the movie about Ward starring and produced by Wahlberg, was about to open. The early reviews were good, and Oscar buzz was mounting, especially around Christian Bale, who played the part of Dickie Eklund, Ward's half-brother. Dickie, a far more sophisticated boxer than Micky, had taught Micky most of what he knew about boxing, but Dickie had squandered his own promise in traditional ways—crack, armed robbery, jail—before embarking on an equally traditional arc of recovery. The canonization in global popular culture that comes with being the subject of a big-time Hollywood movie would square all accounts for Micky, and maybe even for Dickie. "It makes all those days and nights, the b.s., worth it," said Ward. "The hospital visits, the headaches, everything."

Ward is from Lowell, Massachusetts, a former textile-manufacturing capital thirty miles northwest of Boston. When I asked him how he expected the movie to go over there, especially its depiction of his mother as blindly favoring Dickie and of his sisters as a crew of baleful harpies, he said, "Some of them were taken aback when they saw what we were doing, but it is what it is." Wahlberg, who grew up in a large working-class family in Dorchester, stressed the importance of his own local knowledge in assuring Ward and his family that the film would get Lowell right. "I know he took comfort in the fact that I was the driving force behind the movie," Wahlberg said.

Micky Ward (right) and Mark Wahlberg. Courtesy of Stuart Cahill/*Boston Herald*.

Ward, who was forty-five, was not much heavier than his prime fighting weight of 140 pounds. Straight-backed but relaxed, giving brief answers and smiling occasionally, he had the former fighter's aura of residual force. Consequential blows, given and taken, had worn smooth all his sharp edges. Wahlberg, thirty-nine, the bulkier of the two men, talked in longer, more energetic riffs, leaning forward as he described his long effort to bring the movie to fruition. Wahlberg spent five years developing *The Fighter*, but his desire to play a boxer goes back to his early days in show business, as a viewing of his Marky Mark videos from the early 1990s will confirm.

Wahlberg did his best to defer to Ward, but Ward refused to take over, and, anyway, a movie star's idea of deferring does not preclude dominating the conversation. Wahlberg, known in the business as a former knucklehead who matured into a decent guy who gets things done (for instance, he produced the HBO series *Entourage*), clearly wanted to be taken seriously, not only as the prime mover behind *The Fighter* but also as a tough customer. He brought up his youthful brushes with the law, and he told me that the boxers who worked on *The Fighter* had not been in shape for long shooting days, but he had been, having trained for them. He interrupted himself at one point to ask why I hadn't written down something he'd said that apparently struck him as quotable. Ward, for his part, said he had nothing left to prove to anybody. He was getting more requests for appearances and endorsements as a result of the movie, but they were no more than icing on the cake. "I'm pretty smart"—*smaaht*—"on how things go," he said. "I don't need a lot lot"—*luot luot*—"to be happy. My wife and my daughter are all set. Comfortable. I'm satisfied with that."

Wahlberg had at least one further ambition for Ward, however. "Next stop is the Boxing Hall of Fame, baby," he said. Ward looked apologetic. If he is elected, it will be as a sentimental favorite or because the movie puts him over the top as a celebrity, not because he was one of the best of his time, let alone all time. He has become a folk hero—in the subcultural niches of eastern Massachusetts and the fight world, and now, thanks to the movie, in the mainstream of global popular culture—not because he conquered all comers but because his name has become synonymous with a set of virtues conventionally labeled "blue collar": heaping quantities of the amalgam of courage and will called "heart," and a working man's resilience and perseverance. Mark Wahlberg may be a local boy made good, enjoying the fame and fortune accruing to an international movie star, but Micky Ward is the toughest guy in town, the prototypical regular guy, celebrated as such in song, in story, and on the cover of the video game *Fight Night: Round 3*.

The cult of Micky Ward, rooted in the Boston area, is one of many local or regional cults that spring up around a sports figure understood to embody virtues especially tied to a place. But, thanks mostly to the movie, this particular cult has gone global in ways that allow us to more easily trace within its form and content the marks left by large-scale flows of resources, power, people, and meanings. To talk about Micky Ward is to talk not only about some really stirring ass whippings, but also about major historical transformations that extend far beyond eastern Massachusetts.

* * *

Let us begin with the ass whippings. Ward, who retired in 2003, was very good, a reliable pro with a solid chin and a picture-perfect left hook to the body, but he wasn't great; he could be had by quicker, trickier boxers, and by bigger hitters. He never reached the top of his division, he never held a major title, his career record was a respectable but not world-historical 38–13, and he lost two of his three most famous bouts, a trilogy of brawls with Arturo Gatti in 2002 and 2003 that looked like Popeye cartoons, only more eventful.[1]

Neither Ward nor Gatti was among the best in their weight class when they fought, and no title was at stake other than a mythical one: champeen throwback to a half-imagined, hazily remembered golden age when Irish and Italian dreadnoughts unflinchingly exchanged giant-slaying blows that would obliterate lesser men of the sort we have to settle for in our own time. The Ward-Gatti trilogy occupies the apex of the fight world, where that subculture registers in the culture at large via HBO, ESPN, video games, music videos, and other avenues that feed exceptional niche-sport content into the mainstream. Ward is widely admired for his part in the trilogy and, more generally, for how he carried himself in and out of the ring, win or lose.

His apotheosis was the ninth round of his first bout with Gatti, the only one of the three that Ward won. Many observers and fans feel that this is one of the great rounds of all time, and certainly one of the best of the last twenty-five years. Ward dropped Gatti with a textbook body shot early in the round, causing the trainer Emanuel Steward, one of the announcers calling the fight for HBO, to declare that Gatti was finished. But Gatti recovered from abject collapse in his usual lycanthropic manner and the fighters traded punches for most of the round. Gatti battered Ward along the ropes for a while, during which Ward gave him a little hard-case nod of acknowledgment that induced near-apoplexy in Jim Lampley, HBO's blow-by-blow man. Then Ward came on again, heaping so much damage on Gatti in the last minute of the round that the announcers once again declared that he was done. He wasn't, of course. Gatti surged back once more, the fight went the distance, and Ward took the win by majority decision.

The cult of Micky Ward is founded on the material fact of the sanctified body that gave and took such memorable punishment. When he was fighting, Ward was trained down not into a pumped showpiece but into a smooth-muscled and smooth-functioning mechanism that could soldier on through terrible difficulty. His no-frills fighting style made the most of his outsize appetite for hitting by forcing the action until the other guy had to decide if he had it in himself to go all the way. Ward was celebrated for his unfailing willingness to do what he always did in the gym and then in the ring, to work the body and keep coming and put in a full day of labor on the shop floor inside the ropes, no matter what.

Add to the evidence of the flesh a few supporting biographical facts, chief among which is Ward's strong identification with Lowell, once a famously depressed former mill town and now a recovering depressed former mill town. Also, he had a day job on a paving crew, which, like his accent and his polite and faintly embarrassed public manner, was taken as indicative of authenticity. So were the travails of Dickie Eklund, whose spectacularly rough life was examined in the HBO documentary *High on Crack Street* (1995). Dickie's narrative of recovery and hard-won wisdom parallels the narrative of Lowell's comeback: a long decline, bottoming out in the late twentieth century, followed by a hopeful upswing in recent years. Lowell stands for a particularly working-class kind of endlessly game response to hard knocks—and Micky and Dickie, the steady-working brother and the trouble-seeking wildman brother, respectively embody the light and dark sides of Lowell-style toughness.

* * *

The inner rings of the cult of Micky Ward can be found in popular culture on the regional level, beginning in the local fight world, a niche within a niche. Anyone who has spent any time in recent years at the fights around Boston has seen Ward and Eklund working a fighter's corner, or has seen Ward called up from the crowd into the ring between fights to be introduced as a ringside dignitary. On the latter occasions, Ward often finds himself standing next to Kevin McBride, the Clones Colossus, a hulking heavyweight famous all over town for defeating Mike Tyson in 2007. McBride receives good-natured cheers, but everybody knows he was never much of a fighter and caught Tyson at the tail end of a long decline. But wherever Ward goes in the local fight world, people who think of themselves as regular guys and gals choke up with tribal pride at the sight of him. He exemplifies what they like to think of as true local manhood.

Progressing outward from the Boston-area fight world into the cult as local and regional culture, you pass through articles in local newspapers and regional magazines that attend to landmarks in Ward's postretirement life (running the Boston marathon, the making and release of *The Fighter,* and so on) and arrive at the artifact that most purely expresses particularistic Boston-area pride in Ward: "The Warrior's Code," a paean to Ward by the Dropkick Murphys, an Irish American rock band out of Quincy that is strongly associated with Boston, sports, drinking, labor unions, and American Irishness. The band is best known for another song on the Warrior's Code album, "Shipping Up to Boston," which has been employed as theme music by Martin Scorsese in *The Departed* (2006) and by Jonathan

Papelbon of the Red Sox, two guys from somewhere else who turned to the Dropkick Murphys when they wanted to invest their work with a claim to authentic Bostonness.

Part of the appeal of "The Warrior's Code" lies in the earnestly labored quality of the performance: the shouted delivery and straining to make pitch, the awkwardness of the lyrics ("You were born to box in a city that's seen their share"), the stiffness of the clichés ("the quitter never wins"; "a throwback with the heart of a lion"). And part of the appeal lies in the self-presentation of the band, including, in the official video of the "The Warrior's Code," the visual rhyme between interpolated highlights from Ward's ring career and the surging energy of the band and milling fans, which creates a visual claim to peoplehood: we are hard-working regular guys who surge around and do dynamic aggressive things with our bodies, and Micky is our exemplary hero because he's the one who does that in the most spectacular and powerful fashion.[2]

The lyrics also cite Lowell's reputation as a fight town. Like nearby Brockton, or Youngstown, Ohio, it's known as a place that has traditionally produced capable violent men (and extraordinarily resilient, capable women). The song makes reference to Al Mello, Larry Carney, and Billy Ryan, Lowell boxers of yore whose pictures hang above the bar in Lowell's Gaelic Club. Citing the placement of Ward's photo among theirs in that holy location cements the song's claim for him as a throwback: an exemplar of a traditional kind of working-class masculinity associated with Lowell as a hardboiled mill town. And the final lines of the third verse, "A bloody war on the boardwalk/And the kid from Lowell rises to the bell," combine with the image in the video of a wincing, gutted Gatti to place the Ward-Gatti trilogy at the center of the claim for Ward as the bearer of an atavistic set of virtues: a combination of heart and craft that the song associates with being from Lowell and, more abstractly, Irishness. That Irishness resonates with the band's self-presentation, above all the piper in scally cap, honking and screeching with the ancestral beet-faced dignity of the old days and the old ways.

* * *

Fight Night: Round 3 made a start on moving the cult of Micky Ward from niche to mainstream, but *The Fighter* has done it in earnest. The movie's trailers promise a familiar, easily consumed artifact, a sports biopic with melodramatic highs and lows, idealized good brother and excitingly bad brother, loss and redemption, and actors eager to show off their worked-out bodies. While the film delivers all that, the trailers are also a lie. They disguise a smart, nuanced movie as a ham-fisted one along the lines of *Cinderella Man* (2005) or the Rocky franchise.

Take, for example, the moment when Dickie admits to Charlene, Micky's girlfriend, that he has blown his own chance at greatness and that they should pull together to save Micky's. "Okay," responds Charlene, "I'll see you in Micky's corner." One trailer positions this clip to suggest that the struggles over Micky between Charlene and his family are resolved in that moment, reducing it to a precursor of his inevitable triumph in the ring, which is all true as far as it goes, but the trailer selectively flattens a more complex and satisfying moment. In that scene, Dickie and Charlene—played by Amy Adams, who for this role has somehow managed to acquire the upper-lip wrinkle of a disappointed aspirant to better things—pitilessly strip each other of illusions. He tells her that she's mistaken in thinking that she's something special because she went away to college. She failed at it, and now she spends her nights in a bar like everyone else in town. She responds with a hurtful shot of her own: Dickie didn't knock down Sugar Ray Leonard, his principal claim to fame; Leonard slipped, and Dickie's just another big-talking crackhead. They look at each other for a moment, two disappointed hometown losers whose dreams of success in the wider world just make them ridiculous, and then Charlene tells Dickie that she'll see him in Micky's corner. But the trailer leaves out the scene's kicker: outside the truce space of Micky's corner, Charlene adds, Dickie can go fuck himself.

The dramatic premise of that scene and of *The Fighter* as a whole turns on the problem of what it means to be rooted in Lowell. Micky has been made hard by his hard-knock hometown and his hard-knock brother, so in that sense Lowell is the source of Micky's edge in the ring, but Lowell also threatens to drag him down into the loserdom that Charlene and Dickie identify in each other. Undermined by Dickie, their mother, and their horrible sisters, who refer to Charlene as "the MTV girl" because she strikes them as having unforgivable pretensions to cosmopolitanism, Micky comes to realize that merely replacing Dickie as "the pride of Lowell" would amount to failure. With the help of Charlene, Micky has to figure out how to separate the usable aspects of Lowell-ness from the toxic elements.

Success, in this kind of movie, means winning a world title. Rushing toward that pinnacle, the script freely abuses the facts of Ward's career: ignoring losses, puffing up victories over lesser opponents, changing records and weights, turning a marginal belt into a major one. This is typical Hollywood fudging, but done here with thematic consistency. What matters is that Micky goes out into the world beyond Lowell and shows everyone that the local ways, the old-school ways, still carry a charge.

That's also the point of the movie's purposeful intertextuality with HBO. The prospect of being on HBO, which the characters regard as the *ne plus ultra* of engagement with the wider world, frames the movie's meta-problem of how to properly represent the quality of Lowell-ness. Even as Micky angles for a big fight on HBO, a camera crew from the cable network follows Dickie around town, making *High on Crack Street,* in which Dickie will serve as Exhibit A for the drug's pernicious effect on the lives of users. The fight sequences visually mimic HBO house style in the '90s (Wahlberg told me that he brought in the director of the Ward-Gatti bouts for HBO to show David O. Russell, the movie's director, how to do it), but the cleverest and most expressive bit of HBO intertextuality is a sound gimmick that comes during the film's climactic bout, a victory over the Irish ham-and-egger Shea Neary for the relatively trivial World Boxing Union light welterweight belt that the movie treats as if it were the crowning achievement of Ward's career. The film samples lines from the HBO announcing crew's ecstatic call of round nine of Ward-Gatti I, which took place after the action of the movie comes to an end, and places them in their mouths as they call the Ward-Neary bout. The substitution winkingly apologizes for misrepresenting Ward-Neary as a bout worthy of being treated as a big deal, and it offers in compressed shorthand a climax to the story of how Lowell shaped Micky Ward into a paragon of old-school virtues who would go on to attain the status of folk hero, worthy of a big-time Hollywood biopic, by losing two out of three brutal fights to Gatti.

* * *

The Fighter has become the definitive artifact of the cult of Micky Ward, the primary bearer of this local set of meanings to the wider world, and it has fused the cult with a larger set of likeminded stories. The recent boom in Massachusetts-made Hollywood movies has included a subset that, like *The Fighter*, devotes significant effort to achieving a local feel. I'm not talking about a movie like *Paul Blart: Mall Cop* (2009), which was shot in the suburbs of Boston but doesn't try to establish any kind of local identity; I'm talking about *The Friends of Eddie Coyle* (1973) and *The Brink's Job* (1978); *Good Will Hunting* (1997), which set the template for Boston movies to come; *Monument Ave.* (1998); *Next Stop Wonderland* (1998); *The Boondock Saints* (1999); *Mystic River* (2003); *Fever Pitch* (2005); *The Departed* (2006); and, with the maturing of the state's film tax credit, a burst of recent productions: *Gone Baby Gone* (2007); *Black Irish* (2007); *What Doesn't Kill You* (2008); *Shutter Island* (2010); *Edge of Darkness* (2010); *The Town* (2010); *The Company Men* (2010); and *The Fighter* (2010), with more on the way.

Massachusetts woos film and TV production as part of its commitment to cultural economic development. The state film office was founded in 1979, and in the past few years Massachusetts has boasted one of the nation's most attractive film tax credit programs.[3] Policy moves to ease the way of film production are a classic postindustrial economic strategy. The decline of manufacturing opens up a gap that can be filled in part by new industries, including the production of culture, as the New England mill city becomes a backwater in the industrial economy and acquires a new role in the postindustrial economy. The very fact of becoming a backwater enabled and demanded the policy moves that put Massachusetts back in the center of the cultural action as a hotbed of film production, just as (at least as the cult tells the story) the old-school qualities of Lowell as a fight town, a depressed mill town, helped equip Ward to take cultural center stage as an atavistically tough throwback hero.

You can see the arrival of the postindustrial phase in the repurposing of physical elements and the history of the formerly industrial city, as in the many cases of using old factory buildings to house museums, arts spaces, loft housing, convention centers, and resonant places to eat, drink, and shop—thus maxing out the consumer impact of the arts and culture dollar. This is Postindustrial Transformation 101: mill towns that don't make things anymore must turn to providing services, information, images, history, experiences. Scenes like the long shot in *The Fighter* of Charlene knocking on the door of Micky's apartment with dark factory buildings looming in the background exemplify how Boston-area films exploit the possibilities—for cheap production and for making meaning—opened up by material and cultural conditions that typically hold sway in postindustrial cities.

Lowell, with its textile mills turned into museums, national historical park, and unified branding scheme, has become a regional poster child for such transformation. The slow, difficult, incomplete process of turning Lowell into something other than a depressed place where the mills all closed, the process of grafting an interesting city onto a tough town, has gathered enough momentum that the process itself has become a leading feature of Lowell's identity. That's what Micky was talking about when, in a video interview with the *Lowell Sun,* he contrasted the down-and-out Lowell of the 1980s and '90s depicted in the movie with the "revitalized" Lowell of today, "with the downtown area, and the shops outside, and the cafes."[4] Dickie, sitting next to him, added, "Lowell's cleaned up 110% from before," then segued without a rhetorical break from urban revitalization to his own clean and sober status. Staking out an identity with Lowell and a relationship to history, the brothers put the bad old days in the past while also maintaining the link to them that the cult assumes is one principal source of Micky's virtue: that is, they're tough guys from a tough town. The occasion of the interview was the making of *The Fighter,* and they talked about the movie as a nostalgic trip to the tail end of the tough town's golden age of hard times—a journey we can all make, courtesy of the film tax credit.

But to recognize the film tax credit as an example of postindustrial policy explains only why a lot of movies get made in Massachusetts these days, not why some of these movies try so hard to establish a local feel. In everything from obsessively excessive dialogue coaching to minutely parsing local class fractions, they ostentatiously seek to bear the mark of the place in which they were made. Casting calls for *The Fighter* specified boxers and trainers, women with red or blond hair, and residents of Lowell.[5] At least the aura of the real thing matters. Why?

Begin with the fresh attraction of any local texture at all in a self-consciously globalizing age. As time and space are measured in America, and especially in Hollywood, New England cities like Boston and Lowell are strange, ancient places with distinctive physical forms, exotic folkways, and curious languages, like Jerusalem or the cities of the Silk Road. A movie can cite signs of locality—the qualities understood to make Boston Boston, or Lowell Lowell—to give itself an air of authenticity. Remade foreign material translocated to Massachusetts often makes this move in the most obvious ways: for example, *Fever Pitch,* a remake of a British adaptation of a Nick Hornby book about his obsession with the Arsenal Football Club, reduces Bostonness to being a Red Sox fan. Homegrown stories often do it with more subtlety. There's a priceless moment in *Gone Baby Gone* (2007), which is based on a novel by Dennis Lehane (who's from Dorchester), when a little boy on a bike cuts in front of a car and, despite being entirely in the wrong, yells "Go fuck ya motha" when the driver tells him to move out of the way. It's a moment of pure Boston-style unpleasantness—bad traffic skills, bad manners, nastiness to outsiders, refusing to pronounce the r in "mother"—and it's exactly like a shot of a yak herder or a snake charmer in a movie set in Mongolia or India: a moment that's there for the pleasure of tasting exotic locality. One side effect of globalization is valorizing the irreducible, unmeltable, romantically unreconstructed local.

But I think it's possible to be more specific about the attractions of the local as it shows up in Boston and neighboring cities in movies like *The Fighter,* and in a way that helps explain the power of the cult of Micky Ward. These movies tend to focus on a particular layer of locality: the remnants and by-blows of industrial urbanism, the distinctive ways of living that grew up in industrial cities, an order that had its autumnal golden age in the mid twentieth century and was undone by, among other large forces, the deindustrialization of the mill cities that formerly drove the rise of America as a world power, and the change in American immigration patterns that decentered Ireland and Italy and recentered on Asia, Latin America, the Caribbean, and eastern Europe. These are for the most part movies about white ethnics, usually Irish American (like Ward, who fought under the ring name "Irish" Micky Ward), descended from the old "new" immigrants who came to the cities of America, especially on the East Coast, to work in factories, and who fashioned their urban folkways around a familiar neighborhood landscape of factory, saloon, parish church, school, union hall, boxing gym, and the like—the landscape of the urban village. In movie after movie, the camera lingers on the remnants of this landscape, soaring in over the tightly packed roofs of the tough town or the Old Neighborhood, unsteadily tracking the heroes from dive bar to parish church, elegizing the urban order that rose and fell between the late nineteenth century and the late twentieth.

These movies are besotted with the exploration of a masculinity native to such places, and they're also often violent crime stories, in which the surface crime may be a murder or disappearance or rape or robbery, but the sense of deep crime, the profound condition that is uncovered by the investigation of the surface crime, is wrapped up with the decline and fall of industrial urbanism and its style of manhood. They imagine a shrinking yet still vital cohort of white-ethnic tough guys who are exemplary in old-school ways, and therefore more than equal to the challenges presented by the ghetto, the barrio, and new immigration. In that sense, these movies extend the project of the Rocky series: imagining the continuing potency of the Old Neighborhood in a time when that potency is called into question by succeeding urban orders.

In addition to whatever else they're about, these movies want to think about what has been lost or salvaged in the aging-out of industrial urbanism.[6] For both material and symbolic reasons, the urban landscapes and culture of Massachusetts, represented by the triple-decker block or the redbrick factory building or the phantom letter r, have become familiar material with which to do that kind of thinking. And that's true both for homegrown Boston-area artists, like Mark Wahlberg, the Afflecks, and Matt Damon, and for storytellers from elsewhere, like Clint Eastwood, Mel Gibson, and Martin Scorsese, who seek to refresh their mythmaking powers by converging on Massachusetts, of all places, and on the qualities that are presumed to make Boston Boston or Lowell Lowell.

The cult of Micky Ward participates in the movies' project of simultaneous recovery and elegy. The constant labeling of Ward as a throwback with the heart of a lion celebrates the continuing potency of Irishness, an identity that no longer dominates urban culture as it once did in places like Lowell and Boston, and also marks the passing of that identity's ascendancy on the street. The narrative of do-or-die immigrant striving no longer applies to white ethnics in the ways that it once did. Meanwhile, Lowell, for instance, has filled up with so many do-or-die Southeast Asian immigrant strivers that the Cambodian government opened up a consulate there in 2009. (A second casting call for *The Fighter* specified Cambodian men who speak fluent Khmer.)[7] The cult sorrows as well as glories in having found one last white-ethnic paladin, a last Irishman standing, who still embodies the connection to industrial urbanism: a steady-working hero who's good with his hands and perseveres even when outclassed, outgunned, badly hurt, or on the wrong side of history.

The cult of Micky Ward is rooted in Lowell, but for all its local groundedness the cult is also eminently portable, packaged in such various forms as the feature film, the YouTube highlight clip, the song, the music video, the video game, the mash-up-able fight calls of HBO announcers. And the essence of the cult can be deposited in different bodies, which is what the fetishized discussion of dialogue coaching, advice from local experts, and apparently Oscar-worthy questing after Boston-area authenticity that surrounded the making of *The Fighter* was all about. Like the seasonal flu, the cult now rides the flows of international cultural commerce, spreading everywhere. This mainstream canonization couldn't happen to a more modest or unassuming guy than Micky Ward, who has the decency to be vaguely embarrassed about it even as he receives it as his due, payment in full for several lifetimes' worth of hard work and hard knocks.

Notes

1. For Ward's boxing record, see http://boxrec.com/list_bouts.php?human _id=3603&cat=boxer, accessed November 5, 2011.

2. See http://www.youtube.com/watch?v=ebHIxQ_zhNY. Uploaded December 9, 2007.

3. The Massachusetts Film Office claimed an average annual economic benefit of $267,225,000 for the tax credit from 2006 to 2009, with $452 million in direct spending by film productions in 2008 alone (http://www.mafilm.org/mass-film-tax-credit-by -the-numbers/). It also claimed that film production in Massachusetts created 4,972 jobs, which would include at least one for Micky Ward, who has worked as a teamster on film productions.

4. http://www.youtube.com/watch?v=z9WOnxNFYCo. Posted September 10, 2009.

5. http://www.beantownbloggery.com/2009/05/casting-call-fighter.html. Posted May 26, 2009.

6. I have taken up of other aspects of this general subject in other places. On boxing and postindustrial transformation, see, for example, *Good with Their Hands: Boxers, Bluesmen, and Other Characters from the Rust Belt* (Berkeley: University of California Press, 2002). On boxing, place, and local-global dynamics, see, for example, "The Stepping Stone: Larry Holmes, Gerry Cooney, and Rocky," in *In the Game: Race and Sports in the Twentieth Century,* ed. Amy Bass (New York: Palgrave, 2005): 237–62. On film genre and the fall of the Old Neighborhood, see "Praying for Stones Like This: The *Godfather* Trilogy," in *Catholics in the Movies,* ed. Colleen McDannell (Oxford, U.K.: Oxford University Press, 2007), 227–52.

7. http://www.beantownbloggery.com/2009/06/casting-call-fighter-2nd-call-68.html, accessed December 20, 2011.

Afterword

DANIEL A. NATHAN

While I was working on this afterword, my mother gave me an article from a recent issue of *Sports Illustrated*. She ripped it out of a magazine that was in her doctor's waiting room. Titled "In My Tribe," it was written by Terry McDonell, the magazine's managing editor. A series of well-chosen, well-told vignettes culled from *Sports Illustrated* writers (that is, McDonell's tribemates) extolling sport's virtues and "the transcendent moments that lift us," the article is simultaneously sentimental, perceptive, and germane to this project.[1] Many of the best stories in the article are coming-of-age tales, some of which involve intergenerational bonding; they're rich examples of "the game or the team or the athlete as a bridge between generations, the adhesive that binds relationships, the spit that holds families together."[2] At the same time, McDonell and some of his colleagues recognize that sport's ability to promote a sense of belonging moves well beyond families. They understand, for example, that "big-city teams like the Yankees" are "civic metaphors," as are "small-market teams like the Packers."[3] They even go a step further and suggest that sport has something like a "primal ability to connect, to merge, to create community."[4] Though dubious about the "primal" part of this claim, as it seems to me that this is a cultural phenomenon, I think the larger point has merit. As it has historically, sport continues to forge community and identity, personal *and collective.*

Since you made it this far, you know that the fourteen essays in this book examine different sports (baseball, basketball, boxing, football, and so forth), played at different levels (interscholastic and intercollegiate, professional and pickup) by different kinds of people for different reasons. They also discuss varied communities—large, midsize, and small; urban, suburban, and rural; college towns, postindustrial cities, and megalopolises—in more than a dozen states in different regions of the United States. This means *Rooting For the Home Team* covers a lot of territory and, like most books, is selective, not comprehensive. Actually, a comprehensive study of the sport-community-identity phenomenon is not possible. There is simply too much heterogeneity out there. Still, patterns emerge, and as the folklorist Henry H. Glassie puts it, patterns "carry toward meaning."[5]

One thing this collection drives home is that when it comes to sport, meaning is local and not just an individual matter. Communities, too, create meaning. Communities care about and are invested in sports. Communities often seek their identity, comfort, order, and tradition from the sports they play and cheer, host and subsidize. This was true in "Middletown," Indiana, in the 1920s, in big cities like Baltimore, Boston, Chicago, Los Angeles, and Philadelphia, and it's still true in State College, Pennsylvania, even after the devastating Jerry Sandusky sex abuse scandal. In the days after that disturbing news broke, one Penn State student, reflecting on the school and its football team, said: "What was obviously a source of our pride is now a shattered identity."[6] It's not completely shattered, of course. Penn State and Penn Staters still care fervently about their football team, no matter how much things have changed. Football is still one of the primary things that define the Penn State community, for better or worse. Probably both.

One of the most interesting things about the essays collected here is how the contributors conceptualize community and identity differently and the various ways in which they bring these subjects together with sport. Some of the communities discussed here are tightly focused geographically, say, the small towns where high school football held (and holds) sway, or where "six-on-six" girls' basketball promoted a strong sense of community identification. Some are more scattered, like the Red Sox Nation diaspora, "the Chicagoland area," and California's "Southland." Others seem to be crumbling, such as Baltimore and Buffalo, both victims of postindustrialism. What they all have in common, though, is that they are dynamic (think about how quickly some parts of the Penn State community have changed since David Zang wrote his essay) and that sport was and/or is "a significant site for the construction and maintenance of community ties."[7]

Likewise, some of the essays here treat their subjects dispassionately, at a historical and emotional remove. Yet most of them reveal the authors' personal connection to their subject, to different degrees: the spectrum is wide. However, in every case where contributors use the first-person narrative voice or anecdotal evidence, they go beyond their own personal experiences. Back in 2009, when this project began, I gave my contributors license to get personal and be self-reflexive. "Feel free to be creative," I told them, "to be autobiographical, to be interdisciplinary." They responded to this invitation with enthusiasm, but without narcissism or tunnel vision. So, for instance, Susan Cahn's essay is about herself, yes, and her personal sports odyssey, but it's not *just* about her and her experiences; it addresses larger concerns and issues.

Not one to traffic in hyperbole, cultural critic Gerald Early declares: "Sports may be among the most powerful human expressions in all history."[8] That seems right, for many reasons, some of which have been articulated in this book. Time, of course, has something to do with it. Sport, after all, is an extremely old practice and institution, arguably as old as civilization itself, and has been put to many uses, from bread-and-circus spectacles to the promotion of nationalist ideologies to the expression of self. For some, like Hans Ulrich Gumbrecht, author of *In Praise of Athletic Beauty* (2006), the appeal of sport resides primarily in its aesthetic delight and "the feeling of communion which overcomes me as I am rooting for my favorite teams and for my most admired heroes."[9] That "feeling of communion" is at the heart of this book. "Sometimes," Gumbrecht continues,

> the distance between myself and my athletic heroes seems to become smaller than most of us tend to assume in our everyday rationality. Perhaps we should not rule out the possibility that watching sports can allow us to be suddenly, somehow, one with those beautiful and beautifully transfigured bodies. For many years now, I have known how much I enjoyed this vague and powerful feeling. I accept the risk that it might turn out to be an illusion, but at least I want to find out exactly how athletic performance can produce this feeling—or this illusion—of oneness.[10]

The "vague and powerful feeling" to which Gumbrecht refers is sometimes illusory, or at least superficial and fleeting. But as the essays collected here demonstrate, it can also be tangible, deep, and meaningful, something to take seriously. Why? Because the sense of "oneness" that Gumbrecht describes, the "common passion," to borrow a phrase from sociologist Émile Durkheim, that many people experience playing, watching, and cheering sports is more than microcosmic or metaphoric (though it can be those things, too): rather, it captures who most of us are or seem to be, social creatures who yearn for meaning and a sense of belonging.[11] Indeed, a sense of belonging often provides people with the meaning they desire.

In April 2011, I went back to Iowa City, to give a lecture at a symposium on this very subject. Spring was in the air and it felt good to be back. It had been fourteen years since I had graduated and moved away, and more than twenty since I first moved to town. Some things had changed, of course, mostly small things. Some stores and restaurants had closed. Others had opened, as had a terrific new public library. Not surprisingly, given their ages and profession, coaches Dan Gable, Hayden Fry, C. Vivian Stringer, and Tom Davis were all gone; they had either retired or moved on to greener pastures, if that's what you want to call New Jersey, where Stringer coaches at Rutgers University. The basketball season was over and the spring football game was a few weeks away. Nonetheless, the sports-related sense of *communitas* was palpable. Everywhere I walked, there were black-and-gold Tiger hawk logos—they were on every imaginable surface: clothes, glassware, notebooks, towels, and so forth. The local media gave Iowa sports a great deal of attention. The majority of people I met and talked to—fellow alums, current students, professors, waiters and waitresses, store clerks, my airport shuttle driver—brought up Hawkeye sports, if only briefly. It was as if caring and talking about the Hawkeyes was endemic, an important part of the local culture.

For some, it's easy to get sentimental about the ways in which people in Iowa and elsewhere use sport "to connect, to merge, to create community." And clearly, sociologist Garry Crawford and others are right that "this sense of community and belonging is not open to all and fan communities are frequently exclusionary of certain individuals, on the basis of class, disability, ethnicity and gender."[12] What this means, though, is that we—like the contributors to this book—should take the nexus of sport, community, and identity seriously, and should try to be critically alert about it even as we root for the home team.

Notes

1. Terry McDonell, "In My Tribe," *Sports Illustrated,* November 28, 2011, 68.

2. Ibid., 70.

3. Ibid.

4. Gary Smith quoted in McDonell, "In My Tribe," 76.

5. Henry H. Glassie, *Material Culture* (Bloomington: Indiana University Press, 1999), 47.

6. Quoted in Adam Geller, "On Penn State campus, bleeding blue and white," November 11, 2011, accessed December 27, 2011, http://abclocal.go.com/wpvi/story?section=news/crime&id=8428704.

7. Mike Cronin, "Playing Games? The Serious Business of Sports History," *Journal of Contemporary History* 38 (July 2003): 498.

8. Gerald Early, "Performance and Reality: Race, Sports and the Modern World," *The Nation,* August 10/17, 1998, 12.

9. Hans Ulrich Gumbrecht, *In Praise of Athletic Beauty* (Cambridge, Mass.: The Belknap Press of Harvard University Press, 2006), 32.

10. Gumbrecht, *In Praise of Athletic Beauty,* 32.

11. Émile Durkheim (translated by Carol Cosman), *The Elementary Forms of Religious Life* (Oxford, U.K.: Oxford University Press, [1912] 2001), 157.

12. Garry Crawford, *Consuming Sport: Fans, Sport and Culture* (New York: Routledge, 2004), 52.

Contributors

AMY BASS is the author of *Not the Triumph But the Struggle: 1968 Olympics and the Making of the Black Athlete* (2002) and *Those About Him Remained Silent: The Battle over W. E. B. Du Bois* (2009) and the editor of *In the Game: Race, Identity, and Sports in the Twentieth Century* (2005). She teaches history at The College of New Rochelle and directs its Honors Program.

A professor of history at the University at Buffalo (SUNY), **SUSAN K. CAHN** is the author of the award-winning *Coming On Strong: Gender and Sexuality in Twentieth-Century Women's Sport* (1994) and *Sexual Reckonings: Southern Girls in a Troubling Age* (2007) and co-editor of *Women and Sports in the United States: A Documentary Reader* (2007).

MARK DYRESON of Penn State University is the author of *Making the American Team: Sport, Culture, and the Olympic Experience* (1998), the editor of *Mapping an Empire of American Sport: Expansion, Assimilation, Adaption and Resistance* (2013), a past president of the North American Society for Sport History, and a senior editor of *The International Journal of the History of Sport*.

MICHAEL EZRA is professor of American multicultural studies at Sonoma State University and the author of *Muhammad Ali: The Making of an Icon* (2009) and *Civil Rights Movement: People and Perspectives* (2009).

ELLIOTT J. GORN is the author of *The Manly Art: Bare-Knuckle Prize Fighting in America* (1986), *Mother Jones: The Most Dangerous Woman in America* (2001), *Dillinger's Wild Ride: The Year That Made America's Public Enemy Number One* (2009), co-author (with Warren Goldstein) of *A Brief History of American Sports* (1993), and the editor of *Muhammad Ali, The People's*

Champ (1995) and *Sports in Chicago* (2008), among other publications. He holds the Joseph A. Gagliano Chair in American urban history at Loyola University Chicago.

A native Chicagoan, **CHRISTOPHER LAMBERTI** recently earned his Ph.D. in American history from Brown University. His dissertation is a social-cultural history of the Chicago 1919 race riot, titled *Riot Zone: Chicago, 1919,* focusing on labor diasporas, neighborhoods, "whiteness," and masculinity. He has designed and developed Web sites for various history-related projects, and he contributes to a White Sox blog.

ALLISON LAUTERBACH is a Ph.D. candidate in American history at the University of Southern California and a J.D. candidate at the University of California–Berkeley School of Law (Boalt Hall), where she is also on the editorial board of the *Berkeley Journal of Gender, Law & Justice.* She has been awarded research fellowships and grants from the Society for Historians of American Foreign Relations, the Radcliffe Institute for Advanced Study at Harvard, the Lyndon Baines Johnson Presidential Library, and the Center for Law, History and Culture at USC Law, among others.

CATHERINE M. LEWIS is a professor of history, director of the Museum of History and Holocaust Education, and the executive director of Museums, Archives and Rare Books at Kennesaw State University. She is the author, co-author, or co-editor of nine books, including *The Changing Face of Public History: The Chicago Historical Society and the Transformation of an American History Museum* (2005), *Don't Ask What I Shot: How Eisenhower's Love of Golf Helped Shape 1950s America* (2007), and *Jim Crow America* co-edited with Dr. J. Richard Lewis (2009). She is also a guest curator and special projects coordinator for the Atlanta History Center, having curated more than twenty exhibitions, including the award-winning *Down the Fairway with Bobby Jones.*

SHELLEY LUCAS is an associate professor in the Department of Kinesiology at Boise State University. Her areas of interest include women's sport history, gender equity in athletics, and media representations of gender, race, and sexuality in sport.

The author of the award-winning *Saying It's So: A Cultural History of the Black Sox Scandal* (2003), **DANIEL A. NATHAN** has also published essays and book, film, and exhibition reviews in *Aethlon, American Quarterly, Journal of American History, Journal of American Studies,* and *Journal of Sport History,* among other publications.

A former NFL player and associate dean at Oregon State University, **MICHAEL ORIARD** is the author of seven books, including *Reading Football: How the Popular Press Created an American Spectacle* (1993), *King Football: Sport and Spectacle in the Golden Age of Radio and Newsreels, Movies and Magazines, the Weekly and the Daily Press* (2001), *Brand NFL: Making and Selling America's Favorite Sport* (2007), and *Bowled Over: Big-Time College Football from the Sixties to the BCS Era* (2009).

CARLO ROTELLA is the author of *October Cities: The Redevelopment of Urban Literature* (1998), *Good With Their Hands: Boxers, Bluesmen, and Other Characters from the Rust Belt* (2002), *Cut Time: An Education at the Fights* (2003), and *Playing in Time: Essays, Profiles, and Other True Stories* (2012). He writes for the *New York Times Magazine* and the *Boston Globe* and his work has also appeared in *Critical Inquiry, American Quarterly, The American Scholar, Raritan,* the *New Yorker, Harper's, Slate,* and *The Best American Essays.*

An assistant professor at Penn State University, **JAIME SCHULTZ** has published her work in the *Journal of Sport History, Journal of Sport and Social Issues, Sociology of Sport Journal, International Journal of the History of Sport, Aethlon, Sport in Society,* and *Stadion.*

MIKE TANIER is a contributing editor to FootballOutsiders.com, co-author of the *Football Outsiders Almanac 2009* (2009), and a frequent contributor to the *New York Times.*

A professor and former assistant dean of the School of Recreation, Health, and Tourism at George Mason University, **DAVID K. WIGGINS** is the author of *Glory Bound: Black Athletes in a White America* (1997) and has edited or co-edited seven books, including *The Unlevel Playing Field: A Documentary History of the African American Experience in Sport* (2003), *Out of the Shadows: A Biographical History of African American Athletes* (2006), *Sport in America, From Colonial Leisure to Celebrity Figures and Globalization,* Volume II (2010), and *Rivals: Legendary Matchups That Made Sports History* (2010).

DAVID W. ZANG teaches at Towson University, and is the author of the award-winning *Fleet Walker's Divided Heart: The Life of Baseball's First Black Major Leaguer* (1995) and *SportsWars: Athletes in the Age of Aquarius* (2001), and is the producer of the documentary film *For the Love of Soul: A Story of Music, Color, and the Sixties* (2011).

Index

The University of Illinois Press
is a founding member of the
Association of American University Presses.

———————————————————————

Composed in 10.5/13 Chaparral Pro
by Jim Proefrock
at the University of Illinois Press
Manufactured by Thomson-Shore, Inc.

University of Illinois Press
1325 South Oak Street
Champaign, IL 61820-6903
www.press.uillinois.edu